The Diet Dilemma—

Rosemary Stanton is Australia's best-known awarded an Order of Australia Medal for her services to community health and her work involves educating medical students, doctors, teachers and the general public about nutrition. Rosemary is the author of 26 books on food and nutrition, several thousand magazine and newspaper articles and many scientific papers. She is currently an advisor to several research projects and is also the co-author (with Garry Egger) of the highly successful *GutBuster* series.

Rosemary is married with four adult children and is enjoying her role as a grandmother. Her favourite hobby is her country garden—especially the vegie patch.

The diet dilemma—explained

whether to lose, how much to lose,
how to lose, how not to lose

Second edition

Rosemary Stanton

ALLEN & UNWIN

Copyright © Rosemary Stanton, 2000

All rights reserved. No part of this book may be reproduced or transmitted in any form or by any means, electronic or mechanical, including photocopying, recording or by any information storage and retrieval system, without prior permission in writing from the publisher.

First edition 1991
Reprinted 1992, 1993, 1994, 1995, 1996, 1997, 1998
Second edition published in 2000
Allen & Unwin
9 Atchison Street, St Leonards NSW 1590 Australia
Phone: (61 2) 8425 0100
Fax: (61 2) 9906 2218
E-mail: frontdesk@allen-unwin.com.au
Web: http://www.allen-unwin.com.au

National Library of Australia
Cataloguing-in-Publication entry:

Stanton, Rosemary.
   The diet dilemma—explained: whether to lose, how much to lose, how to lose, how not to lose.

   2nd ed.
   Includes index.
   ISBN 1 86508 256 2.

   1. Reducing diets. 2. Weight loss. 3. Nutrition—Requirements.
   I. Title.

613.25

Set in 11/13 pt Plantin Light by DOCUPRO, Sydney
Printed and bound by Griffin Press, South Australia

Contents

Preface ix

1 The great diet hoax continues   1
A gullible public
The 'need' for the new
Profitability
Body image
Why so many diets and diet products?

2 Why lose weight?   12
Who is too fat?
Body Mass Index
Weight versus fat
Body shape
Special problems for women
Special problems for men

3 Why do people get fat?   26
Overconsumption
Underactivity
The role of genes
Structuring the environment
Why diets don't work

4 Health and body fat   38
'Apples' and 'pears'
Coronary heart disease
High blood pressure
Adult-onset diabetes
Gallstones

Cancer
Arthritis and gout
When is weight loss unnecessary?

5 A bit of magic — 48
Selling techniques
Ingredients in weight loss/fat metaboliser products
brindleberry or hydroxycitric acid (HCA) • chitosan • amino acids • L-carnitine • collagen • choline and lecithin • kelp • chromium picolinate • pyruvate • DHEA or dehydroepiandrostenone • *Ginkgo biloba* • capsaicin • guarana • pectin and other fibres • grapeseed extract • escin • sweet clover • evening primrose oil • inositol • conjugated linoleic acid (CLA) • Chinese herbs • St John's wort • other herbs • enzymes • vitamins

6 The diet merry-go-round — 69
Problems with fast weight loss
Self-esteem
Getting off the diet merry-go-round
Weight loss and metabolic rate
Diets make you fat
How the body accumulates and loses fat
Breaking down fat stores
Exercise
The importance of exercise

7 The best of the diets — 88
The goodies
If Not Dieting, Then What? • GutBuster Waist Loss Guide • Trim for Life • Licence to Eat • A Weight Off Your Mind • The Diet that Works • The Pritikin Program • Eat More, Weigh Less
The almost-make-its
Eat More, Weigh Less • The Hip and Thigh Diet • The Complete F-Plan Diet

8 The rest of the diets — 104
Current trendies
The Liver Cleansing Diet • The Zone • Sugar Busters! • Fit For Life • The Montignac Method • Stop the Insanity • Beyond Pritikin
Golden oldies
Dr Atkins Super Energy Diet • The Complete Scarsdale Medical Diet • The Israeli Army Diet • The Egg Diet • The Drinking Man's Diet •

CONTENTS

The Beverly Hills Diet • The Rotation Diet •
Negative Calories • The Grapefruit Diet •
The High Sexuality Diet

9 Other weight loss methods   134
Weight loss programs
Meal replacement products
Slimming drugs
Acupuncture
Surgery
Fasting

10 Changing your eating and exercise habits   163
What are you eating?
Principles of healthy eating
Exercise

11 Planning your new habits   178
Breakfast
Lunch
Dinner
Snacks
Weight plateau
Bingeing and coping with guilt

12 The overweight child   194
Special foods for children
Does overweight matter?
How excess weight begins
Drinks
What to do about excess weight in children

13 Coping with eating out and other distractions   203
Eating out
Guide to different cuisines
Drinks
Entertaining
Holidays
Giving up smoking

Appendix: Useful books and recipe books   219
Index   221

Preface

I wrote the first edition of *The Diet Dilemma* to help readers sort out the confusion surrounding weight loss. My hope was that people—especially women—would realise the futility of dieting. Sadly, the dieting mentality is still with us, so a second edition has become necessary to discuss the latest round of diets and slimming products.

Most women still want to be thinner, and this applies equally to those who are already slim and those who are fatter than is good for their health. Women are also still looking for 'solutions' to normal parts of their bodies. We have seen fortunes made by con merchants who wrap women in plastic wrap to 'dissolve' their fat or sell pills that are supposed to find their way to the thighs and banish cellulite. Clever marketers, promising to get rid of this harmless part of most women's bodies, net millions of dollars, with no proof that their products work. By the time nutritionists and obesity specialists publicly point out that such products are a rip-off, the women have paid their money and the merchants have made their millions.

There are still new diets appearing, some just new versions of old ones. We thought we had convinced people that the old low-carbohydrate diets were useless for long-term weight loss, causing the body to cut back its energy expenditure and making exercise difficult. Now a new lot have surfaced to satisfy those wanting a quick weight loss—even if it doesn't last. The new diets *sound* more authentic because they involve discussions of glycaemic index, a valid principle in its correct context. The diets, however, just add to the load of diets designed for short-term effects.

The most profitable area has been the swag of miracle products, most of which are supposed to increase metabolism or mobilise your fat—some even claiming you need do nothing but swallow the magic.

None of these products work to reduce body fat, but some sound plausible and many are sold by highly motivated multi-level marketing sales people. These people have often been 'converted' to the product or company with offers of easy prize-money for selling, and they use well-established selling techniques to part you from your money in search of the elusive magic bullet to fight fat—real or imagined.

We have a dilemma with body fat. At one end of the spectrum, we need to convince women that looking like a rake is not a healthy or sensible aim. At the other end, populations all over the world growing steadily fatter need help to reduce the health problems that accompany excess body fat. Which group should we concentrate on? The answer is that both groups need help, and I don't see that one should negate the other. We need to help those who are genuinely too fat and help the rest to see that they are not.

Some health professionals think that if we continue to emphasise the very real health problems of excess body fat, we will exacerbate the number of women who want to lose weight—even when their body weight is within the normal range. Others see the much greater numbers of those who are genuinely too fat ignoring their excesses, and believe we must address the problem of obesity.

The average Australian gains one gram of body fat a day. That might not sound like a lot, but it adds up to a substantial national girth, and repair of the damage is a major drain on the nation's health budget. Almost every country in the world is experiencing increases in the number of people who are too fat.

Our main hope lies in prevention. Governments are looking in this direction and there is now a world task force to deal with problems of obesity.

At some stage, someone must be prepared to take part of the blame for fatness. Authors of some diet books blame the liver; others blame wrong food combinations. There is ample evidence that these are not the true culprits, although the psychological boost to individuals in having something else to blame has sold many books espousing these causes.

The real blame must lie with our society, which searches for a 'cure' for obesity yet continues to endorse more foods being produced than could possibly be consumed unless we expand our bodies, and lauds every new labour saving device. We produce foods with lots of kilojoules and inventions that use up fewer kilojoules. We have even dispensed with handles to wind down car windows in favour of energy-saving buttons! Roads are built without footpaths and bicycle paths must give way to cars. Many buildings no longer have accessible stairs and even public transport—which requires some walking to access—is becoming so expensive that its use is declining. Until our society decides to make some strong recommendations about food and

PREFACE

physical activity, widespread success in fat loss will continue to elude us. A motivated individual, however, can take action.

My aim in writing this second edition of *The Diet Dilemma* is to give information about problems associated with excess weight, including the concerns of those who try to treat what they don't have, and to advise against useless diets and weight loss products. I also want to let readers know of the sensible approaches that are available.

There is no easy way for the overweight to lose excess body fat. Anyone who has been fat has a high chance of returning to their previous state. Whether this is because the fat cells sit waiting to fill up again at the first overfill of kilojoules, or whether it signifies an inherited set point, is not yet known. But the evidence points to both genetic and environmental factors.

We cannot change our genes, but we can change the food and exercise environments in which we live. Few studies have looked at long-term success with weight loss. However, in the United States, there is now a National Weight Control Registry. A survey of those listed who have lost more than 30 kilograms and maintained that loss for at least 5 years, found that their secret was to keep to a moderate kilojoule intake and a relatively low fat intake, with fat averaging 24 per cent of daily kilojoules. There is no evidence of magic—success comes through a moderate approach. It's not popular, but it is the only way.

I hope this book makes it easier to see the futility of weight loss gimmicks and crazy diets. There is no Fairy Godmother to wave a magic wand and melt fat. I have no 'cure', but I hope I can enthuse the reader to see how body fat accumulates and why so many methods of getting rid of it fail.

The only way is to learn to like yourself, whatever weight you may be, and then to look after the body you like by moving more, enjoying exercise and balancing delicious and nourishing foods.

Rosemary Stanton

For all who fear they are too fat
and are not
and for those who genuinely are
and have not known what to do about it

1

The great diet hoax continues

THE GREAT DIET HOAX HAS TWO parts. The first is the idea that some diet or diet product will magically melt away fat. The second concerns the idea, held by most women, that normal body fat deposits on particular parts of women's bodies are abnormal or unhealthy. Both ideas give rise to the sale of countless diet books, articles and products that make a mint for their purveyors, and have very little positive effect on anyone else. Their very presence in such numbers also makes a mockery of the real problems associated with genuine obesity.

A GULLIBLE PUBLIC

In spite of all that has been said about the uselessness of different diets and weight loss pills, powders and potions, hundreds of these products continue to sell to gullible people. Some products seem sillier than others, but commonsense seems to go out the window as people desperate to lose weight give the latest method a try. Claims that some pill or powder is *the* easy, fast or healthy way to lose weight means that every new product catches more than its fair share of would-be slimmers.

Over the past few years, the 'quack' slimming market has expanded with many multi-level marketing companies advertising their wares on the Internet and daytime television programs. Many people believe that if there was anything wrong with these products, someone would stop them being peddled by persuasive people. The reality is that people pay to appear on some daytime television programs, and anyone with a product that won't actually poison you can have it listed under the Therapeutic Goods Act (or the Dietary Health and Supplements Act for products being sold from the United States). Such a listing does *not* mean that the product works, and products are not tested before being listed. It is always a case of buyer beware.

The number of overweight and obese people is expanding in both sexes and at all ages. Sales of diet products and programs are also increasing. You might think that the penny would drop and people might realise that the products don't work. But hope springs eternal in the overweight breast and the continued sales of diet products is a testimony to the sales tactics employed by many in the slimming industry.

I don't mean to imply that there are not some genuine people trying to help others. I have written this book so that we can look at diets and diet products to see where hope might lie. Overwhelmingly, however, the slimming industry perpetuates the enormous hoax that it is easy to lose weight by 'taking' something.

With diet pills, powders and product ranges, the choices have expanded. Many no longer concentrate just on slimming. They also offer HEALTH!!! The accompanying hype is horrible and you can generally assume an inverse relationship between facts and upper case lettering and exclamation marks.

The health angle is also profitable because you can sell more products. Lose weight and get healthy sounds good, until you realise that many of these programs hardly mention food and good healthy eating. The 'health' comes from pills. These are usually expensive and if you query why they cost so much, you will usually get a response along the lines of 'surely your health is worth it'. Health is probably our most important asset, but you get it from good genes, good food, exercise, sleep, relaxation and adequate resources for clean water and shelter. You can't buy health in pills or potions.

In reading some of the diet material, you can even get tired eyebrows from the amazement, the continuing outbursts of wonder. If you removed the repetition, the capital letters and the exclamation marks, and cut down the margins a bit, many of the diet books could be reduced to very slim volumes. The brochures that go with many so-called weight loss products would also lose their bulk.

Many of the old diets are still around, and it is likely that between the writing and printing of this book, some will undergo a revival, often sprouting a new name in the process. But the principles of the old diets don't disappear, although some have faded a little.

THE 'NEED' FOR THE NEW

Every year, we get new diets and new diet products. The diets tend to come in cycles. Years ago, we had the low-carbohydrate/

high-protein/high-fat offerings such as Dr Atkins' Diet Revolution. These were gradually replaced by much healthier diets with high carbohydrate, moderate protein and low fat levels such as the Pritikin Program or the moderate GutBuster program. Dietitians and health department campaigns also promote this more moderate approach.

The latest diet books such as *The Zone* and *Sugar Busters!* are back to low carbohydrate eating once more, probably because so many people are unhappy with the slower weight loss from the more sensible programs. They have a new twist, of course, and now invoke the perfectly valid principles of low glycaemic index (GI). However, the diet books extend the GI concept way beyond the proof and into more fanciful areas.

Few people look beyond the first weeks and the glowing testimonials from people who claim to have lost kilos in a few weeks with a low-carbohydrate diet. In fact, the joy of the initial weight loss with these diets turns to sadness as the lost kilos return, usually with some bonus body fat. How quickly we forget that these old low-carbohydrate diets were discredited because of their poor long-term prognosis.

There is also a trend towards diets that claim to cleanse you. The notion that we are dirty or that our livers need to be cleansed appeals to many people who feel that fat is evil. Such diets can also make you feel that you are not to blame for your excess weight. Their message is that you are only overweight because your liver hasn't been working well. If only it were so simple. This too is a hoax, as we discuss later.

There are also many 'food combining' diets, most of which actually promote food 'separating' rather than food combining. Again, the implication is that fat only accumulates because people don't combine their foods correctly. Scientifically, this is nonsense and the authors of such concepts appear to disregard (or perhaps are unaware of) how the process of digestion occurs. Since we are mostly taught little about such things, that is not surprising, but those who write in this vein, claiming to be 'experts', should check some basic facts.

You might think we would have woken up to the fact that diets don't work, but the constant stream of diet books, advertisements for pills and powders and diet success stories in magazines and on the Internet keeps people coming back for more.

PROFITABILITY

The diet merchants promise that your waistline will shrink and your smile will expand if only you follow their advice. It's a cruel and expensive hoax. The main people smiling are the successful sellers of these products as they see their bank balances growing.

Dr Joe Proeitto noted recently in the Australian Association for the Study of Obesity (ASSO) newsletter that the initial Australian shipment of 50 000 boxes of a product called Cellasene sold within the first hour of release. The price was $59/box, so the income from this was a staggering $2 950 000. A second shipment of 40 000 boxes sold almost as fast, netting a further $2 360 000. The Australian distributor of Cellasene told Dr Proeitto that in the USA, 11 million boxes were sold in the first three weeks. At US$40/box, this meant a staggering US$440 million dollars. When you consider there is no proof that this product works, such trust and sales are staggering.

HOW EXPERT ARE THE EXPERTS?

To show how easy it is to acquire 'expert qualifications', a few years ago I collected an order form published in a health food journal to join the American Association of Nutrition Consultants (AANC). I filled in the form in the name of 'Samantha Stanton' and sent it off with the required payment in US dollars. Back came a certificate beautifully inscribed with Samantha's name, announcing she was now a professional member of AANC. Her personal AANC member package included rental car discount coupons and preferred traveller cards for three different US car rental companies, offers of discounts in over 1200 motels and hotels in the USA and information on laboratory tests for hair analysis and other nutritional tests. Had the AANC done even a cursory check on their new member, they would have discovered that Samantha Stanton was our old English sheepdog, now deceased. So always check out great-sounding qualifications.

BODY IMAGE

Most women have been convinced that their bodies need changing in some way—this is the basis for selling aspiration, diets and supposed weight loss products. Whether objective measurements define women as overweight or not makes little difference to most women's desire to lose weight. Women of normal weight want to lose some weight as much as women who are genuinely overweight. Even many underweight women want to be a bit thinner. Some whose bodies would be described as scrawny, if they were farm animals, see themselves as having 'ugly' fat.

Almost every woman now believes that normal female fat deposits on the thighs are abnormal and need to be 'fixed'. In fact, fat on the female thighs is remarkably stable and safe. Unlike fat around the waist, which *is* a health hazard, thigh fat does not cause any health problems, except the emotional ones induced by the promotion of the idea that all women should have the thin or taut thighs seen only on men or children. The same female hormones that put fat on female breasts encourage its deposition on thighs. This is discussed further in Chapter 2.

There is also a tyranny of youth that says men and women should stay young, slender and firm-fleshed whatever their age. Once upon a time, when women reached their 50s, they were acceptable with a few extra kilos. Now women want to wear tight jeans no matter what their age. The Weight Watchers organisation has found their most successful promotions have been based on 'jeans' promotions, and many of their members say that the greatest bonus of reaching their goal weight is being able to wear jeans. You might imagine that greater energy, reduced risk of cardiovascular disease or diabetes, or the lower chance of developing certain cancers, would be uppermost in their joy, but being able to wear jeans overtakes them all. I do not mean to imply that people shouldn't wear jeans or that feeling happy you can fit into jeans is not important—it is the priority such matters are given that seems skewed.

We should be concerned by the health implications for those whose body fat levels are genuinely excessive because there are very real and increasing health problems due to obesity. We should also note that the average Australian is gaining a gram a day, putting more people into the high risk categories of excess body weight than ever before.

But there is a middle position between trying to look as though you are still 20 years old when your real age is 40, 50 or 60, and accumulating a true excess of body fat that increases risk of health problems. Some body fat is normal, only a true excess is a problem. Those whose body fat levels are within the normal range gain little except misery by constantly being told they need some diet or weight loss product. They don't. Only those whose body fat levels are truly too high need to be concerned about this. Even among the poorest nations on earth, where many people die of starvation, many of those who have enough food are becoming obese. These are real problems and they are not helped by the silly idea that we should all look like rakes, or spend our lives trying to lose a couple of kilos.

As we discuss in Chapter 2, the health risks associated with excess weight are non-existent until the excess is considerable. Even then, not all overweight people suffer from any weight-related health problems. The real problem is that we have a majority of the female

THE DIET DILEMMA

population from age 10 to 80 who now believe that whatever their size, it is wrong. This attitude may be good for business in selling diet/weight/slimming products, but it leads many women to hate their bodies and experience guilt feelings every time they eat. Once this occurs, the chances of looking after the body are slim. As Dr Rick Kausman so ably says in his book *If Not Dieting, Then What?* 'it is healthy to be the most comfortable weight we can be, but we also need to be as accepting of ourselves as possible'. If I had my way, all women would be given a copy of the book *Real Gorgeous* by Kaz Cooke. At least we could then laugh at the way women's minds are being manipulated to get them to buy particular products to 'fix' their 'problems'.

The media does not help women's body image with images of supposed perfection. Almost without exception, the bodies we see in advertisements are impossible for the average woman. Indeed, many of the looks are only attainable after considerable efforts by a team of people. One of my favourite quotes was attributed to supermodel Cindy Crawford, who is reputed to have said that 'even she doesn't look like Cindy Crawford when she gets up in the morning'.

Not content with having women disenchanted with their bodies, men are now being targeted by the media, with youthful muscular images of what is considered desirable. At least the image portrayed for men does not rely on them trying to shrink their bodies, as occurs with women. And many men are still able to dismiss images of trim, taut, terrific looking young males with the disparaging comment that 'they're all just kids'. Women's self-esteem has taken a bashing for too long to be able to adopt such a healthy attitude.

Some magazine editors maintain that an image of perfection is 'aspirational' for women. From my perspective, images women know they will never be able to achieve plunge many into an endless round of diets and despondency. Just as the woman of average 165 cm height can't rise to the 185 cm height of many models, neither can most women achieve the long slender look that fashion designers desire.

It would be good if women would use the same criteria to think about their body size as they apply to their feet. If a woman has large feet, she walks into a shoe shop and asks for shoes in a large size. If her feet are wide, she acknowledges this and gets a wide fitting. Everyone accepts that you can't change your feet, so we learn to live with the feet our genes have dictated. In our society there is no stigma attached to the size of your feet, and people generally accept that their feet are big or small, narrow or wide. No one foot is considered to be the standard by which all others are judged.

With bodies, however, we are encouraged not to accept the role that genes play in determining our basic body shape and the size of our hips, thighs or buttocks. It's true that you can overlay what nature provides with extra fat, but even that is governed to some extent by genetics. Ignoring nature can lead to constant unhappiness.

Many people believe that societies which try to control the size of women's bodies basically want to control women. Our society says women should try to be smaller whereas for men the opposite applies. Until recently, most men who did not fit the stereotype ignored it (many did not even know what it was), but there is evidence that many teenage boys are now developing the same kind of problems as teenage girls with self-esteem, because they do not fit the image of the models used in advertising. At least men used in advertisements still come in a greater range of ages than is the case for women. But marketing experts are now trying to create new markets by making men feel inadequate too. Once you have someone in this position, they are willing to buy a range of products to 'improve' themselves. For the dieting/health merchants, the marketing potential is huge, with different products being sold to men and women. One Australian powdered drink mix called 'Huge', sold at high price to men, is unlikely to sell to many women.

Few women can achieve the slenderness of the average model. Many of the models also cannot achieve the desired look without dangerous behaviours such as not eating or throwing up after eating. Many feel guilty if they eat a normal meal, knowing that some modelling agencies want women who are at least 175 cm tall and preferably not more than 50 kilograms in weight. Any woman who achieves such dimensions will no longer menstruate and cannot be considered normal. Models and modelling agencies would help all women if they looked for women of more normal dimensions. Some are starting to do so, but most still opt for impossible body shapes.

The answers to these problems are not simple. And most diet books and diet products do not even begin to address the real issues. Some do, however, and these are discussed in this book, along with the rubbish that deserves to be discarded.

WHY SO MANY DIETS AND DIET PRODUCTS?

Anyone who is tempted to pay for yet another diet or diet product should ask themselves why there are so many of them. There has been a steady stream of diet books for years and there is now a flood of fat metabolisers, slimming powders and other supplements supposed to get rid of excess fat easily and quickly. If any of them worked, why would scientists all over the world still be struggling to find an answer to the growing number of medical problems related to obesity?

In spite of the obvious fact that the thousands of dieting products don't work and most diets are a waste of time, when magazines include a diet they are almost guaranteed to sell their entire print run, bookshops list diet books among their best-sellers and many people are making millions from selling supplements. Everyone wants to try the latest diet or product just in case, this time, someone may have found a magic formula.

All the diets and diet products have one thing in common—they promise you it will be easy. And that little promise guarantees them successful sales. Everyone wants to lose their excess flab without having to make the effort to change the habits and accept the genetic factors that put it there in the first place.

Even when a diet or product fails, most overweight people try another. One woman told me she had spent in excess of $20 000 looking for an easy way to lose weight. Eventually she bought a small book for $3.95 which listed the fat and fibre contents of foods. She filled up on high-fibre foods instead of eating too many fatty foods and lost 110 kilograms. It took her two years, which is what you would expect, but she ate normal foods and stopped looking for a miracle which money couldn't buy.

The worst aspect of failed dieting efforts is that most people blame themselves for what they perceive as their failure. It doesn't occur to them that there might have been something wrong with the method they had been sold. Some also feel stupid for having been so gullible and don't take action because they don't want their foolishness made evident. A lack of self-esteem and self-confidence also prevents many people acknowledging they have been ripped off.

Diets and dieting products are among the greatest and cruellest hoaxes ever foisted on consumers. Even those that promise a money-back guarantee can be fairly sure they will never be called on to repay anything. Most people who try the diet, read the literature or pay huge sums for pills or other products and then find the product does not live up to its promises, are too embarrassed to complain. Besides, they think there must have been some fault in the way they followed (or failed to follow) the program. After all, the brochures and Internet sites listed heaps of comments from supposedly satisfied customers, so if it didn't work for them, it must have been their own fault. Right? Wrong. The testimonials from Mrs LM from Townsville or Amy B from Sydney, claiming their lives had been changed by some diet or pill, so they are 'now having difficulty coping with the admiring looks from males', are worth nothing. Do you really think these people exist? If they are real people, they are usually involved in selling or promoting the product.

For women who are genuinely overweight, their past failure to lose weight with a variety of diets often makes them believe they have some problem with their metabolism. Few overweight women have the confidence to blame the diet instead of blaming themselves.

People do lose weight if they eat less and exercise more, and these are the real reasons why some slimmers succeed. Groups such as Weight Watchers acknowledge that their success stories—who always get full names, not just initials—have found a new way to enjoy good food and to increase their level of exercise. But this is the exception rather than the rule. Most of those selling pills and potions claim their product is the reason for any successes. 'Lose weight while you sleep' says the brochure for one collagen hydrolysate product. The fine print says you must also avoid food for three hours before going to bed, but still some users are convinced the product they have paid for dearly works some magic on their metabolism once they hit the pillow.

How gullible we are! And there's precious little protection for consumers from these products. You can (and should) make a complaint about misleading information to the Australian Competition and Consumer Commission (ACCC) but it's a long drawn-out process. Persistence can bring rewards, however, as occurred when consumers were refunded their money after taking action against Swiss Slimming Clinic, a company which charged them thousands of dollars for a useless body wrap program.

With more than 34 years' experience as a dietitian, it never ceases to amaze me how even those who have tried everything still believe that somewhere there is a magic wand that will work for them. The purveyors of diets have conned a whole generation of people into believing there is some easy way to lose weight, and all you have to do for success is find the method. Many are now hopeful that some new drug will make it all happen.

There is no magic wand. There is no instant cure. And there is no secret formula. Sure, many products do bring an initial flush of success and as we discuss in Chapter 2, there is no great mystery about the first rapid loss of weight that most popular diets can achieve. Nor is there any great mystery about why the first flush of success is almost always followed by a return of the lost weight. There are simple biochemical explanations for such phenomena.

We are caught in a bind. On the one hand, we have a rapidly expanding food industry producing 'goodies', all vying for a space in our finite stomachs. On the other hand, our society is obsessed with slimness, especially in women. So we have the push to get us to eat more and the pull of the promise of exciting possibilities for those who remain slender in the face of such abundance.

We respond by buying more and more food in response to effective persuasion by promotions and advertisements. And the foods that command the biggest advertising budgets are often those that contain the most padding in the form of cheap ingredients such as fats, sugars and artificial additives, and the least fibre and real food ingredients. This keeps manufacturers happy as it increases profits and reduces the bulk consumers need to eat.

We live in what has been called a toxic food environment. According to an article in the *New York Times*, three new McDonald's outlets are opened every day and the company aims to have every American within 4 minutes drive of one of its restaurants. Fast food outlets continue to proliferate in Australia, most selling foods that are high in fat and low in fibre. These products are now available in some hospitals in Australia, at many airports, in shopping centres and service stations, so that few people are ever more than a short distance from them.

Unfortunately, too much of such foods almost inevitably leads to an increased intake of kilojoules—and extra deposits of body fat. This then opens up a wonderful world to the diet merchants. Those who sell supplements, fat metabolisers, meal replacement products, herbal mixtures, slimming pills and formulas, books, magazines or machines to pummel masses of excess flesh, can make millions. And the more you convince your market that your latest weight loss method is fast and easy, the more money you stand to make. Many products also promote healthy-sounding concepts such as building lean tissue or providing energy, and supply extra amino acids, antioxidants or some other normal component of foods with the idea that their product will normalise the body so weight loss becomes easier. Most such concepts are based on one of two false premises: either that we can't get the necessary components from food, or that taking extra will be of some benefit. With compounds such as amino acids, for example, there is no way that supplying a small quantity in a pill is either necessary or useful. Amino acids are the building blocks of proteins and are more than amply supplied in the average diet.

Perhaps the real reason why there are so many diets and diet products, and why so many people are so easily conned, stems from our desire for instant gratification. Our society promotes the idea that we can and should have everything we want. Either through good luck, happy choice of parents or sheer hard work, some people *are* able to have whatever they want in life. Similarly, when it comes to food, some people have the right kind of metabolism or genes or active lifestyle or preference for healthy foods that enables them to eat their fill without gaining a gram. Others spend their lives being happy just to have what they need and some of the things they want, whether it be material possessions or food.

But some people like eating more food than their bodies need, or they prefer the kinds of foods that are dense with kilojoules even though their bodies or lifestyles do not need such excess. Just as we can blame our parents if we don't have the nose or eyes or height we would like, so genetics play a role in how much weight we will gain from a given amount of food. Increasingly, however, we are urged to eat types and quantities of foods that do not match the modern body's needs. The answer to such problems is not to look for a miracle, but to learn what your body needs and then match your intake to those needs. You may be able to increase the amount you eat by raising your level of physical activity, but it may be that you are not able to eat as much as someone who can stay slim without making a conscious effort to do so. That is no different from most other aspects of life.

Excess weight does not appear overnight and it will never disappear that way either. There is no magic wand and no product to melt away fat or mysteriously build muscle. But our first task is to consider what is too fat and what is not.

2

Why lose weight?

WHO IS TOO FAT?

We have no absolute proof, but most experts believe that our ancestors were not over-fat. Throughout most of recorded history, few people have been too fat. When humans have to carry water, cut their own timber, catch, grow or gather their own food and generally live without labour-saving devices, they do not become fat. Excess body fat is a by-product of urbanisation, mechanisation, a sedentary lifestyle and abundant high-kilojoule foods.

There have been some exceptions, and in some societies fat was considered so beautiful that certain members of the community—often the ruler or young women—sat around and were brought large quantities of food, and did become fat. In more recent times, being fat provided an obvious distinction between the working classes (who were thin) and the upper classes (who could afford not to do physical work and to purchase more rich food and so were more corpulent).

Until the 1970s, it was also considered normal for women to be fatter than is thought to be desirable today. This was not a problem, but today the standards of thinness promoted by the fashion, film and television industries, and also by many sections of the fitness movement, are unrealistic, unattainable for most women and often unhealthy. You only have to look at the size of women in movies to note the changing depiction of desirable body size. What some people now consider 'fat' was previously described as 'pleasantly plump'.

In spite of the perceived desirability of being very thin, the average woman, like the average man, continues to grow fatter. This recent phenomenon has accompanied the gradual reduction of physical activity and the increase in ready-made and packaged foods which are easy to

WHY LOSE WEIGHT?

eat. Greater affluence also means that foods once consumed only as special treats are now a regular part of most people's daily diet.

Overweight or obese Australians

Age group (years)	% of males	% of females
9–11	20	26
12–15	28	18
16–18	22	20
19–24	38	26
25–44	62	39
45–64	76	61
65 and over	67	59
19 + (overall)	64	47

These figures are based on the body mass index (BMI), described below, and show that excess weight is a major problem. At the same time, it is important to note that 5.4 per cent of 19–24 year-old females are underweight (BMI less than 18.4) and another 15 per cent have a very low body weight (BMI 18.5–19.9), a level that presents a high risk for future development of osteoporosis. Whenever we talk of the need for weight loss, it is important to remember that we are not talking about an open-ended loss, and it is not relevant for the entire population.

The problem of increasing numbers of people who are overweight or obese is becoming apparent in most countries throughout the world. In many developed countries, there is more obesity among those of lower socioeconomic status and among rural people. The opposite occurs in developing countries, where being overweight is more common among the more affluent and urban members of the population.

The highest incidence of excess weight and obesity occurs in the United States. Unlike Australia, where more men than women are overweight, the United States has more overweight women than men. There is much less obesity in developing countries, but the incidence is climbing rapidly. Less than 1 per cent of people in the Philippines are obese, but more than 10 per cent of those in Chile and over 6 per cent of those measured in 11 major Chinese cities are rated as being too fat. As living standards in poorer countries increase, so does obesity. Some may consider this is a worthwhile price to pay for greater affluence, but better living conditions without obesity are also possible.

BODY MASS INDEX

Life insurance companies realised long ago that there was a relationship between weight and longevity. Fat people died earlier and cost them money. These companies therefore examined the health risks associated with particular weights and heights and came up with tables of ideal weights for particular heights for men and women of various ages which were used to calculate insurance premiums.

As statistical methods have improved, weight for height tables have changed. Most experts now consider there is a range of weight associated with the lowest health risks for any given height, rather than one specific weight. The healthy weight range takes account of different frame sizes so that someone measuring, say, 170 cm will have the lowest risk of ill-health if they weigh between 58 and 72 kg. Those with a small frame may feel more comfortable at the lower end of the healthy weight range while people with larger frames may fit more easily at the upper end. However, it is sometimes difficult to estimate frame size and many an overweight person has discovered a much smaller frame than they had imagined, once they have lost some of their excess fat!

The limits for the healthy weight range are estimated from the Body Mass Index (BMI). You can work this out by dividing your weight in kilograms by the square of your height (in metres).

Medical research shows that a BMI between 20 and 25 is associated with the lowest risk of weight-related health problems. (Some people maintain that an acceptable BMI is 18.5–25 while others who are concerned about the higher risk of osteoporosis in thin people, especially women, believe a BMI of 18.5 is hazardous.) The BMI is only a rough guide but it is some help in establishing an appropriate weight and is useful in developing ranges appropriate for the population. Many young women who consider themselves overweight are not even heavy enough to reach the healthy weight range, and some would like to be lighter still! As we have discussed earlier, many women are poor judges of their own body weight status. However, over the past few years, the burden of excess weight carried by a large percentage of the population in many countries has become a problem for an even greater number of people.

The recent National Nutrition Survey in Australia reported that over 20 per cent of women are underweight, if judged by a BMI less than 20. The same survey also showed an increase in the percentage of both men and women with a BMI above 25. With 64 per cent of men and 47 per cent of women having a BMI greater than 25, we need to be concerned about both ends of the healthy weight range—those who are too heavy, as well as those who are too light. Of the two groups, most health authorities consider the greater number of people who are overweight to be the more urgent problem.

The BMI is usually applicable to those over the age of 18. However, recent research has shown that it may also have some validity for teenagers who are still growing (see Chapter 12 for

WHY LOSE WEIGHT?

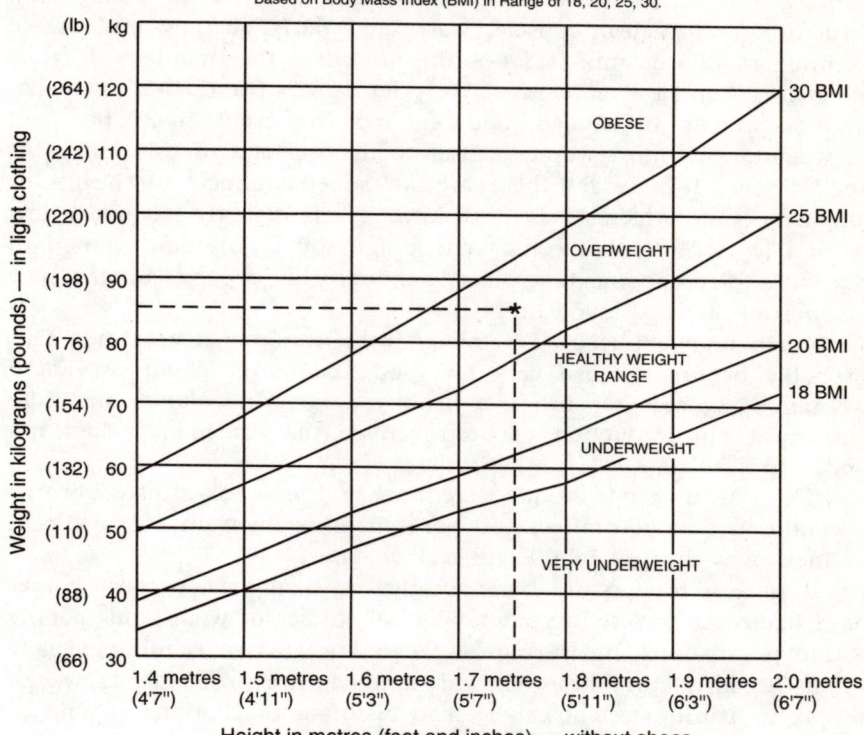

Reproduced with the permission of the Australian Nutrition Foundation Inc.

information relating to overweight children). Normal BMI standards are not appropriate for people with a large amount of muscle, such as body builders or elite sports people, because the weight of their high muscle content may give a BMI above the healthy weight range, even though their level of body fat is low.

Overweight or obese?

There is some confusion about these terms because people in different countries have used different standards to define them. They are now becoming standardised to consider that people are overweight if their BMI is between 25 and 29 and obese if they have a BMI greater than 30. A BMI greater than 35 is sometimes referred to as 'morbid obesity' because of the great increase in health problems associated with it. This book mostly uses the generic term 'overweight'.

WEIGHT VERSUS FAT

Most people talk of 'weight', but weight consists of bone, skin, structural tissues, lean muscle, water and fat. The only undesirable component of this mix is fat—and *only* when the quantity of fat is excessive. Among men, normal body fat ranges from 10–15 per cent of total weight. In women, body fat may represent 20–30 per cent of weight, with most women closer to the top end of this range. At such levels of body fat there are no adverse effects on health or longevity. Elite athletes may have lower levels of body fat, and a low natural level of body fat may encourage some girls and women to become athletes in the first place, although this depends on the type of sporting activity involved.

When body fat levels fall, many women stop menstruating. This probably occurs because very low body fat stores could prevent a woman being able to sustain a healthy pregnancy. Nature therefore cuts back on production of oestrogen so that pregnancy does not occur.

Those with very low body weight are at a high risk of osteoporosis, a condition that now affects 60 per cent of women and 29 per cent of men over the age of 60 (Australian data).

It is easy to measure body weight, especially when most homes have bathroom scales. In epidemiological studies of what is happening within populations, measuring height and weight is useful, especially when the BMI correlates well with many health problems. However, simply measuring weight can lead to distorted perceptions of gain or loss for many individuals.

Scales

Scales are useless for giving an accurate day-to-day measure since they show changes in water and muscle as well as fat. Over the course of any one day, weight fluctuates by as much as a couple of kilograms, depending mostly on fluid balance. It is therefore worse than useless to weigh yourself every day, as you may assume these normal fluctuations have some correlation with body fat levels. Even overnight, the body's fluid levels can easily change by a kilogram. To test this, weigh yourself when you go to bed and again first thing in the morning. The morning weight is usually less than the evening weight because you have been breathing out water vapour and sweating (even if it's not obvious). Fat loss overnight is minimal.

If you must weigh yourself, do it no more than once a week, at the same time of day, preferably without clothes. Make a note of your weight and you may detect a pattern after a few weeks.

Try to resist the urge to weigh yourself every day, or, worse still, several times a day. Most people who do this follow one of two courses of action. They weigh themselves, see there has been a loss and feel so good they reward themselves with some food or drinks as a 'treat'. Any sudden drop in weight will almost certainly be due to changes in fluid so the celebration is likely to be premature. Others step on the scales, see no change and feel so despondent that they decide they may as well drown their sorrows—again, in food and/or drink. It may be that the person has gained some muscle from exercising (muscle weighs more than fat) or has a temporary increase in fluid after drinking a cup of coffee and the fact that the scales have not altered has no bearing on what is happening to their body fat. Eventually a fat loss will show up on the scales, but it won't be apparent over a short time interval.

Tape measure

Probably the best way for many people to measure success is to use a tape measure round the waist. Or judge by your belt. The most dangerous place to store fat is around the waist and on the upper body. It is also the easiest place from which to lose fat. Whether it is better to measure the ratio of waist to hip, or to go just by waist measurement is still not clear, but there is evidence that a waist measurement greater than 90 centimetres for a woman or 100 centimetres for a man is a risk factor for health problems.

Clothes fit

One of the best ways to determine if you are losing body fat is to judge by the fit of your clothes. As you lose fat, your clothes become too big. This can happen even without a loss of weight—for example, if you are losing fat but gaining muscle. As muscle is denser than fat, it weighs more but takes up less space.

The naked eye

Theoretically, one of the best ways to determine whether you are too fat is to take an honest look at your body. In practice, however, most women find fault with their bodies, no matter what they look like. It is, however, a good method for a trained person to use with overweight children. A child who is too fat looks too fat.

Height-weight charts

These have been superseded by the healthy weight range charts using BMI.

The pinch test

Inaccurate as it is, using your thumb and forefinger to pinch a fold of skin from your back just below the shoulder bone gives some idea of fatness. The fold should be less than 2.5 cm in thickness.

Skinfold measurements

Many gyms and fitness centres use callipers to measure skinfold thickness at various sites in the body and then calculate body fat from their measurements. It takes considerable expertise to use skinfold callipers accurately, and more than 100 equations have been produced to predict body fatness from skinfold measurements. All are inaccurate, and you should ignore anyone who claims otherwise.

Other methods

It is difficult to measure body fat easily and accurately, even under laboratory conditions. Underwater weighing (also known as densitometry) is usually regarded as the best method, but is not completely accurate. You can also buy scales that measure the resistance to a flow of current through the body in a technique known as bioelectrical impedance, giving a body fat reading. Their makers claim they are accurate.

In laboratories or hospitals, ultrasonic technology (computed tomography or CT scans) can be used to measure the thickness of fat and muscle at particular places in the body.

Why measure body fat?

For elite athletes who may need maximum lean body mass for their height and weight, measuring the proportion of the body that is fat may have relevance. For the rest of the population, it is almost certainly less relevant and sophisticated methods of measuring fat content have not solved the problem of deciding what are appropriate levels of body fat. Some gyms and fitness centres also measure body fat levels to show how well clients are progressing. Under such circumstances, you need to be sure that their methods of determining body fat are sufficiently accurate.

BODY SHAPE

There is a great variation between what constitutes excess weight and different people's perceptions of it. Much of the variation is due to cultural norms and fashion. Some cultures expect women to retain their prepubescent boyish figures whereas others prize body fat on women. For example, among the Tuareg tribe in Africa, a fat woman is greatly admired and young women are fed vast quantities of milk so they will become an acceptable size for marriage!

Whenever I mention this to Australian women, they want to know where this Nirvana is! To give up the battle of the bulge—which may or may not exist—seems like heaven to many women who are obsessed with the tyranny of slenderness. The absurdity is that many women who are striving to weigh less in western societies are not overweight by any objective criteria. They simply believe that whatever size they are, they should be thinner. Wallis Simpson is reputed to have said, 'a woman cannot be too rich or too thin.' I have no expertise on the joys or hazards of being too rich, but there is a growing body of medical evidence concerning the hazards of women becoming very thin. Extremes of weight in either direction cause health problems. Most women, however, are less interested in the hazards of extremes of weight and concerned only with the appearance of fat. We all need some fat. It gives us padding, protects vital organs, and produces shape in the body which most previous generations have found attractive.

Even in the 1950s and 1960s, women who were considered normal had more fat than is fashionable today. Watch some old movies and note how well-rounded the screen goddesses of the day were. Swimmers and athletes from 20 to 30 years ago would have been banned by some modern sports coaches. And a study of the entrants in Miss World contests and other beauty pageants showed they have been getting taller and lighter every year.

In stark contrast with the images portrayed as 'perfect', the average woman in western countries is much bigger, both in height and weight, than in earlier generations. The sizes in women's clothes have altered from previous standards so that a size 10 garment is now made to the measurements once considered as size 12. The clothes are still labelled as size 10 because manufacturers know that most women are influenced to buy clothes that appear to be as small a size as possible. Some women will even buy a garment not because they especially like it, but because they can fit into something marked as a size smaller than what they usually wear!

It all sounds ridiculous. But women are faced with models of perfection that few can achieve. For some it is not the amount of fat they carry which worries them, but the number on the scales. A low figure reassures them they are all right. Even some slim women are only happy if they feel they are losing weight.

In modern western society, the ideal female body has more fat on the breasts and less on hips and thighs. This has probably been idealised because it is an unusual shape for women, most of whom have more fat on the lower body—hips, thighs and buttocks. Anything uncommon is considered desirable—in many aspects of life we prize what is rare. In most areas of life, however, we do not damn the normal and convince its owner of its inferiority.

The media cannot escape responsibility for the obsession about body shape. The slender models with their trim, taut buttocks and thighs may be only fourteen or fifteen, although their age is rarely mentioned. Neither is the fact that some of them are unhealthily thin. Boyish figures are in vogue, and those who don't have them naturally are expected to diet to achieve this 'look'.

The full-bodied female form has always been associated with fertility. There is a biological basis for this, since very thin women have lower oestrogen levels and will not ovulate regularly. This becomes apparent in the very low birth rates in countries where women are thin and malnourished because of famine.

It might also help women to talk to farmers. If their animals were in the same condition that many women strive for, they would be worth little and the farmer would be considered neglectful of their welfare.

Some psychologists hold the view that in times when women are striving to show equality with men, fashion demands that they become thin. This reduces their fertility and gives them a greater ability to compete with men in the workplace (since they do not have to take time off to have babies). Whether this is correct or not is a matter of opinion. However, it is a fact that the images of women now portrayed as 'normal' do not fit reality. Some 95 per cent of women on television and shown in the print media have body weights below the average. This means we are constantly being given unrealistic role models.

The facts are that women need to carry more body fat than men since they have specific areas where female hormones dictate fat deposition. These include the breasts, tummy, hips, buttocks and thighs. Many people accept that women should have extra fat on the breasts but believe fat in other places is undesirable (see 'Apples and pears' in Chapter 4). A certain amount of fat in each of these areas is under the control of genes and female hormones. There is no physiological need to try to remove it by dieting unless it is excessive—*as judged by objective criteria*.

SPECIAL PROBLEMS FOR WOMEN

Fashion tyrannises women. Whatever size most western women are, they want to be smaller or to alter their basic shape. In summer, when swimming costumes and skimpy clothing reveal more of the body, a rash of diets appears in magazines and weight control organisations do their best business. Women who are overweight strive to do something about it and those who are not overweight think they would look better if they were a little thinner.

My advice to women who feel their bodies are the wrong shape is to surround themselves with prints of the great master painters. Rubens and Renoir and their fellow artists, not to mention Norman Lindsay, never painted women with the boyish figures now considered desirable (but usually unattainable). They preferred fuller figures with well-rounded thighs, tummies and buttocks. Few of these models were overly fat although they may have been in the upper half of the healthy weight range.

From a health point of view, extreme self-induced slimness in women is not only unnecessary, it is a health hazard, just as excess body weight—generally apparent in women when BMI is over 25—can create a health hazard. The major problem of a BMI of 26 is that, without changing the balance between what is consumed and what is used up for metabolism and physical activity, it will almost certainly gradually increase until it reaches a point where the risk of health problems also increases.

For many women who are overweight, being the providers of food can cause problems. For example, many women's magazines place great emphasis on their recipe pages, and a lot of women enjoy reading them. It often seems ironic that a magazine may feature the latest diet for women on one page and recipes for scrumptious-looking cakes on the next. What are women supposed to do? Cook the cakes and feed them to others while they stand and watch?

Many women try these very tactics. Some buy special diet meals for themselves or use expensive packaged foods from some diet centre. At the same time, they are expected to provide more robust meals for the rest of the family. Is it any wonder that women feel resentful and confused?

Many a man with definite weight problems will sit down to a hearty meal prepared by his female partner, while the woman—who is trying desperately to lose weight herself—tries to spread food thinly over her own dinner plate. Such a dichotomy leads many women to 'pick' at foods, to eat leftovers and to surreptitiously 'sneak' various foods. None of these habits leaves women feeling too good about themselves. Nor do they end up achieving any real reduction in kilojoules which would help them lose weight.

Perhaps the only way to deal with such problems is for others in the family to take on some of the responsibility for thinking of what to eat, doing the shopping, cooking and clearing away afterwards. After all, women have taken on many of the roles previously left to the 'breadwinner'. With fewer household responsibilities, women would not be so constantly around food. They might also be able to use some of the extra time which would become available to do some exercise. The importance of exercise is discussed in Chapter 10.

Some men also sabotage the efforts of women who are genuinely overweight and are trying to lose weight. They bring home boxes of chocolates, speak of salads and vegetables as 'rabbit food', demand 'real' food (meaning large quantities of meat or pies) and sulk when women go out to exercise. Only a minority of men may act in this way, but it is almost as though they prefer their woman not to change. There may be some justification for their view, as there are documented reports that there is a high divorce rate among women who were once overweight but gain self-esteem and lose weight.

Cellulite

Cellulite is a term coined in 1973 by the owner of a New York beauty salon that specialised in skin and body care to describe deposits of dimpled fat on the thighs and buttocks of many women. Since then, cellulite has become a household word and millions of dollars have been spent trying to get rid of it.

Contrary to the claims of some selling cellulite 'cures', cellulite is not 'toxic wastes trapped beneath the skin'. Nor is it a problem of poor circulation or failure to eliminate fats or something that can be massaged, pummelled or creamed away. Recent statements that pills will remove cellulite 'from within' are without proof, although that has not stopped amazing sales.

'Cellulite' is not a medical term and doctors state that it is just ordinary fatty tissue. Strands of fibrous tissue connect the skin to deeper tissue layers and also separate compartments that contain fat cells. When fat cells increase in size, these compartments bulge into the underlying skin layer, producing the familiar pattern of dimpling, variously referred to as 'citrus peel', 'quilting', 'waffle' or 'hail-damaged'. Studies show that women have a diffuse pattern of irregular and discontinuous connective tissue just below the skin surface, whereas men have a more continuous, smooth layer of connective tissue.

When specimens of regular fat and cellulite taken using a needle biopsy are given to pathologists for analysis and comparison, they can find no difference between the two. Researchers at Rockefeller University have used ultrasonography, microscopic examinations and fat-metabolism studies to compare cellulite and other skin areas in healthy adult subjects. They have concluded that certain characteristics of their skin make women more prone than men to develop cellulite, but there are no significant differences in the appearance or function of the fatty tissue or the blood flow between affected and unaffected sites within individuals.

'Anti-cellulite' products on sale include loofah sponges, mitts made from cactus fibres or horsehair, creams and gels to 'dissolve' cellulite, liquids to put in your bath, rubberised garments, exercise machines with brushes and rollers, body wraps and toning lotions. Salons offer women treatment with electrical muscle stimulation, vibrating machines, inflatable hip-high pressurised boots, 'hormone' or 'enzyme' injections, heating pads and massage. All such treatments are expensive and there is no evidence that any are effective.

The greatest sales have been for anti-cellulite supplements containing a mixture of ingredients. One of the highest selling products, Cellasene, contains grapeseed bioflavonoids, *Ginkgo biloba*, evening primrose oil, fish oil, dried sweet clover, kelp (*Fucus vesiculosis*) and soy lecithin. Each of these ingredients is discussed more fully in Chapter 5.

The product was developed by an Italian chemist named Gianfranco Merizzi. It is to be taken twice daily (or three times a day for an 'intensive' program) for two months, and then once daily for maintenance. It costs $59 per box and advertising material claims it 'works from within, nutritionally, to help fight cellulite at its source'. This defies logic. There is no way these pills can be taken by mouth and then find their way to a particular area of the body where they might exert an effect, especially since not a single one of their ingredients has any relevance to body fat. Nor is there any good evidence that taken together these ingredients can have any effect on body fat.

The chief executive officer of the company marketing Cellasene claims that three clinical trials sponsored by the company had demonstrated a 90 per cent success rate, but they would not submit their results to scientific journals because they did not want to reveal the amounts of each ingredient in the formula. In fact, if they had results from a properly conducted trial, they would not be obliged to disclose such information—only their methodology and results.

THE WESTERN WOMAN'S OBSESSION

Many surveys from different countries have backed up the female obsession with slimness. A recent study of underweight young Australian women found that 42 per cent wanted to be slimmer still, while 43 per cent were happy with their underweight size. There was no difference between those from different ethnic groups. Other Australian surveys have shown that about three-quarters of women at the lighter end of the healthy weight range want to be lighter still.

THE DIET DILEMMA

> More than 75 per cent of American teenage girls see themselves as overweight, 55 per cent report that they are 'terrified' about being obese, almost half are preoccupied with body weight and nearly 40 per cent are on diets to lose weight—yet one in six of these girls was found to be at least 20 per cent below ideal body weight.
>
> A Canadian study found that girls who thought they were 'just right' were 5 per cent below the Canadian average weight for their age. This study also reported that schoolgirls who thought they were fat were only 3 per cent above the average weight for their age. Another Australian survey found that of the 24 per cent of teenage girls who saw themselves as being too fat, 7 per cent were more than 10 per cent below standard body weight for their age. Almost 9 per cent of these underweight girls were actively trying to lose weight.
>
> The desire to be thinner is not confined to teenagers and young women. Women up to 85 years of age have reported that they would like to be thinner. The majority of thin men, on the other hand, report that they want to be bigger. In spite of our pretence at non-discrimination, most people still believe a man should have some 'size' to him. Women are expected to be small and slender—and, presumably, non-threatening because of it.

SPECIAL PROBLEMS FOR MEN

The discussion so far has assumed that most of the problems about weight lie with women. This is not the case, of course, as men experience problems too.

One of the greatest problems for men is to accept that they are overweight in the first place. Men have more health problems associated with their fat because it occurs around the waist and on the upper body. In Australia, many men and women regard the bulge above the belt as a 'beer gut' and do not recognise it either as fat or as a problem. Some men are rather proud of it! Some even believe that it is not fat, but a swollen stomach resulting from consuming a large volume of liquid. It is *just fat*. It feels solid because the fat cells are stuffed tight with fat.

Some men like to cultivate a large body as a mark of importance, although this attitude is disappearing. Whereas an overweight woman will be regarded as 'having let herself go', an equally overweight man will be seen as a 'big man'. Size used to be regarded as a sign of success—and still is in some communities—but most companies now see corpulent executives as a high risk investment. There is little point in investing a lot of time, effort and money in an executive if his career is likely to be shortened by health problems associated with his size.

It is refreshing, however, that fewer men than women are obsessed about weight (in themselves or in their female partners). Among teenage boys, however, there is a trend to low self-esteem among those who do not have significant muscle development.

The major problem regarding body fat in men and women is this: it can be difficult to get men to accept that they are too fat and it can be difficult to get women to accept that they may not be too fat.

3

Why do people get fat?

EXCESS BODY FAT LEVELS ARE INCREASING in most western societies and also in many developing countries. In most countries the incidence of excess weight rises with age in both men and women. However, the rise tends to occur at an earlier age in men. Recent Australian data shows that 38 per cent of men aged 19–24 are overweight or obese (as defined by Body Mass Index) compared with 26 per cent of women of the same age. By 25–44 years of age, 62 per cent of men and 39 per cent of women are too heavy. The proportion of fat men remains high and at all ages is greater than for women.

The number of children who are overweight is increasing rapidly worldwide, in most western countries, Asia, South America and the Pacific Islands. The fall in physical activity is one obvious cause, but as diet becomes more westernised in many countries, the number of overweight children increases. Excess weight in many children is a comparatively recent phenomenon. In my own schooldays there was usually one fat child in a class—but rarely more than one. In sharp contrast, about one-quarter of school-aged Australian children are now considered too fat.

There are three inter-related factors involved in why people get fat:

- They consume more (in food and drinks) than they need.
- They use up less energy in physical activity.
- They have a number of genes that predispose them to obesity.

OVERCONSUMPTION

Overconsumption may take two forms:

- Eating and drinking a greater quantity than necessary, or

WHY DO PEOPLE GET FAT?

- Eating and drinking foods which are more concentrated in their energy (or kilojoule) levels than necessary.

Greater quantities

On holidays, or at festive times such as Christmas, it is common to eat and drink more than usual. Returning to a normal lifestyle and eating patterns, most people find they gradually lose any excess weight they have gained during their temporary 'stuffing' period. Generally people are aware of such short-term changes in eating patterns and can make appropriate adjustments for them, although some get into the habit of eating until they feel almost uncomfortably full.

More fats and sugars

A much more insidious problem results from the food supply gradually becoming more and more concentrated in kilojoules. Every stomach has a finite capacity and most people feel satisfied when their stomach holds a particular volume of food. However, the normal feeling of satiety can be tricked if the volume of food stays the same but the energy density increases. For example, compare a modern-day fast-food meal of hamburger, French fries and a soft drink with a fillet of grilled fish, steamed potatoes and a serving of vegetables; both meals may appear the same size and be equally satisfying. The fast-food meal, however, may have three times as many kilojoules as the fish and vegetables because it is loaded with fats.

Many modern foods have high levels of fat which are not always apparent. The major difference with many foods is that we do not see the fat so we do not know it is there. For example, who would guess that:

- a croissant has as much fat as 17 slices of bread;
- a fast-food burger has one and a half times as much fat as an old-fashioned burger;
- a typical bowl of some brands of toasted muesli has more fat (and saturated fat, at that) than a fried egg and some bacon; or
- a slice of quiche with salad can have 5–6 times as much fat as a piece of grilled steak and some vegetables.

Adding sugar is another way to increase the energy density of food without changing its volume. A cup of tea with added sugar is no more filling than a cup of tea without added sugar. A can of soft drink with sugar is no more filling than one which is artificially sweetened, but the added sugar in both cases increases the kilojoules substantially. Sugar itself will only be converted to body fat if you consume very large quantities, but sugary foods can easily supply enough kilojoules for the body to prevent it burning the kilojoules from fat. Sugar also makes fat taste nice and so encourages its consumption in cakes, biscuits, pastries, sweets, desserts and chocolates.

Alcohol is not converted to body fat either. The body always burns the kilojoules from alcohol before it burns anything else. But if you keep drinking, you may supply your body with so many kilojoules that it doesn't burn those from fat, converting them instead to body fat.

In western countries, increasing concentration of kilojoules in foods is one of the major causes of excess body fat in people of all ages. We do not necessarily eat *more* than earlier generations, but the *types* of foods and drinks we consume have changed.

Manufacturers of foods high in sugars or fats commonly maintain that their product only contributes 2–3 per cent of the sugar or fat in the average diet. But it all adds up. With many thousands of these concentrated food products available, and most being heavily promoted, weight gain is not surprising.

Processed foods

Although the majority of women now work outside the home, most still shoulder responsibility for the bulk of household tasks, including buying and preparing food. With so much to do and so little time in which to do it, women have gladly accepted a helping hand from a food industry which gives them many ready- or semi-prepared foods. Unfortunately, most of these foods are higher in fat than the foods they would have cooked themselves. Few people are aware of this fact, and most assume that meals consisting of modern foodstuffs have less fat than the old-fashioned meals featuring bacon and egg breakfasts, roast dinners with large serves of meat and dessert, and snacks such as bread and cheese.

Foods are more concentrated for the sake of profit. Manufacturers take a raw material and turn it into what they call a 'value added' product. This often means adding cheap fillers—usually fat and/or sugar—to the basic ingredients. For example, a fillet of fish is 100 per cent fish. By processing the fish into fish fingers, the manufacturer may use only 50 per cent fish and can add 50 per cent of 'added value' in the form of starch mixture and coating, which includes a high percentage of fat. Eating the fish fingers does not give any greater satiety than eating the fish, but the kilojoule value of each 100 grams of fish fingers is more than double that of the original fish. The 'added value' has been for the manufacturer, not the consumer. It is more appropriate to refer to 'added value' as 'padded value'.

Adding a cheap coating, which can soak up fats, to a food gives the greatest increase in the concentration of kilojoules since fats have more than twice as many kilojoules as either carbohydrates or proteins. Although its effects are much less than those of fats, refined sugar also adds concentrated kilojoules, especially in drinks. Manufacturers add 'value' to water by turning it into soft drinks, converting a no-kilojoule liquid into soft drinks with 700 to 800 kilojoules per can. Quenching thirst with soft drinks rather than water can thus provide many extra kilojoules.

For the health-conscious consumer of soft drinks, manufacturers have provided flavoured mineral waters and sports drinks. The former have almost as much sugar as regular soft drinks. Sports drinks have about half the quantity of sugar and are suitable for those engaged in high level or endurance sports, but many are consumed by people sitting at their desks or watching sporting events.

People buy 'value added' products because they are convenient and because advertising encourages us to do so. On the one hand, our society is being exhorted to be slim; on the other, we are exposed to more advertising and promotions for fast foods, snacks, soft drinks and other sources of extra kilojoules than any previous generation. Most women are also burdened with too many tasks and find it difficult to fit all their chores and responsibilities into the limited time available. Many turn to prepared meals instead of cooking at home.

Advertising and affluence have also led us to expect to eat and drink a greater variety of items than any previous generation has indulged in. This could be a good thing—if we exploited the variety of fresh fruits and vegetables, seafoods and low-fat products available. For too many people, however, variety means three flavours of ice-cream in the freezer, several types of chocolate biscuit in the cupboard, different crunchy snack foods each day and a large selection of alcoholic and soft drinks always waiting in the refrigerator.

Foods which were once reserved for special occasions have now become everyday items. For example, cream was once served only occasionally, now it is a regular food; chocolate mousse was a dessert when visitors were present, now children eat pre-packaged chocolate mousse as a snack; sweets were bought as a once-a-week treat, now they are a regular part of many people's daily intake; pastries were an occasional extra, now they are a regular indulgence with morning coffee.

Teenagers used to satisfy their appetite surges with piles of bread or apples. These days, few teenagers eat more than one sandwich, so they fill up on sweets, iceblocks, crisps and other junk foods. The 'extras' are much higher in kilojoules than the old staples.

Children may also exert pressure on parents to include foods such as crisps and other packets of snack foods in their school lunch box. Some studies show that 50 per cent of children take packeted snack foods to school each day. The same research shows that the children who eat the most snacks eat the least fruit.

Some food manufacturers have contributed to a decline in fruit consumption among children by advertising campaigns claiming that fruit is messy and time-consuming, implying or even overtly stating that their processed fruits made into individually-packed rolls are much more convenient.

Eating out

Most people now buy their lunch whereas once they took sandwiches from home. An increasing number buy breakfast from fast-food outlets or stop for a coffee and croissant on their way to work. Fast food several times a week at night, and regularly for lunch for many men, is becoming the norm. Restauranteurs who once struggled to get by on people's once- or twice-a-year 'big night out' now happily greet their regular customers each week. In some areas, the business lunch lives on, even though with less lingering than was the case a few years ago when entertaining clients at meals was a tax-deductible expense. Many young people without children cook only rarely and eat out or buy takeaway foods for almost all their meals. Single males are particularly likely to do this. On holidays, many people who would once have cooked their own food in the kitchen of their rented flat or house now buy takeaways, or eat in fast-food establishments or restaurants. In most cases, the kilojoule level of a purchased meal is greater than that of the food you cook for yourself.

If you cook pasta at home, you probably drain the pasta and top it with a sauce. You eat the pasta straight away, so it does not clump together, as it would if you left it for a time. The pasta you buy from take-away food shops sits waiting for some time, but it does not stick together because it has been well doused with oil. Even in good restaurants, the pasta is heavily coated with oil before you get it. You think you are ordering a dish high in carbohydrate, but you are getting one high in fat.

In Australia, one-third of the food dollar is now spent on foods prepared ready to eat outside the home. Almost without exception, these foods have a higher fat content than the same foods would have if they were prepared in the home kitchen. You can't always see the fat, but it's there.

Chefs report that mashed potato is very popular in restaurants, yet sales of potatoes for home cooking are down. Although many people now understand that potatoes themselves are not fattening, they feel guilty adding the big lump of butter and the full cream milk that produces good mashed potatoes. If they eat mashed potatoes in a restaurant, however, they can't see the butter (which will be even more than they would have used at home) and so enjoy the end result without seeing or thinking about what made it so delicious.

Meals or snacks?

There is probably no universal answer to the endless debate over whether it is best to eat three straight meals a day or whether a series of smaller snacks is preferable. Studies have shown some advantages, in reductions in blood cholesterol and small benefits in weight loss, when subjects are fed a series of small snacks rather than the same number of kilojoules at major meals. However, in all these studies the subjects were given their food in a very structured program. There is little data on the advantages or disadvantages of snacking versus meals in people who choose their own foods but we do know that, left to choose their own snacks, most people indulge in foods high in fat and sugar.

Quantity or quality?

People in France tend not to eat between meals. Cafés and restaurants close between lunch and dinner, except for drinks. If you miss lunch in Paris, expect to wait until dinner for food. It is difficult to spot anyone in Paris who is overweight. Do their eating habits have anything to do with this?

French people sit down to eat. They do not eat on the run. Everything and everyone stops for a proper sit-down major meal at lunchtime. The evening meal, by contrast, is usually light—a salad and bread in summer, soup and bread in winter. Children often have yoghurt and fruit for their evening meal. The only exceptions are when people eat their evening meal in a restaurant.

In France, Italy and some other European countries, people tend to praise quality more than quantity. French people care about flavour and serving sizes are quite small. A similar pattern is seen in Japan, where tiny—but exquisite—portions of food may be consumed. In both countries, fast foods are increasing, but do not dominate the diet. This may change within the next generation.

Although in many parts of France and Italy foods may be rich, the richer the food, the smaller the serving. Vegetables are never shunned and meat portions are small. Bread is also served with every meal and fills people up so they are unlikely to eat until the next meal. If you buy an ice cream in a cone in the summer in Europe, it is fairly expensive and you get one small scoop—about one-third the size of a typical serve in Australia. Both women *and* men are also very fashion conscious, dress well and expensively and consider it undesirable to be obese.

By contrast, in the United States, the quantity of most food portions is enormous. Even a sandwich may be piled with 16 slices of cold meat; when you order a coffee, you have the choice of an enormous mug or an even larger disposable container. Some recent analyses in New York showed that a typical tuna salad sandwich has 43 grams of fat, a chicken Caesar salad slightly more at 46 grams, a hamburger with fried onion rings has a massive 101 grams of fat and a porterhouse steak dinner tops the lot, with 125 grams of fat.

Australia fits somewhere between these extremes. Restaurants and cafés do not offer gigantic servings and most people would assume that a large quantity meant lower quality. But there is a tendency to follow the North American pattern of eating at all times of the day and night, which might be part of the reason why excess weight is increasing.

UNDERACTIVITY

Humans evolved in an environment where there was not a lot of food and we had to expend energy to capture or gather most of it. Overeating and underactivity were rarely possible for our ancestors.

Previous generations had plenty of kilojoule-burning physical activities which are no longer part of the typical daily routine. Most people no longer carry water, chop firewood, build their own dwellings, or bury their rubbish, as people did several generations ago. We do not even walk as much as people did 20 or 30 years ago, and in many modern buildings the stairs are accessible only as a fire exit and using them triggers an alarm.

These days, we also specialise and so leave many tasks for experts (who use machines to carry out their work). We design kitchens to save energy, install lifts in buildings and home units and try to avoid expending physical effort at every opportunity. We press buttons, gently manoeuvre machines and use so many labour-saving devices at home and at work that few people can now be classified as being in 'active' work. We even use remote control devices for such simple tasks as opening doors and gates, opening and closing car windows and turning off the television or compact disk player.

Many people, especially women, are so busy that they find it hard to fit in time for exercise. Even housework, which has not diminished in quantity, has become much less labour intensive. We no longer scrub floors, haul washing from coppers and wring it by hand, shine surfaces by vigorous rubbing or beat cakes by hand. We do not even carry the groceries home each afternoon. We have machines, cleaning and polishing solutions which we wipe on and wipe off, and we drive cars. These things save time, and they save energy.

I am not suggesting we return to back-breaking work. Having to spend many hours working outside the home as well as inside prevents such an option, even if we did find delight in such pursuits. However, we need to realise that our modern lifestyle is far less energetic than that of our parents and grandparents. As a result, we now have much less chance to burn up the kilojoules from our fat-laden foods.

We are also much busier in many ways. So much is expected of most people that they can no longer find the time to walk anywhere. Even for distances as short as a kilometre, most people will opt to drive rather than walk. Many people also spend time driving around a carpark looking for a space close to the door so they won't have so far to walk. The usual reason for a lack of activity is to save time, although you can usually park on the outskirts of a carpark and walk to the door in less time than it takes searching for that elusive spot near the entrance to office or shops. And what do we do with all the time we have saved? Much of it is spent sitting watching television or in front of a computer. Once upon a time we would have followed much more active pursuits. The average child now spends several hours a day watching television or sitting in front of a computer. Previous generations of children spent many of these hours playing actively.

We do not even let our children walk anywhere. We drive them, using reasons of safety or time as an excuse. We have become a nation of couch potatoes.

Europeans do much more walking than Australians—at least in cities. Public transport is good and so is widely used. Many buildings do not have lifts so people walk up stairs. Most homes are multi-storey; for those in units, again it is a matter of walking up stairs.

The decrease in physical activity is at least as much to blame for the expanding waistlines of the nation as the foods and drinks we consume. Many experts claim that the lack of exercise is the greater problem, because exercise not only burns up kilojoules but regulates appetite. Several studies have shown that physical activity normalises appetite. Physical activity also increases the amount of muscle or lean tissue in the body and this tissue burns more kilojoules than fat, which burns little.

THE ROLE OF GENES

The role of genes in obesity is often debated, especially the relative roles of genes, food and physical activity. Studies with identical twins show that genes are important, especially in those who are very overweight or were overweight from an early age. When pairs of twins are overfed under experimental conditions, they all gain weight, but some sets of twins gain more than others. Within each pair of twins, weight gain is similar, so there is no doubt that inherited factors make it easier for some people to gain weight than others. There is no simple role for genes—many are involved, and the number identified as playing a role continues to increase. However, even though genes are an important factor, they are only relevant when you take in more kilojoules of energy than your body is using.

The common belief that some people are fat because they have a sluggish metabolism is an oversimplification of the role of genes. In fact, larger, fatter people use more energy for their metabolism than smaller, thinner individuals. The idea that 'glands' are responsible for excess body fat is rarely correct. Many specialists working in the area of obesity say they see only a small number of such cases in a lifetime.

Genes have not been responsible for the rapid rise in the incidence of obesity throughout the world. It takes many generations for genetic changes to become apparent, and obesity has increased dramatically in just a few years.

There is no doubt that we need to consider genetic makeup, and scientists will continue to search for the genes responsible for controlling weight, in the hope that they may be able to make changes or come up with an anti-obesity drug to control genetic factors. But a search for the genes involved in obesity does not mean we should stop looking at other aspects of excess weight. Searching for a gene for obesity and doing nothing else is a bit like searching for a gene to work out who will get lung cancer if they smoke, but not bothering with anti-smoking campaigns.

STRUCTURING THE ENVIRONMENT

We started to prevent people smoking inside buildings when we realised how damaging smoking is. We may have to accept that overweight and obesity are also health problems and that we should structure the food and exercise environment accordingly.

We could make some foods more attractive and include many more government funded promotions for healthy foods like fruits, vegetables, breads, grains and fish. While not forbidding others, we could make them more difficult to get or more expensive in places like school canteens. We could also increase the tax on snack foods and fast foods, subsidise the cost of fresh fruit in canteens in schools and workplaces, stop advertising junk foods when children are the major television audience and make physical activity easier by installing bike paths, separating carparks from work buildings, having steps prominent and accessible and encouraging children and adults to play sport for fun rather than for competition.

Such suggestions are usually greeted with sarcastic remarks about 'food police'. But with health problems related to excess weight increasing and costing the community more—including those problems experienced by people who are *not* overweight but are made to feel as if they are—we may need to at least try such programs. At the very least, we should implement moves to make towns and cities safer so that adults and children can walk or cycle without the threat of harm.

WHY DIETS DON'T WORK

Most weight loss diets do little to change body fat. You can lose weight with almost any of the popular weight loss diets, at least initially. However, many of these diets are designed to achieve their weight loss through a loss of water and lean muscle tissue, both of which are normal and important components of the body. Since muscle weighs more than fat, any loss of muscle will give a faster decrease in the reading on the scales than a true loss of fat.

Most people like the psychological boost of being able to say how much weight they have lost after a week or two of the diet, but the overall effect when most—or all—of the lost weight inevitably returns is depressing. Many people think they have failed once again, and instead of blaming the diet think it was their fault. Some distance themselves from feelings of guilt and failure by blaming it on their metabolism.

There is no mystery to the sudden initial drop in weight with almost all fast weight loss diets. Most achieve it by restricting carbohydrates. Once you cut down on bread, potatoes, pasta or rice, your body is no longer supplied with the major fuel for its muscles. Over the next few days (or hours, if you exercise vigorously), the stores of carbohydrate in muscles (known as glycogen) are used up. Since the average person has 500–700 grams of glycogen in their muscles, the loss of this accounts for some of the initial weight loss. However, every gram of muscle glycogen is stored with nearly three times its weight in water, so the total loss of weight is quite substantial. The muscles have lost their main source of fuel—and you feel tired and unable to continue with exercise—but the scales show a fairly dramatic result.

Along with the water loss from muscle, any very low kilojoule or low carbohydrate diet will cause the kidneys to excrete more sodium and potassium than usual. These mineral salts are lost in urine and take some of the body's water with them, causing a further loss in weight. Losses of other minerals such as calcium, magnesium and phosphorus may occur too, and the loss of these, as well as the loss of water, may be responsible for the muscle cramps that often accompany stringent efforts to lose weight.

Many very strict diets fail to supply enough food to last until the next meal. Without enough food, the blood glucose level falls and the body's first attempt to reverse this situation is to send out hunger pangs. Food quickly restores blood glucose and the hunger pangs disappear. If you do not eat anything (and most strict diets forbid anything between meals), the feeling of hunger disappears after a few minutes because the body quickly converts some glycogen stored in the liver to glucose. Once that has been used—usually in about 30 to 40 minutes —you feel another hunger pang. If you again ignore it and do not have something to eat, you use up more of your liver glycogen. This process is repeated several times until the liver glycogen supplies are exhausted.

The body needs to maintain a basic level of glucose in the blood because it is the only fuel the brain can use under normal conditions, and the body always tries to protect the brain. So, ever resourceful, the body puts its next survival mechanism to work and breaks down protein to replenish its flagging blood glucose. With very strict diets, or with diets that do not include enough protein and kilojoules to last you between meals, lean body tissue (mostly the body's muscle) is broken down to replenish blood glucose. This leads to further weight loss—but there have been many reports of people on very strict low carbohydrate diets suffering permanent health problems, even death, because the protein has come from some vital structural tissue. Kidney damage is also possible under these conditions and is the major reason why most strict diets warn people to drink plenty of water.

Many mildly overweight people ignore the warnings against very low carbohydrate diets because they assume that damage will only occur in people who are massively obese. In fact, most deaths in dieters have occurred in people who were only slightly too fat. The reasons are not yet understood.

Muscle is dense and heavy, so losing muscle produces a fast weight loss, at least initially. Once the body breaks down protein to convert it to glucose, it must get rid of the nitrogenous waste products. This occurs through the kidneys and requires a lot of water, leading to further weight loss, but also partial dehydration in those who do not drink enough water. Loss of muscle tissue may give a good-looking response on the scales, but not on the slimmer!

Lean muscle tissue is the firm part of the body that keeps you looking good. The haggard look many people experience when dieting is partly due to loss of lean muscle tissue. Extreme fatigue and dislike of exercise occur because the muscles have lost their fuel supply (glycogen). It is biochemically impossible for the body to spare its lean muscle tissue and convert fat into glucose instead. Some sellers of supplements claim their products help this happen, but they do not understand the biochemical impossibility of it.

Reducing the body's glycogen, muscle and water is the basis for almost all fast weight loss diets. Whatever name they are given, an analysis shows they are low in carbohydrate, and hence cause fast weight loss from muscle loss. The body cannot burn fat fast, and the fast weight loss so many people desire is impossible without a loss of lean muscle tissue.

Fast weight loss diets that were very low in carbohydrate were popular for many years, then dropped from the limelight as people realised that foods such as bread, potatoes, rice and pasta were not fattening. They have now returned, as we shall see in Chapter 8. Diets low in carbohydrate or kilojoules cause the body to cut back on its energy expenditure. It does this under the influence of an enzyme called lipoprotein lipase, which helps conserve fuel supplies, but also promotes fat storage and restricts body fat being mobilised—exactly the opposite of what is needed to lose body fat.

With any very low calorie diet, ketones are formed for the brain to use for energy when it is short of carbohydrate. As ketones accumulate in the blood, they lower its pH level, creating acidic conditions which interfere with the body's ability to regulate temperature. This makes exercise hazardous. High levels of ketones also cause headache, lack of energy, nausea and vomiting.

You may lose weight with a fast weight loss diet, but the proportion of fat in your new flabby body is actually higher than before you started. You may find your body looks floppier. Loss of water and muscle is ineffective for reducing most of the hazards associated with excess weight, and can be dangerous. The loss of lean muscle tissue means you are likely to gain fat more easily in the future.

If you just want to lose weight, you could cut off your leg! No one in their right mind would see this as a viable method. Yet otherwise rational people are happy to lose weight by reducing equally important components of the bodies—their muscle and water. Instead of aiming for weight loss, we should look for fat loss. It won't be as fast, but it will be safer and more likely to improve health and appearance.

4

Health and body fat

'APPLES' AND 'PEARS'

While accepting the health risks of being overweight, we must appreciate that some body fat is normal and desirable. There are also health risks associated with being underweight, especially for women. Health problems made worse by excess body fat also depend on the distribution of the body fat. Having too much fat is a much greater hazard if the excess fat is on the upper body. Fat around the abdomen, chest, arms and neck is a health hazard. Fat on the lower body is much less risky. Most overweight people fit into one of two basic body shapes: 'apples' or 'pears'.

'Apples' carry their excess around the waist and on the upper body, especially on the chest, around the shoulders, neck and face. 'Pears' are larger on the lower half of the body with more fat on the lower 'tummy' area, hips, buttocks and thighs. The apple shape is more commonly found in men and in post-menopausal women. Younger women tend more towards the pear shape. Male pears are rare.

ARE YOU AN APPLE OR A PEAR?

The best way to determine if you are an apple or a pear is to take the ratio of your waist:hip measurements. If the ratio of these measurements is greater than 0.9, you are at high risk of the health problems mentioned below.

HEALTH AND BODY FAT

> For example, if your waist measurement is 80 cm and your hips are 85 cm, the waist:hip ratio would be 80 ÷ 85 = 0.94.
>
> This would put you in the high risk group for health problems. However, if your waist measurement was 70 cm and your hips 90, the waist:hip ratio would be 0.78 and you would be less likely to have any health risk associated with high body fat levels.

The fat in particular areas of the body is present in different types of fat cells. Upper body fat is present in large fat cells which become 'stuffed' with fat. The fat may sometimes feel hard because it is largely saturated fat. (Saturated fats in foods are hard; unsaturated fats are soft.) Some men mistakenly believe this hard fat is muscle and are almost proud of it.

The only good thing about upper body fat is that it is relatively easy to remove with sensible eating and exercise. However, upper body fat is a particular hazard when it is close to body organs (called visceral fat). You can't necessarily see visceral fat, but those who are fat around the waist tend to have lots of it.

Smokers, whether fat or thin, have a higher proportion of their body fat in the abdominal area. They tend to be 'apples' and this adds to their risks of poor health.

Lower body fat cells are much smaller, softer and contain more unsaturated fats. The fat in these cells is much more resistant to removal through sensible eating and exercise, although increased physical activity will increase the muscle content and hold the fat more firmly.

Most of the health risks associated with excess weight are confined to the apple shape. It is fat on the upper body which increases the risk of coronary heart disease, high blood pressure, diabetes, gout, gallstones, certain types of cancer and sleep apnoea. Being pear-shaped is not a risk for any of these conditions. Health risks are associated with excess body fat when waist measurement is greater than 100 centimetres in men and 90 centimetres in women.

At this stage, medical researchers are not sure whether the risk to health associated with upper body fat is caused by upper body fat itself or whether some other factor causes both the health problems and the upper body fat. One group of researchers has shown that men have a different distribution of muscle fibre types than women. They have also found that women with the apple type body have the same type of muscle fibres as men. They therefore conclude that some factor causes both the fat distribution and the health problems associated with it.

Whatever the cause, it is clear that those who are apples need to reduce their body fat whereas pears can relax. Somewhat ironically, those who carry excess fat on the upper body tend to ignore it while the poor pears spend much of their lives being miserable about their body shape, even though it is medically much safer.

Until recently, excess body fat was seen only as a risk factor for other health problems, but in 1998, obesity was declared a disease and an international taskforce was set up to tackle the growing obesity pandemic throughout the world.

GOOD REASONS FOR LOSING WEIGHT—PHYSICAL

Excess body fat is a health hazard. Those who dispute this are often overweight themselves and look for some justification not to lose their excess fat. Some have chosen to read only specific articles in medical journals. Health problems associated with excess weight include:

- coronary heart disease
- high blood pressure
- diabetes (adult-onset type)
- gallstones
- some cancers
- arthritis and gout
- joint problems, especially in the spine and knees
- varicose veins
- increased hazards if surgery required
- sleep apnoea

Some of these health problems are a greater risk than others. Some shorten life while others decrease the quality of life.

In looking at the health risks of excess body fat, it is important to understand that these occur only in those who are genuinely overweight. A BMI between 20 and 25 is not associated with any health risks, and those who fit within this category should not consider their weight as a health problem. The major problems associated with a BMI below 25 are psychological ones, caused by the feelings of inadequacy and low self-esteem engendered by a society that worships slenderness and whose fashion industry has decreed that the pear shape familiar to most women is undesirable. Our society needs to take a more appropriate view of body weight, aiming to do something about those who are genuinely too fat and helping those whose weight is not associated with physical health problems to relax.

> ### PSYCHOLOGICAL PROBLEMS ASSOCIATED WITH OBESITY
>
> There are also a great many psychological problems for fat people living in a society which considers 'thin' to be normal. Overweight children, especially, suffer jibes and discrimination from their peers. Studies have also shown that overweight people of all ages are discriminated against in employment, promotion and education. Such problems are appalling and we should strive to eliminate the discrimination against fat people. Being fat does not mean people have defects in personality.

CORONARY HEART DISEASE

For some years, medical researchers thought that excess body fat was only a risk factor for coronary heart disease because of its effects on other risk factors such as high blood pressure, high levels of cholesterol and triglyceride fats in the blood. There is no doubt that excess body fat does increase these risk factors, but excess upper body fat itself is a separate and definite hazard for heart disease, especially in those under the age of 50. Those who have high levels of body fat also have lower levels of the protective 'good' cholesterol called high density lipoprotein (HDL).

Excess body fat is one of the early factors in the chain of events leading to heart disease. It is also an independent factor for premature heart disease and influences the way the heart pumps blood, the volume of blood in various blood vessels, the activity of the heart fibres and the concentrations of relevant factors in the blood.

Since the late 1960s, the incidence of deaths from coronary heart disease has been falling in some countries, including the United States and Australia, although this decrease has now levelled off and has done so at a level much higher than that in many countries in the Mediterranean region and parts of Asia.

Some critics of the idea that excess body fat increases the risk of heart disease cite the fact that heart disease rates decreased while the incidence of excess weight increased. This ignores the fact that heart disease is due to many factors, of which excess upper body fat is one, along with smoking, high blood pressure, high levels of blood fats and physical inactivity. The large number of middle-aged men who gave up smoking in the 1970s, and better treatments for high blood pressure and blood fats, are responsible for the decrease in coronary heart disease. The continuing increase in excess weight helps explain why coronary heart disease rates are no longer decreasing.

Medical researchers now agree that excess body fat is a separate risk factor for heart disease. If more people of both sexes and all ages decreased their upper body fat, we could expect coronary heart disease rates to fall. It is still our greatest killer.

For those who lose their excess upper body fat, levels of triglycerides and cholesterol in the blood will fall, and the protective HDL cholesterol my increase.

HIGH BLOOD PRESSURE

There is no doubt that excess body fat increases the risks of high blood pressure. Not everyone with high blood pressure is too fat, nor does everyone who is too fat have high blood pressure. However, considerably more people with upper body fat have high blood pressure compared with those who are thinner.

Apart from using drugs to control blood pressure, the most effective way to reduce high blood pressure is to lose any excess upper body fat. With effective fat reduction, many people no longer need drugs to control blood pressure and almost all can reduce the dose of drugs needed (with medical supervision). Losing excess body fat is more effective in reducing high blood pressure than reducing salt intake, even though this is also important.

ADULT-ONSET DIABETES

Insulin is a hormone which takes glucose from the blood into the body's cells where it can be used to provide energy to the cells. In childhood diabetes, the body stops producing insulin altogether. In adult-onset diabetes (also called type 2 diabetes), insulin is produced but either the quantity made is insufficient or the action of the insulin is blocked. Either way, the result is that glucose accumulates in the blood (giving a high blood sugar measurement) until some 'spills over' into the urine, where simple tests can identify it. Meanwhile the cells are starved of the glucose they need for energy.

Diabetes is due to a genetic problem but the condition may never show up if the person does not become overweight. Up to 90 per cent of people with adult-onset diabetes are overweight and this type of diabetes is increasing rapidly in most countries of the world in parallel with increases in body weight.

In some overweight people, the quantity of insulin produced may be sufficient only for someone of normal weight. The action of the insulin may also be blocked by a layer of fat around the membrane of the body's cells. Once the overweight person loses some body fat, their diabetes virtually disappears.

Being overweight is sometimes associated with producing too much insulin. No one is sure whether excessive insulin causes weight gain or whether the accumulation of body fat sets up a resistance to the action of insulin which the body tries to overcome by producing more insulin. However, more than half of all overweight people have some degree of intolerance to blood glucose and diabetes is a potential problem for them.

Most people with diabetes have abnormal levels of fats in the blood. Weight loss for all people with diabetes should therefore stress the reduction of saturated fats in the diet. They should consume more high-fibre foods, and reduce their consumption of fast foods and other foods high in saturated fat, such as fried foods, biscuits, cakes and pastries. Those with adult-onset diabetes should also restrict alcohol, as the body burns less fat when alcohol is present. A small amount of alcohol in conjunction with a low-fat diet is generally no problem.

The ideal fat intake in diabetes may differ between people. Some studies have found that people with diabetes have better control of their condition with a diet moderately high in monounsaturated fats rather than the diet typically recommended, which is very low in all fats and much higher in carbohydrates. However, since monounsaturated fats can still increase body fat levels, it is important that they be consumed in place of other food sources of kilojoules, not in addition.

Sugar provides kilojoules but has virtually no important nutrients. Problems with sugar occur when large quantities are consumed (as in soft drinks) or where it is accompanied by saturated fats (as in cakes, desserts, biscuits, chocolates). General advice to people with diabetes is to avoid highly concentrated sources of refined sugar, although the small quantities of sugar present in high-fibre foods are not a problem. Cutting total kilojoule intake will help with weight loss.

It is important for people with diabetes to include foods that do not release their glucose too quickly into the blood. Such foods are said to create a low glycaemic load and include legumes, oats, barley, many fruits, yoghurt (preferably reduced-fat varieties) and wholegrain (not wholemeal) breads and cereals. Researchers are still debating whether the glycaemic load of the diet affects body weight or just influences blood glucose control, but either way, it makes sense to avoid foods that create a high glycaemic load.

YOU AND DIABETES

People who are mildly overweight have twice the risk of developing diabetes as people of normal weight. For the moderately

> overweight the risk increases to five times, while severely overweight people have ten times the chance of developing diabetes. In all cases, it is only excess fat on the abdomen and upper body which increases the risk of diabetes.

GALLSTONES

Gallstones can occur in thin people who have too high a proportion of their diet in the form of fat. However, gallstones are much more common in people with upper body fat.

When the body is converting excess food to fat, more bile is produced in the liver and stored in the gall bladder. This increases the risk of gallstones. Once gallstones have formed they must be removed, or shattered by ultrasonic treatment. Weight loss will not remove gallstones but it will help in their prevention.

CANCER

Most of the cancers related to being overweight are related to various hormones. They include breast cancer, cancer of the endometrium, uterus and ovary in women, and of the prostate in men. There is now clear evidence that bowel cancer (colo-rectal cancer) is also more common in overweight people.

The American Cancer Society studied 750 000 men and women and found that underweight men, but not underweight women, had higher death rates from cancer than those of average weight. This was mostly related to lung cancer. The study also showed that both overweight men and overweight women had higher than average mortality from cancer, but this effect was much greater in women.

In men, excess weight is associated with more bowel cancer and more cancers of the pancreas and stomach. Other studies have also shown the link between bowel cancer and excess weight, especially where the weight is associated with a high-fat diet and low levels of physical activity. In women, excess weight is most strongly associated with breast cancer and also with cancers of the uterus, ovary and endometrium. Many other studies have since confirmed the link between breast cancer and excess weight. Women with more fat produce greater quantities of oestrogen and some hormone-related substances.

Most, but not all, studies have shown that breast cancer in women over 50 years of age is more common among those who are overweight. A few studies have shown an increased risk of breast cancer even in younger women who are overweight. A Californian study found that a major factor for breast cancer in post-menopausal women was weight gain between age 20 and the menopause. However, several studies have shown no association with weight and breast cancer in women before menopause. Most researchers have concluded that weight gain is a risk factor for breast cancer in women after the menopause but not in younger women. It has also been shown that older women who lose weight gain some protection against breast cancer.

A number of studies have shown that the dietary culprits for breast cancer are the total fat consumed and animal protein. Others dispute any relationship with fat intake and a slight reduction in the amount of fat eaten does not seem to be effective in reducing risk. Only when the fat in the diet is decreased below about 20 per cent of the kilojoules is there protection from breast cancer. This is a slightly lower level of fat than that which reduces the risk of coronary heart disease.

Animal studies have shown that mammary tumours grow much more slowly when the animals are given less fat in their diet. Since few people have any use for a lot of fat in the diet, it makes sense for those with breast cancer and those wanting to prevent it to eat less fat. The lower kilojoule level in a low-fat diet will also reduce body fat levels and further reduce risks of breast cancer, at least in post-menopausal women.

The American Cancer Society and other similar organisations have recommended that women avoid having very high levels of body fat. The dietary factor relevant to hormone-related cancers in women, and to excess weight, is fat. Some types of dietary fibre (especially insoluble fibre in wholewheat and bran products) may give some protection against the effects of a high-fat diet.

BODY FAT AND OSTEOPOROSIS

Osteoporosis is one major health problem with an inverse relationship to body weight. In other words, it is much more common in those whose body weight is low. This is the major reason why most health authorities put a lower limit on their healthy weight range.

A large or sudden drop in body fat levels will decrease a woman's levels of the hormone oestrogen. At menopause, the production of oestrogen slows to a stop and leads to a substantial

THE DIET DILEMMA

loss of calcium from the bones. If the bones are not dense enough to start with, post-menopausal women with low oestrogen levels develop osteoporosis, or weak, porous bones. Osteoporosis is a major health problem in western societies in older people. However, the body does not distinguish between different causes of low oestrogen levels, and a woman whose oestrogen levels fall because of low levels of body fat can begin to lose calcium from her skeleton even while she is young.

There are two major types of bone: cortical bone and trabecular bone. The cortical bone predominates in the long bones of the limbs while the trabecular bone is the spongy bone which exists in the spine.

Women who believe 'thin is beautiful' to the extent that they stop producing adequate levels of oestrogen can do permanent damage to the spongy bones in their spines. There is not much beauty in having a spine which is bent and painful, as elderly women who develop this condition through the depletion of oestrogen that occurs with ageing can attest.

A woman who has not yet reached menopause can tell if she is not producing adequate amounts of oestrogen because her periods stop. If this continues for some months, the risk of permanent damage to trabecular bone increases.

Many women body builders 'cut back' just before a competition to reduce their body fat to as low a level as possible. Their periods stop but often resume when they regain more normal weight after the competition. At this stage, we do not yet know whether 'off again, on again' periods due to changing oestrogen levels cause any permanent damage to bone density.

Other factors are also involved in bone density and there is some evidence that phytoestrogens (plant oestrogens) in products such as soy and linseeds, and also the types of omega-3 fats in fish, may help bone density. But there is no doubt that extreme thinness, whether by nature or by design, is a risk factor for this condition.

ARTHRITIS AND GOUT

Osteoarthritis is a condition of wear and tear on the joints which is inevitable as we grow older. Rheumatoid arthritis is a more serious type of arthritis in which the joints become inflamed. All types of arthritis are more severe in overweight people as the excess weight increases the strain on many of the joints involved.

Gout is a form of arthritis in which uric acid accumulates in the joint, usually in the big toe, and causes extreme pain. It is much more common in overweight people, especially those with high levels of blood fats.

Alcohol causes problems for those with gout because the kidneys are so busy getting rid of the breakdown products of alcohol that they do not excrete uric acid.

Anyone with gout should lose weight slowly. Fast weight loss will lead to a rapid breakdown of lean body tissue—and the waste products from this tissue as well as waste products from a loss of fat must be excreted by the kidneys. Under such conditions, the kidneys will not excrete uric acid properly and fast weight loss will cause a flare-up of gout.

There are obviously good reasons to lose excess body fat. As with most aspects of life, however, some caution is needed and weight loss is not suitable for everyone—especially those who have little excess fat to lose.

WHEN IS WEIGHT LOSS UNNECESSARY?

As discussed in Chapter 2, there are important reasons why women who are not overweight by anyone's standards, except their own, should not lose weight. When women's body-fat levels drop too low, their ovaries produce less oestrogen and the body thinks it has reached menopause. It responds with large losses of calcium from bones.

There are also no good medical reasons why young women with a pear-shaped distribution of body fat should try to lose weight. There are some good reasons why such women should *not* attempt weight loss. The most important of these is the problem of failure.

If you are not overweight on the upper body but think your hips, thighs and tummy are too fat, there may be little future in attempting to reduce these areas. Spot reducing is impossible. Some women whose upper bodies can only be described as 'scrawny' try to starve their recalcitrant thighs into skinny obedience. The fat does not budge until the woman has become so thin that her periods stop.

If you ask yourself what is to be gained by the misery attached to such dieting efforts, the answer is nothing! Constant efforts at dieting may even make you fatter!

5

A bit of magic

SELLING TECHNIQUES

There is no easy way to lose body fat and many people have realised that most diets don't work. In response to this we have a plethora of salespeople claiming that the answer to the diet dilemma lies in their magic pills, powders and supplements. Some put out scientific-sounding brochures, often supplying books or reprints, supposedly from scientific journals. You can now buy dozens of supplements that are supposed to help you lose weight, metabolise your fat and protect your muscles and health with their added ingredients. Many are sold in normal commercial outlets, others are available only from distributors for multi-level marketing (MLM) companies. The Internet has also opened up vast markets for MLM marketers and for individuals selling supposed weight loss supplements.

MLM companies use persuasive campaigns using well-practised selling techniques to recruit salespeople. These people are first convinced by other distributors to try the products themselves. If they like them, they are exhorted to spread the gospel, encouraging their network of friends, relatives, acquaintances and other satisfied users to help sell the products to their friends, relatives and acquaintances. For your role in helping those under you become established as distributors, you receive bonuses. As you might expect, the financial rewards can be great for those at the top and your income increases as you encourage more people to sell the product(s). It sounds a lot like the illegal practice of pyramid selling, and although the differences between MLM schemes and pyramid selling seem marginal, most MLM methods of operation scrape inside the law. Schemes are illegal if:

1. Participants are rewarded primarily or substantially for recruiting others.
2. Recruits must purchase goods or services to join the scheme and those who recruit them get a reward but the goods or services purchased are grossly overpriced or are of no value.
3. The goods and services become irrelevant or peripheral and the major emphasis is on recruiting rather than selling.

If judged by their appropriateness for weight loss, many of the supplements sold as weight loss products would fall into category 2. However, regulatory bodies have said that MLM schemes will not be treated as illegal pyramid selling schemes if:

(a) participants are rewarded on the basis of sales of products only, including those they make and those made by people they have recruited into the scheme; and
(b) the products are genuine products for which there is a genuine demand and they are not grossly overpriced.

The guidelines also state that they recognise that many MLM schemes will charge high prices for products. For the customers, however, any questioning of the high prices is regarded almost as an insult. Sellers are trained to say 'Isn't your health worth it?', followed by a spiel on the priceless nature of good health.

MLM companies sell strategies as well as their products, citing product savings from the elimination of 'middlemen'. In fact, many products cost much more than similar products on sale in normal retail outlets. MLMs also stress that the financial success you will enjoy grows as you help others to become successful, claiming this is superior to the 'dog eat dog mentality' in normal marketing. The sales hype neglects to mention that as you continue to take money from friends, relatives and acquaintances, and encourage those on the rung beneath you to do likewise, the market must eventually diminish for someone. In fact, those at the bottom of these schemes make very little money, while the real entrepreneurs at the top can make millions.

Health food shops and some pharmacies also sell heaps of slimming products of dubious value. Even the suburban supermarkets have shelves of so-called fat metabolisers and herbal weight loss teas, usually sold in their 'health' section.

Historically, most slimming products claiming amazing results arrive with a burst of publicity and quietly disappear some time later. A few years ago, we had glucomannan tablets that were supposed to swell up and stop overweight people from eating. Unfortunately, some products increased in size before they reached the stomach, blocking the oesophagus. In some cases, surgery was urgently needed to remove the obstructing block of solid fibre.

There were also starch-blocker pills that were supposed to prevent the body converting starches to fat. They disappeared when the undigested starch caused considerable gastrointestinal distress as it found its way out through the bowel. In any case, research shows that starch is only converted to body fat when you eat very large quantities—a difficult task since starchy foods are filling. Most of the starch in foods is burnt for energy and only the accompanying fat is usually converted to body fat.

Over the years, slimming aids containing vitamin B_6, iodine (usually from kelp or some other type of seaweed, now often sold as the more exotic sounding *Fucus vesiculosis*), vinegar and lecithin seem to be perennial favourites. They have been joined by an array of new compounds, each of which claims to be *the* magic way to get rid of excess body fat.

Before taking a look at any evidence that might back up weight loss claims for some ingredients, it is worth noting that the listing of any product by the Therapeutic Goods Authority (TGA) in Australia, or the Dietary Supplement and Health Education Act (DSHEA) in the United States does not mean the product is *effective*. As long as a product does not contain known toxic ingredients, and the manufacturer pays the registration price, any product can be listed. There is no onus on the seller or the TGA or DSHEA to prove that the product works. No one checks such things, and if you are told that a product has been given 'approval' or has some special status because it is listed by these authorities, be sceptical and realise that something shonky may be afoot.

To expand the market, or possibly to gain credibility, many products now claim to build muscle, protect health or provide antioxidant protection as well as aid weight loss. In most cases, the claims are not sustainable, although many now contain antioxidants. Contrary to the claims of those marketing these supplements, the thousands of antioxidants present in natural foods can supply all the body needs. There is no evidence that taking extra antioxidants helps weight loss. Any substance that does act as an antioxidant can also have the opposite effect at high doses. Vitamin C provides a simple example of this, with a moderate dose acting as an antioxidant, but a large dose having the opposite effect and functioning in an undesirable pro-oxidant.

INGREDIENTS IN WEIGHT LOSS/ FAT METABOLISER PRODUCTS

Brindleberry or hydroxycitric acid (HCA)

Brindleberry (or *Garcinia cambogia*) is a fruit native to parts of Asia. Its rind contains a substance called hydroxycitric acid (HCA) which can be extracted and dried to a powder. Many weight loss products make claims that either brindleberry extract or HCA help prevent the synthesis of body fat.

The claims are based on the supposition that hydroxycitric acid stops the action of an enzyme called adenosine triphosphate-citrate [pro–3S]-lyase, said to be necessary for the synthesis of fat. As with many of the 'wonder' weight loss compounds, enthusiastic salespeople sold products containing brindleberry (or *Garcinia cambogia* or HCA) before any trials had shown it was effective in treating excess weight.

Some early trials of hydroxycitric acid claimed promising results. But a closer inspection shows that these trials involved small numbers of subjects, did not have a control group, ignored the influence of confounding factors such as diet and exercise, and many were reported only by those selling products containing hydroxycitric acid.

In 1998, a scientifically valid trial of hydroxycitric acid from brindleberry extract was done, with 135 people given either 1500 milligrams of hydroxycitric acid or a placebo plus a high-fibre, low-kilojoule diet. The results of the study, reported in the *Journal of the American Medical Association*, showed there was no difference in weight loss between those taking HCA or the placebo. Weight loss was due to the diet the subjects followed, not the supplement. The researchers also measured body fat, but there was no difference in the percentage of weight loss from fat in those taking HCA.

The bottom line: Don't waste your money on brindleberry extract, *Garcinia cambogia* or any mixture which claims success from hydroxycitric acid. Such preparations only result in weight loss if you also cut your kilojoules—and this is responsible for any weight loss.

Chitosan

Chitosan is made from chitin, a polysaccharide compound found in the shells of prawns and other crustaceans or extracted from certain fungi (*Aspergillus*). It has wide industrial application because it can adhere to particular compounds. Oil spills in the ocean are treated with a complex mixture which includes chitin or chitosan. Chitosan is also used as a bonding agent in dentistry and as an anti-fungal agent, and pharmaceutical companies sometimes use it to help carry active drugs in capsules and tablets. It can also be used to flocculate the fat from whey left over after making cheese.

Because of its use in mopping-up oil spills, it seemed possible that chitosan given to humans might 'stick to' and remove cholesterol from the body. This indeed proved to be the case in animal studies and chitosan does reduce cholesterol levels in rats, mice, chickens and rabbits. Its action is a bit like that of a commonly-used cholesterol-reducing substance called cholestyramine.

In some strains of lean mice, chitosan also lowered blood glucose. However, when fed to a type of mouse that is overweight and has diabetes and high insulin levels, there was no effect.

In reducing cholesterol, however, chitosan also creates some hazards. In the animals studied, their blood levels of vitamin E dropped alarmingly, many minerals were no longer properly absorbed and the bones of rats lost a lot of calcium. Another study which gave mice chitosan by mouth found that the good bacteria in their intestine decreased. The authors warned of the dangers of chitosan.

In humans, any of the adverse effects seen in animals would be potentially serious. Vitamin E is an important antioxidant. Adequate mineral absorption is vital and loss of calcium from bone would accelerate conditions such as osteoporosis. 'Good' bacteria maintain the health of the large intestine, overcome 'bad' bacteria and are thought to decrease serious diseases such as bowel cancer. Loss of valuable bacteria could create long-term havoc.

These potentially serious hazards are reason enough to avoid taking chitosan, but they become especially important when you consider that there is not a single study showing that chitosan causes weight loss in humans and one study showing it had no effect. We also know that drugs used to reduce cholesterol do not reduce body weight. And there is no way that chitosan could attack fat already on your hips, thighs or any other place.

If chitosan had any action in preventing fats being absorbed, it might prevent future weight gain. If it could do this, any fats eaten and not absorbed would have to be excreted and would create foul-smelling fat-containing faeces. As well, fat-soluble vitamins (A, D, E and K) would be lost and there would be less absorption of essential fatty acids as well as a loss of valuable antioxidants and anti-cancer compounds from fruits and vegetables.

Given the hazards already described when chitosan is given to animals, and the fact that if chitosan did prevent fats being absorbed, it would have undesirable health implications, it is a substance that should be left for industrial applications.

The bottom line: Given the known hazards when chitosan is fed to animals, the potential loss of vitamins, good bacteria and antioxidants, plus the lack of any verifiable evidence that chitosan causes weight loss, this is one to avoid.

Amino acids

Tablets and powders marketed as fat metabolisers contain amino acids, including one or more of L-arginine, L-carnitine, L-ornithine, phenylalanine, methionine and the branched chain amino acids valine, leucine and isoleucine. Amino acids are the building blocks of proteins and the average western adult consumes 80 to 120 grams of protein a day. This protein contains quantities of amino acids well in excess of daily requirements.

Once we swallow a protein food, it is partly broken down by digestive enzymes in the stomach. Enzymes in the small intestine complete the breakdown to the constituent amino acids. Some of these amino acids are transported in the blood to the body's cells where they are used for the growth and repair of tissues and organs. Any excess amino acids are available to be converted to glucose or, rarely, to body fat. Amino acids are important but it would be a biochemical mystery if they could help remove excess body fat. It would also be interesting to know why the excess amounts of amino acids which result from high-protein western diets do not bring about some loss of weight. The answer from those selling amino acid supplements is that their products have a better combination of amino acids to prevent conversion to body fat. However, amino acid supplements have no advantages and no specific effect on the breakdown of body fat or fats in foods. There is no biochemical reason to include amino acids in products that claim to be fat metabolisers.

Claims that amino acid supplements or fat metabolisers will help preserve lean body tissue in those trying to lose weight are also not valid. Strict diets without enough carbohydrate and protein do lead to loss of lean body tissue, but the solution is to avoid such hazardous diets. Adding amino acids from supplements to a foolish diet does not make the diet safe or desirable.

Some people have claimed that the amino acids ornithine and arginine can increase growth hormone and hence lead to increased levels of lean body tissue, which can then burn more kilojoules of energy than fat tissue. However, the research techniques used by those making these claims are poor and cannot be duplicated by those using better techniques and equipment.

There are no dangers associated with taking amino acids present in most fat metabolisers because the quantities of individual amino acids are small and insignificant in comparison with those available from food. By contrast, some higher dose amino acid preparations sold to athletes and containing larger quantities can cause stomach cramps and diarrhoea.

The bottom line: Don't be taken in by fat metabolisers or amino acid supplements. They have no effect on body fat.

L-carnitine

This amino acid is supplied in ample quantities from food but is also made within the liver, kidneys and brain from other amino acids. It is found in every cell in the body and is needed for fats to be burned to provide energy in body cells.

Sellers of supplements extrapolate from L-carnitine's role to assume that extra L-carnitine will cause the body to burn more fat. Unfortunately, the assumption is wrong.

L-carnitine rose to fame when it was used by the Italian soccer team before they won a historic World Cup game in 1982. Since then, a wide variety of claims have been attached to L-carnitine and it commands high prices even though there was and is no evidence that the Italian soccer players' victory had anything to do with this supplement.

Carnitine has been well studied. When college swimmers in the United States were given 4000 milligrams of L-carnitine a day, their lap times were no different from those on placebo. Cyclists given the same dose for 14 days also showed no improvement in performance and other studies have confirmed these findings. No study has reported loss of weight, body fat or cellulite from L-carnitine.

Researchers have found that the body exerts strong control over the quantity of L-carnitine taken up from the blood by muscle cells. When extra carnitine is supplied in pills, the blood levels may rise, but the amount in the muscles, where it is needed, do not change. The final quantity of L-carnitine we need and use remains the same, whether we make it ourselves or take it in an expensive supplement.

Most fat metabolisers contain 50 to 2000 milligrams of L-carnitine, which does no harm and no good. L-carnitine also exists as a D-isomer, however, and if this is taken as a supplement it interferes with the body's ability to use its own L-carnitine. One study found that L-carnitine increased the rate of rancidity of fats within cell membranes in the body. As this is an undesirable effect, it makes sense not to take large doses of L-carnitine.

The bottom line: This non-essential amino acid is more likely to burn a hole in your wallet than burn off your fat. Don't waste your money.

Collagen

Included in a product that claims to magically help you lose weight while you sleep, collagen hydrolysate contains the amino acids arginine and proline. Collagen can be extracted from bovine gelatine and the hydrolysate is simply hydrolysed collagen, or a degraded form of protein. Collagen is found in connective tissue and claims that taking it will build muscle and increase metabolic rate are not based on any reliable research.

The idea that a product that forms part of connective tissue can be consumed and find its way to the body's own connective tissue shows a complete misunderstanding of the way the body works. If you were to take collagen hydrolysate, the body would digest it and add its amino acids to those that come from meat, milk, eggs, fish, bread, legumes, nuts or any other protein source. The body uses these amino acids to repair damage, build tissues during periods of growth and provide the material for muscle fibres to increase and become thicker during exercise. However, the idea that you can consume connective tissue and the body will somehow be able to send it to your own connective tissue is as absurd as thinking that if you eat chicken wings, you will grow wings.

Muscle does not spontaneously generate with extra protein from either foods or a supplement. Muscle can only develop when it is used in exercise, or during periods of growth. To use muscle, the tissue must be supplied with adequate quantities of both protein and carbohydrate. But sitting down and eating these nutrients won't do a thing for your biceps or any other muscle in the body. It *is* correct that consuming protein while on a very low carbohydrate diet can help prevent the loss of lean muscle tissue which will otherwise occur to generate blood glucose (via the process of gluconeogenesis), but the obvious remedy for this is not to follow a low-carbohydrate diet in the first place. Such diets are unbalanced and that is why they are not recommended.

The products containing collagen hydrolysate make a particularly silly claim that you must take the product last thing at night on an empty stomach for it to be effective. This is nonsense, although the additional requirement not to eat for the last three hours of the day will cut most people's kilojoule intake enough for them to lose weight. But it's the lower kilojoule intake that helps, not the expensive product.

The brochures that accompany these products also claim that the 'calories in fat are released and filtered out of the body by the kidneys'. This is a biochemical impossibility. Fat cannot be filtered out of the body by the kidneys.

Most collagen products also contain pyruvate, L-carnitine, *Garcinia cambogia* (brindleberry), alpha lipoic acid, chromium picolinate and *Aloe vera*. None of these has any ability to burn fat or build muscle and *Aloe vera* has laxative properties that can be undesirable.

The bottom line: Avoiding food for three hours at night may help with weight loss, but you can do that without buying an expensive and useless supplement.

Choline and lecithin

Choline and lecithin are found in a variety of foods, including egg yolk, soybeans, peanuts and liver. Both are also made by the body as needed.

Choline is an essential part of a substance called acetylcholine, which transmits messages between nerve cells, especially in the part of the brain that controls memory. Lecithin is a phospholipid, a combination of phosphorus and fatty acids, and is involved in the digestion, absorption and transport of fat around the body. Some people have assumed that taking extra lecithin will keep fat moving around the body, so that it does not settle in fat deposits.

Both choline and lecithin are supposed to help memory, but tests do not support the idea that taking extra quantities of either will help a failing memory. Nor is there any evidence that lecithin or choline will help prevent fat deposits or assist weight loss. One Swedish study conducted over a two-year period found that a supplement of protein, kelp, vitamin B_6 and lecithin had no effect on weight loss. Another study in pigs (which have a similar digestive system to humans) found that giving them extra lecithin had no effect on the way they digested and metabolised fat.

A few years ago in California, a man developed a bezoar—a large indigestible ball—in the stomach after taking large quantities of lecithin. It required surgical removal. Excess choline also causes problems when bacteria in the large bowel convert it into trimethylamine, a substance with a fishy smell given off as an unpleasant body odour.

The bottom line: There is no evidence that lecithin or choline will help you mobilise or lose fat. Give them a miss.

Kelp

For many years, various types of seaweed have been touted as cures for obesity. The latest inclusion in cellulite and slimming preparations is *Fucus vesiculosis*—brown seaweed. Like other types of seaweed, it is rich in iodine, a mineral needed by the thyroid gland, which controls metabolic rate. The rationale for taking extra iodine from kelp or seaweed is that it might increase production of the hormone thyroxine and stimulate the body to burn more kilojoules for metabolism.

In fact, the body almost always has biofeedback mechanisms to control such potential changes to its glands. The human thyroid gland can tolerate wide fluctuations in iodine supply and if larger quantities are ingested, the thyroid cuts back on its production of thyroxine. This can produce the opposite effect from that desired.

In cases of iodine toxicity, hyperthyroidism may occur and can result in weight loss, but there is no evidence that the quantity of iodine in usual doses of supplements containing kelp can lead to changes in metabolism or weight loss. In those who consume excessive quantities of products containing iodine, adverse changes may occur in the nervous system, leading to constant crying, insomnia and nervousness, but no change in body fat or cellulite.

A lack of iodine causes hypothyroidism which may result in weight gain. But the converse is not true and weight gain is rarely due to hypothyroidism.

The bottom line: There is no advantage in taking kelp or other forms of iodine for weight loss. If anything, iodine can have the opposite effect.

Chromium picolinate

Supposedly proven in clinical trials as a way to 'lose the fat, keep the muscle', chromium picolinate has become a popular supplement. Its main support comes from enthusiastic salespeople who promote it as an aid to increasing muscle mass and decreasing blood glucose, and for weight loss.

Chromium is a mineral which plays a role in the metabolism of proteins, fats and carbohydrates and increases the effects of insulin, a hormone that takes glucose out of the bloodstream and into the cells. Some support for taking extra chromium came from a study in China where very high doses of the supplement were given to people with diabetes, with some benefits that were not apparent at lower doses. Unfortunately, other studies in people with diabetes have not duplicated these benefits.

A small study in Germany gave 36 obese people a daily supplement of either 200 micrograms of chromium picolinate, 200 micrograms of chromium yeast or a placebo, as well as a very low-calorie diet, for eight weeks. All groups lost lean body tissue (muscle), but the researchers claimed that the 12 people on chromium picolinate increased their lean body mass over the following six months. The difference was not really significant and with no details of how much exercise the subjects did, one could not reasonably promote the supplement on the basis of this study.

Another two studies in 1989 gave football players chromium picolinate and claimed that they lost body fat and gained muscle as a result. Unfortunately, the researchers did not measure body fat accurately, relying on skin callipers and calculating lean body tissue and fat from their measurements. Since that time, with more accurate ways of measuring different aspects of body composition, the initial enthusiasm for chromium picolinate has fallen, although the researcher involved continues as a consultant to those marketing chromium supplements.

A rigorous 1998 study of 20 wrestlers given 200 micrograms of chromium picolinate a day, and using sophisticated equipment to look at body composition, found no effect from the supplement compared with placebo.

In 1996, another study of 36 men involved in weight training and given chromium chloride or chromium picolinate daily for eight weeks also found no beneficial effect on body composition or strength.

In 1995, the Naval Research Centre in San Diego studied the effects of daily supplements of 400 micrograms of chromium picolinate in 79 men and 16 women who exceeded the Navy's percentage body fat standards. They found that the supplement had no effect on body weight, body fat or lean body tissue.

Yet another study at the Pennsylvania State University gave 900 micrograms of chromium picolinate a day to 35 overweight people and found no increase in muscle mass and no changes in insulin, glucose or blood cholesterol levels. There was a similar lack of effect on lean body tissue and other parameters in a 1999 report on 18 men aged 56 to 69 years.

In the United States, one company selling chromium picolinate has been ordered to stop making claims that their supplement causes weight loss, increases muscle mass, burns fat, increases metabolic rate or lowers blood fats or glucose. They have complied with this directive, but many other companies selling the same compound continue to make similar claims.

There are some potential problems with chromium picolinate. Inorganic chromium has a low toxicity but when combined with organic molecules, as occurs in chromium picolinate, it is absorbed more rapidly. One study in hamsters showed that chromium picolinate, in doses equivalent to those which many people take, damaged DNA. Other forms of chromium did not have this effect. There have also been documented reports of kidney damage from chromium picolinate, and substances similar to picolinic acid (known as analogues) have altered the metabolism of neurotransmitters in the brain. Anyone prone to behavioural disorders should therefore take great care with chromium picolinate, at least until its safety has been properly evaluated.

The bottom line: The studies continue, but their results all show that chromium picolinate has no ability to help weight loss or increase muscle. Chromium does play a role in glucose metabolism, but at this stage there is no evidence that most people with diabetes lack chromium and would benefit from chromium picolinate. With possible side effects, the message is caution.

Pyruvate

Another weight loss 'cure' from the United States, pyruvate is supposed also to build muscle. Dr Ronald Stanko, a researcher from the University of Pittsburgh, holds the patent for one pyruvate product and is a staunch advocate of its usefulness in weight loss and exercise. He has published several trials in which he claims that pyruvate is effective for weight loss. There are also claims that taking extra pyruvate will build muscle, reduce blood fats and act as an antioxidant.

Pyruvate is a compound produced by the body whenever it breaks down glucose or glycogen to generate energy. In anaerobic activity (short, sharp actions where there is no time for oxygen to be involved in the production of energy), pyruvate is metabolised to lactic acid. In aerobic exercise (longer sustained activity where oxygen is available), pyruvate is further broken down to carbon dioxide and water, and more energy is generated.

In spite of the claims made, the evidence that pyruvate supplements will help weight loss or muscle development is poor. The studies reported by Stanko used small numbers of people for very short periods of time. In one study, eight obese women were given a very low-kilojoule diet of 1300 kilojoules (about 300 Calories) a day for three weeks, then given a more normal diet plus a supplement of pyruvate and dihydroxyacetone for the next three weeks. A control group of nine women was given the same diet but their supplement contained a placebo of polyglucose. Stanko reported that the women who got the placebo regained 1.1 kilograms more than those on the combined supplement. As the women were extremely obese, these differences are slight, especially in the context of the very short time frame.

In other studies by the same researcher, one group of 13 women given a diet of 2100 kilojoules (500 Calories) plus a similar supplement lost 0.9 of a kilogram more than a control group, while a group of 14 women on 4200 kilojoules (1000 Calories) plus the supplement lost an extra 1.6 kilograms.

Each of the studies claiming weight loss were done by the same researcher, using a few very obese women who were confined to bed and given stringent formula diets for several weeks. The claims that pyruvate specifically reduced body fat are not valid since the instrument used to measure body fat does not give reliable results of body fat levels.

Although the research notes that the studies are preliminary and must be confirmed in studies in other people, brochures and information about pyruvate omit this. They also fail to mention that the quantities of pyruvate used in the studies ranged from 28 to 90 grams a day, whereas most pyruvate pills on the market contain less than 1 gram. At least at this level the pills are unlikely to have any adverse effects.

Claims that pyruvate builds muscle and improves exercise performance are based on similarly small trials. Again the trials come from just one researcher and cannot be considered valid until repeated by others, using more subjects over longer time periods. The fact that the subjects suffered from flatulence and diarrhoea is a concern.

There is no evidence that pyruvate supplements function as antioxidants or reduce blood fats.

The bottom line: There is no good evidence that pyruvate helps weight loss or fat loss or can meet the claims currently made for it. The clinical proof cited is not conclusive and there is no data about the effects of pyruvate supplements given to ordinary people eating and living under normal conditions. Skip the hype and save your money.

DHEA or dehydroepiandrostenone

Marketed as a way to lose body fat and increase lean body tissue, DHEA or DHEA-sulphate is sold through multi-level marketing companies or through the Internet. Its sellers claim it is an elixir of youth, that it rejuvenates your sex life, prevents heart disease and reduces the risk of cancer. Some also claim it can cure AIDS and lupus. Some health food shops in the United States also sell a wild yam extract, with claims that it contains DHEA. The compound, however, does not exist in plants and the body cannot convert plant steroids into DHEA.

DHEA is normally manufactured in the adrenal glands and ovaries. Before birth, the foetus makes DHEA and it also stimulates the placenta to form oestrogen during pregnancy. Production stops at birth, recommences at about 7 years of age, peaks at 30, and declines slowly thereafter.

Studies in rats suggested that DHEA might protect an overfed rat from becoming obese, and that mice given DHEA avoid the usual fall in immune function that occurs with age.

These studies gave rise to human trials, but the results were less positive than they were with rodents. The University of San Diego gave DHEA or a placebo to 9 men and 10 women, aged between 50 and 65. The men taking DHEA had a slight decrease in their body fat mass, but the women had a small increase. No changes were found in basal metabolic rate, bone density, fasting insulin, glucose or other biochemical factors, and no significant adverse effects were noted. Two other small trials did not show positive results. In one, 40 healthy older people were given 50 mg DHEA a day for two weeks, in another, 36 seniors were given DHEA at the same time as they received a flu shot. The groups getting DHEA had no advantages over a placebo.

Dr Samuel Yen, an endocrinologist who is conducting research on DHEA, strongly discourages the use of over-the-counter DHEA, while researchers from the Department of Obstetrics and Gynaecology at Baylor College of Medicine in the USA note that DHEA 'should be used judiciously, if at all'. Part of the caution may be due to the fact that in one study, 14 out of 16 rats given DHEA developed liver cancer. Human studies have also reported heart palpitations in those taking DHEA and post-menopausal women with high natural levels of DHEA have a higher incidence of breast cancer. More exhaustive testing is needed before recommending this compound.

As DHEA can be converted to testosterone in the body, it is banned for sportspeople. Several sportspeople who have taken DHEA have been picked up on routine drug tests and banned from their sport as a result.

The bottom line: Caution needed. Wait for more research before trying this one.

Ginkgo biloba

The leaves of the ancient ginkgo or maidenhair tree are widely used in fat metabolisers, cellulite cures and weight loss preparations. Their inclusion is somewhat strange as there is no suggestion in any medical reports that *Ginkgo biloba* has any effect on body weight.

Studies have shown that *Ginkgo biloba* has some modest effects in improving blood flow and this may be why the herb is added to so-called cellulite cures, although, as discussed in Chapter 2, there is no evidence that cellulite results from poor blood flow or can be eliminated if blood flow improves.

There are also claims that ginkgo improves memory. Do weight loss promoters think this might be an advantage for those trying to remember to exercise, perhaps? Unfortunately, there is no good evidence that *Ginkgo biloba* works to enhance memory. One study claimed that a huge dose given to 8 young women improved their memory for series of numbers but another gave 12 women the same high dose and found no memory changes. A study of people with impaired memory found no advantages in 12 out of 13 memory tests.

The bottom line: There is no evidence that this herb helps with weight loss or has any effect on cellulite. It's also unlikely that it will help you remember to exercise or watch what you eat.

Capsaicin

The heat of chillies and capsicums comes from capsaicin. This substance is now being sold through health food shops as a slimming aid. There is some evidence that capsaicin may be of use, although the studies relate only to eating chillies, not to taking an isolated compound in a pill.

As you know when you eat hot chillies, they stimulate a painful response, which many people find pleasurable. The response comes because capsaicin stimulates neurones which in turn may increase production of endorphins (the compounds that produce runner's 'high') and, more relevant for weight loss, increased levels of epinephrine, which stimulates conversion of protein to glucose and also the breakdown of fat. Capsaicin's effect on neurones can also increase production of a substance called cholecystokinin, which is produced in the intestine and stimulates the action of the hormones insulin and glucagon. Some researchers have therefore theorised that capsaicin might be of benefit for weight loss.

Studies in rats have found that spicy food can raise body temperature and increase the amount of oxygen the body uses. One study found that humans given a first course containing plenty of chilli and spices ate less for the rest of the meal. Whether this is directly due to the effects of capsaicin or possibly related to the taste buds getting satisfaction from the strong flavour is not known. There is no evidence that capsaicin in a capsule has any beneficial effect.

The bottom line: If you like eating spicy foods with plenty of chilli, go ahead—at least it will taste good and it just might help.

Guarana

Guarana is made from the seeds of a climbing shrub (*Paullinia cupana*) native to South America. The seeds contain methylxanthine alkaloids, the major one being caffeine. In Brazil, guarana seeds are ground to a paste and mixed with hot water to form a popular beverage with two to three times the level of caffeine found in coffee. Guarana also contains some antioxidant compounds which may be valuable.

Tests in the United States of supplements claiming to contain guarana have found that many do not contain authentic guarana but have caffeine from other sources, without the true antioxidants that the Indians have long believed prevent gastrointestinal upsets.

Caffeine stimulates the central nervous system and increases alertness, at least until the body becomes habituated to the dose. It also allows the body to use free fatty acids for energy, preserving carbohydrate stores in muscles and, in theory at least, allowing for prolonged exercise. Unfortunately, some studies show this effect is more likely in those of normal weight than in obese people.

However, caffeine can stimulate metabolic rate and may have some use in weight loss, although the effect diminishes with repeated use. Eight studies have examined the effects of caffeine in weight loss, although only one study added caffeine and compared its effects to a placebo. In this study, caffeine had no effect on body weight. Of the remaining studies, only those which combined caffeine with ephedrine (see p.67) showed any effect, and the side effects included insomnia, jittery feelings, changes in heart rhythm and increased risk of heart attack and stroke. Such combinations are therefore undesirable. No studies have specifically examined guarana in humans although one study in animals found no changes in weight. Toxicity is related to dose and low doses appear to be non-toxic, except in early pregnancy.

Guarana, like coffee, has a diuretic effect which may cause apparent short-term changes in body weight through fluid loss. Such changes do not represent loss of body fat.

The bottom line: Guarana appears to be safe in small doses, but has no real benefits for weight loss. The major danger lies in not knowing the dose in some supplements.

Pectin and other fibres

Pectin is a form of soluble fibre included in many weight loss and cellulite preparations, presumably because foods high in fibre are filling and may help people feel satisfied with less food. In fact, there is no evidence that fibre supplements lead to lower food intake. The inability to stop eating when they are full is a major cause of obesity in many people.

However, it makes sense for everyone, whether trying to lose weight or not, to eat foods high in fibre. Such foods are also good sources of other nutrients. There are no proven benefits from the very small amounts of fibre included in weight loss supplements.

One small study claimed that taking 5 grams of pectin could delay gastric emptying and increase satiety, but the subjects were not overweight.

Another type of soluble fibre—guar gum—has been trialled over a 14-month period in some Dutch women who were also asked to follow a very low-calorie diet. The gum had no effect on their weight, blood pressure, cholesterol levels or the amount they ate.

The bottom line: Pectin won't do any harm, but is unlikely to have any effect on weight.

Grapeseed extract

Another ingredient in many cellulite and weight loss preparations, grapeseed extract, contains antioxidants called proanthocyanidins. Taken in grapes, these antioxidants may have some beneficial effects—even more if the grapes are first fermented into wine—but they have no effect on body fat, weight or cellulite. There isn't a shred of evidence that this ingredient will change body fat or cellulite.

The bottom line: No danger but no benefits.

Escin (or horse chestnut)

The horse chestnut seed contains a substance called escin. This compound helps circulation, which is presumably why it is included in anti-cellulite preparations. There is no rationale for this and no evidence that cellulite is caused by poor circulation or cured by increasing circulation.

The bottom line: Sounds good, but has no effect.

Sweet clover

Clover is a source of phytoestrogens (plant oestrogens), and is being extensively researched for possible beneficial effects in menopausal women and men at risk of prostate cancer. There is no evidence that it has any effect on body weight or cellulite, and no reason why it should.

Claims that it will prevent fluid build-up are not yet proven and, in any case, excess body fat or cellulite are not due to fluid retention.

The bottom line: There may be some advantages to health from sweet clover pills (although this is by no means proven at this stage), but don't bother taking it for any effect on weight or cellulite.

Evening primrose oil

The oil derived from the evening primrose is a rich source of the omega-6 polyunsaturated fatty acid called gamma linolenic acid. It is also produced from linoleic acid, the major fatty acid in polyunsaturated vegetable oils (corn, safflower, sunflower, soy bean, sesame, grapeseed), polyunsaturated margarines and mayonnaise, walnuts, seeds (sesame, sunflower, pumpkin) and oats. Few people lack linoleic acid in their daily diets and many researchers believe an excess of omega-6 polyunsaturates relative to the level of omega-3 polyunsaturated oils (found in fish, linseeds and canola oil) is undesirable. It is difficult, therefore, to understand why supplementary evening primrose oil is included in cellulite products. It does have some use in a particular type of eczema that occurs in small children who lack sufficient quantities of the necessary enzyme to convert linoleic acid into gamma linolenic acid, but this has little to do with weight or body fat.

The bottom line: Harmless but irrelevant for loss of body fat (including cellulite).

Inositol

Another ingredient in many weight loss preparations, inositol is a phospholipid that can be made by the body from glucose. Contrary to popular belief, it is not one of the B-complex vitamins. Skeletal muscle contains high concentrations of inositol, which has given rise to a belief that taking extra quantities will increase lean body mass and decrease body fat. One study that examined this theory reported no benefits and there have been no studies looking at its use in weight loss. There is no theoretical reason why inositol would be involved in weight loss.

The bottom line: No problems, but no benefits.

Conjugated linoleic acid (CLA)

CLA is a polyunsaturated fatty acid with 18 carbon atoms and two double bonds. The positioning of the double bond in its molecule makes it different from linoleic acid, the major polyunsaturated fatty acid in safflower, sunflower, corn, soy bean and grapeseed oils and margarines. Dairy products are major sources of CLA.

According to those selling CLA, it helps burn fat and decreases breakdown of lean muscle tissue. As a side benefit, it is supposed to prevent heart disease, breast cancer and skin cancers—and there is indeed some evidence of these possibilities. In one study with rats, CLA also normalised impaired glucose tolerance.

In rats, mice and chickens, CLA appears to decrease body fat by increasing metabolism and decreasing the animals' desire to eat. There is no evidence that these effects occur in humans and no studies have shown any help with loss of body fat.

The bottom line: More research on humans needed. Taking supplements is unwise when safety tests and toxic levels have not been established for humans.

Chinese herbs

A variety of Chinese herbs are promoted for weight loss. There is no evidence they are effective but there is evidence of serious harm. Several reports from Belgium have described severe kidney failure occurring in women taking slimming preparations containing Chinese herbs. Possible problems include the preparations containing herbs other than those stated, presence of toxic herbs or herbs in toxic quantities, and the lack of standards for what goes into such preparations.

The bottom line: With no studies showing the usefulness of Chinese herbs for slimming purposes, and some known dangers, plus the difficulties of tracing the source of some ingredients, avoid these products.

St John's wort

There is some proof from controlled trials that St John's wort (*Hypericum perforatum*) has anti-depressant properties and is appropriate in measured and known quantities in properly-diagnosed cases of mild to moderate depression. There is no evidence that St John's wort has any ability to assist loss of body fat, nor is there any evidence to suggest that excess body fat is a result of depression—but this is presumably why the plant or an extract of it is an ingredient in some slimming preparations and cellulite cures. Although some people take comfort in sweet and fatty foods when they are feeling low, many other people who are depressed fail to eat and grow thin as a result.

St John's wort was named for St John the Baptist, possibly because it blooms in the Northern Hemisphere at the time of year celebrated as his birthday. It acts in a similar way to prescription drugs called monoamine oxidase inhibitors. Like these drugs, it may cause sudden and severe changes in blood pressure if combined with foods high in tyramine. For this reason, as well as the fact that self-diagnosis of depression is unwise, St John's wort may not be a suitable ingredient in over-the-counter preparations.

There is no information about the quantities of St John's wort in some slimming preparations, and with no proof that it has a role in weight loss and little evidence of its safety in long-term use, it is not appropriate for it to be included in slimming and cellulite preparations.

The bottom line: This herb may be appropriate when used in known quantities and prescribed for mild depression by a qualified doctor or herbalist, but it has no role for weight loss.

Other herbs

Some slimming preparations, especially powdered drink mixes, contain herbs such as *Verbena officinalis* (blue vervain), *Chrondrus* extract (Irish moss), *Rheum officinale* (rhubarb), *Glycyrrhiza glabra* (liquorice), *Juglans cinerea* bark and other types of bark. Each of these compounds has either a diuretic or laxative action and their use may therefore promote loss of water through increased urine or faeces. Diuretics and laxatives have no effect on body fat levels and can have undesirable effects, including loss of valuable nutrients such as potassium, magnesium and other minerals.

Some products sold by multi-level marketing companies in the United States, and products available from the Internet, also contain *ma huang*. This Chinese herb is banned in countries such as Australia (and also for Olympic and most other athletes), but is available in the United States where it is also present in some slimming teas, drinks and meal replacement products. It is also used in some countries on prescription as a treatment for asthma.

Promoters of *ma huang* claim it will increase metabolic rate—and this may indeed be true. However, the herb contains ephedrine—an amphetamine—a 'pep' substance which can produce severe, even fatal reactions. There have been several cases of stroke, some fatal, in people taking this herb in slimming preparations. The reactions occur because ephedrine increases heart rate, constricts blood vessels and can lead to a sudden and violent increase in blood pressure. It also causes headaches, insomnia, changes in heart rhythm and memory loss.

The bottom line: Avoid all products that contain—or might contain—these herbal ingredients. This is especially important for athletes, as some substances included in slimming/muscle building products are included among banned substances. Never take any supplement unless you are absolutely sure of its contents and it comes from a recognised laboratory or retail outlet where it can easily be tracked down if undesirable side effects occur.

Enzymes

Various diets claim that the enzymes in particular foods (especially pineapple or pawpaw) will break down fat. Pawpaw, for example, contains an enzyme called papain which breaks down protein fibres in meat and is sometimes used in meat tenderisers. Papain is also added to beer to prevent a 'haze' forming when the beer is cooled. But that does not mean that pawpaw's enzymes will somehow act on body fat.

Enzymes act as catalysts for many chemical reactions within the body. All living foods contain natural enzymes. Animals, including humans, also produce digestive enzymes in the stomach and small intestine. Enzymes are protein substances and most have quite specific actions to break down particular food components. For example, some protein-splitting enzymes in the stomach begin digesting proteins in the acid environment of the stomach; the pancreas produces secretions containing a variety of specific enzymes which break down fats, carbohydrates and proteins.

The enzymes in foods are digested along with any other protein in the food. Once digested they no longer function as enzymes. Even if the pawpaw enzyme could make its way past the digestive processes, it would not have any effect on body fat. Enzymes may sound fascinating and almost 'magical', but they have no part in weight reduction.

Vitamins

Many diets recommend vitamin and mineral supplements, often because they do not contain a healthy balance of foods which would ordinarily supply these nutrients. Vitamins take part in many of the biochemical reactions in the body. Some, such as many of the B-complex vitamins, are involved in the breakdown of carbohydrates and proteins for energy. However, taking extra vitamins does not mean that more carbohydrates and proteins will be used for energy.

Vitamin B_6 is often promoted as a vitamin for weight loss. B_6 is involved in protein metabolism and helps form chemical substances involved in transmitting impulses in nerves and the brain. It is also vital for healthy red blood cells. A deficiency of vitamin B_6 is rare. Symptoms include mental depression, convulsive seizures, severe skin problems, a type of anaemia, and weight loss. This does not mean that people who feel a bit unhappy will feel better if they take B_6. An excess of vitamin B_6 can damage nerve endings in the fingers and feet, making walking difficult. How the myth developed that extra B_6 could help weight loss is a mystery, although it has sold a lot of vitamin B_6 supplements! Some people with excessive thyroid gland function sometimes need extra vitamin B_6. Since many people incorrectly blame excess fat on a malfunctioning thyroid gland, this may be where this crazy idea began.

A sensible diet can provide all the vitamins the body needs. There is absolutely no evidence that extra vitamin B_6, or any other vitamin, has any slimming power.

6

The diet merry-go-round

PROBLEMS WITH FAST WEIGHT LOSS

Most diets do not appear to work over the long term, although almost any will work over a few weeks. It is therefore important not to judge a diet by its supposed 'success' over 3, 4 or 6 weeks. It is often said that only about 5 per cent of dieters maintain their weight loss after a year or more. The source of such a figure is hard to come by; it seems more like an educated guess since the statistics on long-term success with various weight loss diets have not been recorded, and it is difficult to track people over long periods of time. Some weight loss organisations have now started keeping long-term records of the weight of their clients but reliable long-term results have not yet been published.

It is hard to gauge the success of various diets because those who lose weight and keep it off successfully no longer seek help from dietitians and doctors. Some weight loss organisations such as Weight Watchers keep some of their 'success stories' on as lecturers and keep contact with others through their Maintenance Program. But even a program such as this—which aims to give people advice on how to make permanent changes in their eating and exercise habits—will find that many of the successful clients no longer need them. Thus the '5 per cent success rate' is difficult to verify.

However, most dietitians and weight loss organisations can testify to the fact that many of their clients go from one diet to another. They lose weight initially, regain it, try another diet—and so on, their weight going up and down like a yo-yo. For most dieters, every drop in weight is followed by a greater gain and their weight climbs steadily. The yo-yo effect may be more harmful to health than staying fat in the first place. Some studies have shown that down-and-up body weight causes blood fats such as cholesterol to increase, although other researchers maintain there is little evidence of long-term adverse effects on blood fats.

The diet merry-go-round sets up an impossible situation. The person who is overweight never gives up hoping for a miracle and so will always give the next diet a try. Part of the problem is the attitude of dieters. Full of enthusiasm, they go 'on' yet another diet, assuming that after a while, when they are thin, they will be able to go 'off' the diet. This 'temporary' attitude enables people to endure all kinds of foolish eating patterns. If someone tells you to live on pasta or pineapples or some protein powder, diet drink or herbal mixture for three weeks or even three months, with the promise that it will 'cure' your fatness, you may well give it a try. It sounds so much easier than having to change your total pattern of eating and exercise.

The carrot offered to the dieter is almost always the promise of fast weight loss. 'Get it off fast', 'get the diet over and done with quickly', appeals to most people much more than the long, slow, steady methods of permanent change promoted by dietitians. Even Weight Watchers—an organisation which promotes soundly based and long-term changes in eating and exercise behaviour—sometimes puts out a bait offering a faster start to their sensible weight loss program.

Fast weight loss has nothing to do with good health. The only time it is useful is in the massively obese person who requires surgery and must lose weight to avoid the hazards associated with the high dose of anaesthetic which their large body would require. Fast weight loss by any means may be essential in this case.

For most people, fast weight loss is related to the very human desire for instant gratification. The fact that fast weight loss is not permanent does not even sway those wanting a quick fix. They cannot look beyond the initial fall in the reading on the scales. What happens later is of no current concern. And there is always the hope that once they weigh less, life will become suddenly rosy and they will have no problem adopting a healthier eating pattern. Alas, it does not work that way.

The desire for fast weight loss is related to the reasons for losing weight in the first place. For most women, the major reason is appearance and self-esteem. But, as was noted in Chapter 3, fast weight loss may leave you looking haggard and flabby. Nor is it compatible with permanent weight loss. You can expect an inverse relationship between the speed of weight loss and its permanence. Fast weight loss simply doesn't last.

SELF-ESTEEM

Many overweight people—and many women of normal weight—have low self-esteem. Problems with some who are genuinely overweight are caused by society's attitude to large people. The overweight are discriminated against at school, in employment and by the opposite sex. They are assumed to be more self-indulgent, less attractive, less disciplined and lazy. An Australian magazine aimed at larger women went out of business because advertisers did not want their products associated with larger people. Another magazine editor was sacked because she featured larger models and refused to run silly diet stories. The manufacturers of various products usually advertised in women's magazines seem to assume that larger people, especially larger women, have no interest in fashion, cosmetics, hair care, cars or even electrical appliances. The lack of self-confidence apparent in many overweight women is therefore hardly surprising.

Our society also imposes many physical problems on large people—and some of these apply equally to those who are very tall as to those who are fat. Airline seats cannot accommodate large people. Turnstiles are made for slim people. Many public toilets are constructed in such a way that fat people find it difficult to fit inside the cubicle. Caravans assume people are no more than a certain size. Many cars cannot accommodate the larger figure. Chairs may break under their weight. For fat people, the hardships of living in our society can have a devastating effect on self-esteem—many stay home and try to hide from society, often taking comfort in eating, which, of course, makes matters worse.

There are also problems of self-esteem for the normal weight woman who thinks she is fat. Few women live up to the image portrayed as the ideal or desirable female shape. As we have discussed earlier, many normal (and even underweight) women see themselves as imperfect. This gap between society's fantasy and reality decreases women's self-esteem. It is simply impossible for a woman in her 40s or 50s to look like someone decades younger. Yet women have such unreal expectations largely because the main role models to which they are exposed are young, very slim, smooth skinned, perfectly groomed, presenting an appearance incompatible with the lifestyles of most real women. Lacking self-confidence, many women think all their dreams and hopes will materialise if only they can lose weight.

Women who fit this mould abuse their bodies, either with dieting, fasting, bingeing or a combination of these practices. Lacking the self-confidence to tell the world 'this is me and this is the way I am', they jump on the diet merry-go-round. When the diet fails to deliver the magic they want, they try the next one, and the next one, and so

THE DIET DILEMMA

on. Many spend thousands of dollars on supplements, fat metabolisers and other supposed weight loss cures, as discussed in Chapter 5.

While some overweight men have similar problems to overweight women, most tend to see their larger size in a different light. Some large men enjoy the fact that they take up more space, and use their size as a sign of power. Some even use it to command respect, especially from their subordinates. Others perceive their corpulence as a sign of their largeness of spirit, their love of having a good time and their generosity. Few of these men make any attempt to diet. Even though their weight may be a very real health hazard, they use it to their advantage during their (shorter) lifespan.

HOW TO GET OFF THE MERRY-GO-ROUND

1 Try to like yourself the way you are.
2 Accept that people come in all shapes and sizes.
3 Accept the fact that fast fat loss is impossible.
4 Be prepared to change your eating and exercise habits—but only to the extent that you can live with the changes.
5 Be prepared not to be perfect.
6 Stop thinking that sticking to a diet is 'good' and breaking it is 'bad'.
7 Stop looking for the latest miracle diet.

GETTING OFF THE DIET MERRY-GO-ROUND

Like yourself the way you are

To get off the diet merry-go-round takes courage and self-confidence. First of all, you must learn to accept and like your body the way it is. Even before embarking on a permanent change in eating and exercise patterns—which is the only way to eventually change your fat level—you must accept your worth as a person the way you are now. Until self-esteem improves, it is almost impossible to start the long, slow road to looking after your body's needs for food and exercise.

Many people want to put the cart before the horse. 'Once I lose my weight,' they maintain, 'my self-esteem will improve.' It doesn't work because that attitude is indicative of a basic dislike of yourself. And it is only when you have a great deal of respect for yourself that you will begin to look after your body properly. This applies to those who are genuinely overweight. It also applies to those who are not overweight but think they need to diet.

Some people need help from a psychologist to improve their self-esteem. Women whose husbands or boyfriends maintain their power by destroying a woman's self-confidence need to distance themselves from such men, either emotionally or physically, if they are to achieve success and learn to respect themselves. Other women of normal weight may need to learn to listen to their husbands and boyfriends when they keep telling them they are not too fat. Some people can change these attitudes on their own; others need professional counselling. Some overweight men, especially young men and those who are very obese, may also need help in establishing their self-esteem.

Accepting differences

In the 1950s it was considered undesirable for women to be taller than about 5 feet 4 inches (about 163 cm). Tall women were supposedly less attractive to men and magazines of the day carried advice about how to dress so that you appeared shorter. You were also advised to be seated when 'Mr Right' walked into your life. Tall women were expected to wear low-heeled shoes so their height would not make them look too dominant. Most young women find it hard to believe such absurdities. Fashions have changed, models are tall and young girls now want to be taller. Women today cannot believe that women once wanted to be short.

However, even though women of the 1950s were expected not to exceed moderate height, there was much less emphasis on how fat they should or should not be. The tops of the legs and the buttocks were always hidden under clothing (even swimming costumes had a modest 'skirt' across the front), so no-one worried about problems of 'cellulite'. The ideal female shape was quite curvy with the waist being much smaller than breasts and hips. Slim hips were assumed to be the province of boys.

We now accept that women come in different heights and there is no stigma attached to being tall. Instead, society now expects all women to conform to some mythical perfection of small size in hips, buttocks and thighs. Tummies are expected to magically assume a concavity rather than the normal convexity.

Dietitian Dr David Crawford has spent some years studying women's attitudes towards their bodies and their thoughts about weight. He has found that few women are satisfied with their bodies and the area they dislike most is the tummy. He found that of those women trying to lose weight, 89 per cent wanted slimmer tummies; 80 per cent wanted smaller hips; and three-quarters wanted smaller thighs, buttocks and waist. Even among slim women who were not trying to lose weight, almost half wanted flatter tummies.

We will never get off the diet merry-go-round until we accept that women will never be all the same size or shape. Nor will dieting magically produce some mythically perfect body. Just as women in the 1950s could not control their height and had to accept it, we now need to accept that we will never all be the same size around the waist or hips or thighs. In other words, we must learn to accept our basic body shape—which is determined by genetics, just as height is. Those who are genuinely overweight can lose fat, but this is only likely to happen when they start to concentrate on something other than a dislike of their bodies. You can only lose fat consistent with your basic body shape. If your mother had big hips, you probably will have them too.

It is only when you like yourself that you will take time to attend to your body's needs, whatever they are. These may include giving yourself permission to eat a particular food because you really feel like it, making your own choices of what and when you will or won't eat—rather than having a diet dictated to you—or taking time out to go for a walk. Those who continually ignore their own desires and follow other's prescriptions often become resentful and turn to food for comfort.

Accepting gradual weight loss

Fast weight loss is not fat loss. There are no miracles. You would think that after reading of so many hundreds of diets and weight loss 'cures', people would realise there is no easy solution—but it hasn't happened yet.

Advertisements for various weight loss methods manage to give the impression that *this* latest diet, supplement, powder, pill, potion, chocolate, herbal mixture, drink or health bar is *the* answer to every fat person's prayer. In fact, if you adopt a sleuth-like attitude and read the fine print in advertisements for slimming products, somewhere, usually in very small print, you will see the words 'if taken in conjunction with a calorie-controlled diet'. That is the catch. The product itself 'works' only if you also control what you eat. Cleverly designed advertisements manage to disguise such truths.

In Australia, no food can legally be claimed to be a 'slimming' food or one that will bring about weight loss. Yet many people believe that eating certain foods will actually cause them to lose weight. Grapefruit is the old favourite, while others think they will lose weight if they drink low-kilojoule drinks, eat lots of hardboiled eggs, or even eat margarine instead of butter!

Changing your eating and exercise habits

If possible, consult an accredited practising dietitian who will have the skills to go through your current eating and exercise habits and decide which of your habits need changing and which changes you can make in practice. If you are in doubt about a person's qualifications, check with the Dietitians' Association of Australia.

There is no point in vowing to make changes which are impractical—to eat foods you don't want or don't like, or to take up an exercise program that is uncomfortable or impractical. You should also realise that not everyone needs to make the same changes. There is no one ideal eating pattern, just as there is no one exercise pattern which suits everyone. You need to find something which you can do happily.

Being imperfect is OK

Strict diets almost always lead to breakout binges. Often the slimmer feels so guilty for eating a whopping slice of chocolate cake, or whatever, that she reasons that having broken her diet, she may as well make a total pig of herself. The result is guilt.

A sensible eating plan does not mean you never have another piece of chocolate cake, although it may mean not eating chocolate cake every time you feel hungry. Nor does a pattern of exercising more mean you must never miss a day of exercise, although it will mean not missing weeks or months at a time. Moving is more important than formal exercise and incorporating more movement into your day is often easier than finding time to go to the gym or pool.

Not feeling guilty

What you eat and drink and how much or little you exercise is your choice and no-one has the right to judge you for it. This pattern of feeling guilty when you are 'bad' may be appropriate to childhood but is out of place in an adult.

If you decide to eat some fatty or sugary concoction, that is your right—there is no big brother watching you to pronounce you good or bad. The concept of good or bad assumes someone else has given you orders about what you may or may not eat. The moment someone says you can't have something, it is human nature to want it. Chapter 10 discusses a variety of ways to make small, gradual changes in your eating and exercise habits, according to what suits your lifestyle.

Avoiding miracle cures

Remember that there are no miracles but there are many people who will try to sell you one. Learn to judge a diet or weight loss method according to the guidelines below:

HOW TO PICK A GOOD DIET PROGRAM

Before you are tempted by yet another diet claiming to be the answer to the dieter's dilemma, test out the diet with the following quiz. If you find even one 'yes' answer to the following questions, reject it. There is no magic wand.

- Does it promise fast weight loss?
- Does it claim to be effortless?
- Does it claim to be new or revolutionary?
- Does it claim that you do not need to exercise?
- Does it claim to have a magic ingredient of any sort?
- Does it involve buying special powders, pills or meal replacements?
- Does it claim you can eat anything you like as long as you take a particular product?
- Does it cut out carbohydrates found in bread, cereals, grains or potatoes?
- Does it promise that you can eat unlimited quantities of meats, cheese and eggs?
- Does it promise that special garments, passive exercise machines (where you do nothing), injections or vitamins will help weight loss?
- Does it tell you that you must eat an exact range of foods with no substitutions allowed?
- Does it imply that you can eat as many kilojoules as you like and still lose weight?

WEIGHT LOSS AND METABOLIC RATE

As discussed in Chapter 3, most wonder diets cause a weight loss by reducing water and fuel (glycogen) in muscles, which leads to a loss of lean body tissue (muscle). The scales show a reduced reading—at least for a few weeks. Once you go off the diet (and most are too boring to stick to for long), the body becomes rehydrated and you gradually replace glycogen in muscle tissue, along with its normal content of water. Initially, more glycogen and water will be stored than normal, causing weight to rise to a level higher than before the diet.

The effect is similar to the result achieved by some long-distance sportspeople who deliberately deplete their muscles of glycogen and then eat lots of carbohydrate to give themselves bigger glycogen stores than usual so they can run, row, swim, or whatever, for longer before feeling exhausted. This is the technique known as carbohydrate loading. (Few sportspeople now practise it as they can achieve equally high glycogen levels with a consistently high-carbohydrate diet.)

Glycogen is the major fuel for exercise and the only fuel for any short, sharp exercise such as sprinting, hitting a tennis or golf ball or lifting a weight. When glycogen stores are depleted, you do not feel like exercising at all. In fact, glycogen depletion leaves you feeling lower than an earthworm. The major reason why sportspeople no longer use glycogen-loading techniques is that they hate the enforced inactivity during the glycogen depletion phase.

Changes in glycogen and water balance are temporary. The main problem for slimmers who use a low-carbohydrate diet to deplete glycogen is that they feel weak and exhausted when they try to exercise.

However, fast weight loss diets also cause a loss of muscle tissue itself. Muscle is active tissue, which means that even when it is not being used in exercise, it uses up kilojoules. Fat tissue needs almost no kilojoules for its maintenance.

Metabolism

Metabolism refers to the series of chemical changes which keep the heart beating, the brain functioning, and the liver, kidneys, lungs and other vital tissues carrying out their normal life-supporting functions.

The basal or resting metabolic rate (BMR or RMR) is the energy used for metabolism when you are lying at rest at a standard temperature, not having eaten for some hours (digesting food uses up extra energy) and not having had any significant muscular exertion for several hours. Metabolic rate can be determined by measuring the amount of oxygen the body uses. Newer techniques using 'heavy' water (containing doubly-labelled isotopes deuterium and oxygen-18) which allow carbon dioxide production to be measured, indicating how much energy is being used.

The energy used for basal metabolism is measured in kilojoules or calories (4.2 kJ = 1 Cal). It is a little like the energy a car uses when it stands idling, and it varies from person to person. Men usually use more kilojoules in metabolism because they have a larger surface area and more muscle than women. If we compare a lean man and a lean woman of the same age and height, he will have more muscle than she and, consequently, he will burn up more kilojoules even when they are both standing still.

The amount of energy used for metabolism varies from around 3400 kJ (about 800 Cals) to 7500 kJ (about 1800 Cals). Some of this variation is due to the factors listed in the box on the next page; some is due to individual variation. However, the most important factor governing the energy used for basic metabolism in adults is the amount of muscle.

Physical activity uses up even more energy, as discussed below. This may vary from almost nothing in an inactive person to 12 000 or 17 000 kJ a day in someone undergoing extremely strenuous physical activity. Moderate physical activity uses 1200–1500 kJ per hour. (Note: 1 Calorie = 4.2 kJ.)

FACTORS AFFECTING BASAL METABOLISM

- surface area (the larger your surface, the more energy you burn)
- the amount of muscle (the more muscle, the higher the metabolic rate)
- age (younger people use more energy than old people)
- whether you are growing new tissue (children, adolescents, pregnant women and those recovering from injuries such as burns have higher metabolic rates)
- temperature of the body (a fever increases metabolic rate)
- air temperature (in cold weather, metabolic rate increases to keep the body warm)
- whether you have eaten or are fasting (eating increases metabolic rate, fasting lowers it)
- lactation

DIETS MAKE YOU FAT

With fast weight loss diets, there is a loss of muscle. This reduces the amount of energy used. A person whose weight was stable on, say, 7500 kJ a day will need less than this amount of energy after following any fast weight loss diet. If that person goes back to eating her old amount of food (on which she neither gained nor lost weight), she will now gain weight.

This is the danger of women dieting when they are not even too fat in the first place. The diet causes muscle loss, increases the relative proportion of body fat and reduces the amount of food the woman can eat in the future. After a series of such diets, the woman's kilojoule requirements may be so low that it becomes almost impossible for her to maintain her weight. The dieting has made her fat. It is bad enough for someone who was previously fat to become fatter after dieting. It is even worse for the previously slim woman—who only thought she was fat. After a succession of diets, her fears will be fact.

Fasting and skipping meals also reduce the kilojoules used for metabolism. Diets which tell you to constantly eat less become counterproductive. They also make physical activity more difficult.

HOW THE BODY ACCUMULATES AND LOSES FAT

To understand how body fat accumulates, we need to look at the way foods are digested and used by the body.

When we eat, foods are broken down by the process of digestion in the gastrointestinal tract, with the bulk of digestion and almost all absorption of nutrients occurring in the small intestine.

After chewing and swallowing foods, they pass via the oesophagus to the stomach where their presence stimulates gastric juices containing hydrochloric acid to begin a churning process to break the foods down into a thick, creamy, acid liquid. Partial digestion of some proteins occurs in the stomach but fats and carbohydrates are not digested here.

The presence of food in the stomach stimulates the stomach walls to release hydrochloric acid which breaks foods into smaller particles. Small amounts of acid are released according to the contents of the stomach—the acidity of foods is much less than the acid produced by the stomach. Some people imagine that there is a pool of hydrochloric acid sitting in the stomach which is diluted if you drink a glass of water. Others believe the acidity of citrus fruits causes some reaction. A few food components, such as malic acid in coffee, may increase the production of acid in some people. Some people also find an apple eaten on an empty stomach makes them feel hungry. This may also be due to the weak acids found in apples.

The major purpose of the stomach is to act as a holding chamber. The food is churned about and the chewed particles are mixed with acid, mucins (which lubricate the food), water and secretions containing enzymes which start digesting some protein molecules. A substance is also produced which attaches itself to vitamin B_{12} and is essential to allow this vitamin to be absorbed when it reaches the small intestine. Foods which have not been thoroughly chewed may cause indigestion.

Apart from the breakdown of some protein, little digestion occurs in the stomach. There is no truth in the idea that fruit eaten with any other food will lead to foods putrefying and fermenting in the stomach, as is claimed by the authors of *Fit For Life*. Fruits are digested, like all carbohydrates, in the small intestine, whether they are consumed alone or in combination with other foods.

If there is no food in the stomach and you have a glass of some fizzy alcoholic beverage (such as champagne, gin and tonic, or whisky and soda), some of the alcohol can be rapidly absorbed from the stomach, giving a sudden rise in blood alcohol levels. Food in the stomach delays the absorption of alcohol.

From the stomach, small amounts of food are squirted through to the small intestine. Foods which are mainly carbohydrate pass through quickly. This is why you soon feel hungry after a meal of, say, rice and vegetables, or straight fruit. Protein and fat delay the emptying of the stomach. This is not a problem, is not abnormal in any way, and helps prolong the satiety of a meal. If you eat only carbohydrate you soon feel the need to eat again. This can be a problem if the only foods which come to hand between meals are snacks such as biscuits, cakes, pastries, lollies or chips. It would be much wiser to include some protein at a meal than to be tempted to eat nutritionally poor snacks between meals.

When it leaves the stomach, the liquid food mass goes to the small intestine where bile from the liver neutralises the acidity from the stomach. Enzymes from pancreatic and intestinal juices then break down carbohydrates to simple sugars (such as glucose), proteins to amino acids, and fats to fatty acids, monoglycerides and glycerol. The digested food plus vitamins and minerals are then absorbed into the cells in the highly folded lining of the intestine.

From the intestinal lining, fats pass to the body's lymph system and into the blood. Amino acids and sugars are taken to the liver which distributes them to the cells. Dietary fibre passes to the large intestine where helpful bacteria break it down, releasing acids which provide a source of energy directly to the cells of the large intestine. The bacteria multiply by the million in this process and their spent bodies, plus any undigested fibres, such as lignin, are excreted in the faeces.

In the body's cells, glucose and fatty acids undergo oxidation and release energy. There is some evidence that some types of fats are more readily oxidised and used for energy than others.

To a small extent some amino acids may also provide energy. The cells have a finite requirement for energy which is dependent on how hard they are working. Once the cells have as much energy as they need for metabolism, activity and growth, any excess fatty acids are converted to body fat—a form of stored energy. Many people have too much 'stored energy', but it is fat, not 'toxic wastes' or 'undigested' food, as some popular diet books claim.

In digesting food, the body certainly uses energy. The 'cost' to the body in digesting, absorbing and using proteins means that about 24 per cent of the potential energy from protein is used up. About 5 per cent of the potential energy from carbohydrates is lost and 7 per cent of that in fats. These losses have been taken into account when calculating the number of kilojoules of energy available from different nutrients. Thus, within the body, a gram of fat provides 37 kilojoules (or 9 Cals); proteins provide 17 kJ (4 Cals) per gram and carbohydrates 16 kJ (4 Cals) per gram. Alcohol provides energy at the rate of 29 kJ per gram.

Once the amino acids, fatty acids and sugars have been released into the blood, they are available to be used as required. The amino acids go first to repair tissues, form hormones and antibodies and, if appropriate, allow for growth or the production of milk (in breastfeeding women). Any amino acids not required for these essential purposes are taken to the liver. The body does not like using amino acids for energy, but it can break down excess quantities, producing molecules that can be used in the glucose energy cycle of the body.

The fatty acids are available to be used for energy and people who are physically active will burn these. At this stage, it appears that saturated fats are not as readily used by the body for energy as unsaturated fats. Omega-3 fats, such as those found in fish, are used in the body's nerve and brain cells and in cell membranes and are not converted to fat. Other unsaturated fats are also more likely to be used than stored. However, when the diet is high in fat, leftover fats are converted to body fat. This is a simple process for the body and requires little expenditure of energy. It therefore happens easily and often.

The sugars which come from the breakdown of all kinds of carbohydrates have a number of functions. Some replenish the blood glucose level. This is the brain's only source of fuel and so the body gives it first priority. Blood glucose is also a source of energy for all body cells. When the blood glucose level rises, the hormone insulin is released from the pancreas. This helps glucose move from the blood into the cells.

To protect the blood glucose level, some sugars are made into glycogen and stored in the liver. Should the blood glucose level fall below its optimal level, and the person not respond by eating some carbohydrate, the liver glycogen is quickly converted to glucose.

Some sugars are also converted into glycogen which is stored in muscles. Once in the muscles, this glycogen cannot escape to be turned back into blood glucose. Muscle glycogen is available only for the muscles. Exercise will use up this glycogen and more carbohydrate from the diet will restore the levels for the next lot of exercise. Those who exercise often, and eat more carbohydrate, can store almost twice the usual level of glycogen in muscles. This means they can then exercise for much longer periods without feeling tired. As they exercise, they increase the size of the muscle fibres and burn up more kilojoules in basic metabolism. Conversely, those who avoid carbohydrate foods soon deplete their muscles of glycogen and find exercise very tiring.

If the sugar supply is greater than the body's need for blood glucose, liver and muscle glycogen, carbohydrates increase the body's metabolic rate and warm the body. In theory, excess carbohydrates can be converted to body fat, but in practice this rarely happens because carbohydrates are used as the preferred source of energy. Any accompanying fats will not be used, however, and will therefore be converted easily to body fat. Starchy carbohydrate foods such as bread, grains, cereals, potatoes and legumes, or foods such as fruit, in which the natural sugar is combined with dietary fibre, are often recommended in preference to refined sugars. Studies have shown better long-term storage of muscle glycogen derived from starchy carbohydrates, although immediately after exercise, quickly digested sugars provide an advantage by being rapidly digested and used to replenish such stores. Sugar is a carbohydrate food, but as it has no protein, essential fats, minerals, vitamins or dietary fibre, it is really only useful immediately after exercise.

For those who are trying to lose body fat, it is much harder to overconsume carbohydrate foods which are rich in dietary fibre, such as wholemeal bread, wholegrain cereals, fruits, potatoes and beans, because the accompanying fibre makes the foods filling. By way of contrast, a can of soft drink contains about 40 grams of sugar, but is no more filling than water. To get the same quantity of carbohydrate from wholemeal bread would mean eating 3 or 4 slices. Dietary fibre is a natural obstacle to overeating.

Alcohol provides a large number of kilojoules. As alcohol is basically toxic, the body gets rid of it as fast as possible. Alcohol's kilojoules are therefore always burnt before those from any other foods, but any accompanying fats will not be used and will be added to the body's fat stores.

The body can expand its fat stores to almost unlimited lengths. Any excess of food can be converted to fat. However, the body finds it easiest to deposit excess fatty acids from fats into its fat depots. To change proteins or carbohydrates to body fat requires much more effort and the body prefers to use proteins to repair tissues, and carbohydrates to fuel muscles and provide for physical activity.

One kilogram of body fat represents an energy store of over 32 300 kJ (approximately 7700 Cals). This sounds like a lot but it is surprisingly easy to achieve. A small bar of chocolate (100 grams) has around 2220 kJ. That means one small bar of chocolate, in addition to your normal food intake, once a week, would theoretically lead to a weight gain of 3.5 kilograms a year. In fact, the body is rarely so exact but you can see how easy it is to gain weight from just a small amount of extra fat.

The situation with carbohydrate foods is not as simple. Eating more carbohydrate is likely to lead to a greater increase in energy expenditure than eating a fatty food like chocolate. In theory, eating about 100 medium potatoes would lead to an increase in weight of one kilogram. In fact, since you could not eat so many potatoes at once, the small intake from one potato at a time would be used for physical activity. Carbohydrates do not accumulate in the body.

BREAKING DOWN FAT STORES

Each day, the body needs energy to keep its basal metabolism normal, to digest food, keep warm and provide for growth and physical activity. The fuels used to power these processes are a mixture of fatty acids (from fats we eat or from body fat) and carbohydrates (blood glucose and glycogen).

The process of making energy is a bit like the combustion of a fire. To make a fire, you need to start with some small sticks and a match. Once the small sticks begin to burn, you add bigger sticks and when the fire is going strongly you can add logs. You cannot start a fire by holding a match to the logs.

The production of energy in the body is also a combustion reaction. Carbohydrates are like the sticks which get the fire going. Fats are like the logs which will burn once the sticks have the flames licking.

If we eat fewer kilojoules of energy than we need for the body's metabolism and activity, the body will mobilise some of its fat stores. However, to burn the fat, we must first get the fire going with some carbohydrate. Diets which cut back severely on all foods, and especially on carbohydrates, make the body slow down. Eating very little to create a greater deficit causes the body to respond in a protective way by reducing its rate of metabolism and burning up fewer kilojoules. It is as if it says 'if you're not going to feed me, I will take care not to burn up too much energy'. This mechanism is useful for survival in a famine, but not much use to those wanting to lose weight.

As we have seen, if we eat too little carbohydrate and run out of glycogen, exercise becomes difficult and we also burn fewer kilojoules (as well as feeling too tired to do much). If the body tries to convert carbohydrate into body fat, it takes about four times as much energy to do so as it takes to convert the fat we eat to body fat. For this reason, the body prefers to use carbohydrate to power the muscles for exercise than turn it into fat. Dietary fats, on the other hand, are easily converted to body fat.

EXERCISE

The most variable feature of our kilojoule use is physical activity. The number of kilojoules most people expend in physical activity is now lower than at any previous time. Physical activity burns up kilojoules, the number depending on the type of activity, the length of time you spend doing it and the size of the person doing the activity. It takes more energy to move a large person than it takes for someone of smaller size and weight. It may take so much energy to move a very large body that the person compensates by moving very little.

Someone lighter can often move more and move faster and therefore burn up more kilojoules overall. However, the potential for a larger person to burn up kilojoules is much greater than for a small person. For example, a 50 kg person playing an average game of volleyball will use up 630 kJ (150 Cals) whereas someone of 80 kg would use up 1000 kJ (240 Cals). Playing more vigorously burns more kilojoules. A 50 kg person walking for one hour would burn up around 1000 kJ (240 Cals) while our 80 kg subject would burn around 1600 kJ (380 Cals). Walking might seem to be less energetic than volleyball, but it is constant, whereas volleyball involves jumping, running and time standing waiting.

In practice, if a large person does exercise to lose body fat, he or she will have an advantage over a smaller person. The difficulty can sometimes be to convince large people that they should undertake suitable exercise.

The best kilojoule-burning activities tend to be those which can be carried out over a longer period of time. Walking, cycling, dancing, jogging or aerobics are excellent kilojoule-burning activities. Using a skipping rope is of less benefit as few people can skip for more than a couple of minutes. Some people look up tables listing the number of kilojoules they can expect to burn per hour in some activity—and become disheartened. In the example above, walking for an hour will burn up 1600 kJ—about the same number as in a smallish piece of chocolate cake. The walking takes an hour, the chocolate cake only minutes to eat. However, exercise has other advantages which you should consider.

THE IMPORTANCE OF EXERCISE

Exercise increases metabolic rate. Even hours after finishing exercise, the body will still be burning more kilojoules than when it is at rest. This is partly explained by the fact that exercise 'gets the body going' and partly by the increase in muscle which exercise promotes.

Exercise also increases the rate of weight loss later rather than sooner. Most overweight people have been conditioned to think they must lose weight fast at first. In fact, with a program of sensible eating (see Chapter 10) plus exercise, weight loss gets faster after some weeks. This is especially likely in those who have previously had little exercise. More exercise increases the amount of lean muscle tissue and this muscle then begins to use more kilojoules. Muscle cannot develop overnight so it may be some weeks (or occasionally a couple of months) before any effect is noticeable.

As a bonus, exercise seems to normalise appetite. Many people think they will feel hungry if they start exercising. They may, but studies show that those who exercise eat an amount closer to their body's real needs. Appetite and food intake are often mismatched in the inactive. At high levels of exercise, as occur in marathon or cross-country runners or cyclists, appetite does increase. Such people may have an energy intake as high as 21 000 kJ (5000 Cals). This matches their output and they are always slim. Those who report feeling hungry after exercise have been found to eat less—they sit down eagerly to a meal but actually stop eating sooner.

Without exercise, the body's appetite-control mechanism does not seem to work properly. It is only with regular physical activity that we have any instinctive knowledge of how much food the body needs. Farmers are well aware of this. Animals left to graze and eat at will do not increase their body fat levels to any great extent. Animals to be fattened must be penned. Once their physical activity is curtailed, they eat much more. It is much the same with humans: with our reduced physical activity, it is as though we have all been 'penned', thus we eat more food than our bodies require, and grow fatter.

Fidgeting

There are some among us who seem to be unable to sit in any one place for more than a few minutes. They cross and uncross their legs, try a dozen different positions for their arms, and wriggle around on their chairs like small children. Confined in a bus or plane, they drum their fingers, twiddle their thumbs and shuffle their feet, making other people exhausted just from watching their never-ending 'fidgets'. You may have noticed that these obviously restless people are usually thin. With their almost hyperactive lifestyle, that's hardly a surprise.

Other people appear to move very little. They sit still, walk slowly, are unruffled and exude an air of calm peacefulness. Sometimes such people are fat. This may be because it takes so much energy to move their heavier bodies that they have subconsciously adopted a less active pattern of daily living. But we do not know whether the extra weight or the calm movement came first.

Recent research suggests that most people have a pattern of

spontaneous activity which seems to be genetically preprogrammed. A special radar system which detects small movements has been used to study physical activity, including small imperceptible movements and has found large variations in the amount of energy used for 'fidget' type activity. Within a group of 134 subjects, fidgeting accounted for anything from 395 to 3750 kilojoules (100 to 900 Cals) a day. The higher levels of fidgeting activity would certainly be enough to stop most people ever gaining weight.

Fidgeting may be a genetic trait. Some people make more small movements throughout life than others. Whether you learn to move more by being around fidgety parents, or whether you are born with muscle fibres which prefer to make many movements, is not yet known. Current research indicates that some people are programmed to stay fairly motionless, a few exhibit the almost hyperactive tendencies described earlier, while others come somewhere in between. As you might expect, those who fidget the most have an inbuilt way of burning up excess kilojoules and, consequently, tend to be lean.

The major benefit of the inborn fidget mechanism seems to be to help control body weight. If you carry out sufficient small movements to burn up 3750 kJ a day, you will probably never grow fat, even if you have no obvious sport or exercise. There is also the possibility that the fidgeting activity influences the appetite control mechanism so that food intake closely matches the body's needs.

Before you assume that your genes may have got the better of you, remember that conscious physical exercise can easily burn up as many kilojoules as fidget activity. It may be a nuisance having to plan to include exercise, but almost everyone has to make extra efforts in some areas of their lives to achieve what comes naturally to others.

Active, programmed physical activity may even bring benefits which exceed those of the fidgets. Exercise not only helps control metabolism and body fat levels but also works wonders for the heart and arteries. It also improves general circulation and helps with relaxation.

It has been known for years that those who are leanest move the most. In a classic experiment, Professor Jean Mayer, world obesity authority, measured the difference in energy output between lean and fat teenagers playing tennis. To the casual observer, all the players were equally active. However, through the use of special camera techniques, Professor Mayer established that the fatter players moved much less than their leaner peers. Other studies have shown that the lean move faster making beds and doing other household tasks.

For cardiovascular fitness, you need to do some continuous form of exercise, such as walking for 30 to 40 minutes, swimming or running. For fatness, however, movement is more important than exercise, and the benefits of movement for fat loss accumulate. Just by walking up stairs, leaving your desk often, getting up out of the chair every time you want to change the television channel, mowing your own lawn, hanging the washing on the line rather than placing it in the dryer, parking at the edge of the carpark and walking to the shops, you can incorporate movement and help with weight loss. You can also plan for some extra small movements. While watching television, try sitting with your legs straight out for a few minutes (use the advertisement time) to strengthen tummy muscles. Stand up and move around often; do a few stretching exercises while the ads are playing; knit; do some foot exercises. While waiting at traffic lights, tighten up the muscles in your buttocks, flex your biceps, push yourself against the steering wheel.

Most thin people either exercise or do not eat a lot, when their total food intake is considered. However, there are always a few people who do not seem to fit either category. They eat a fair amount, do little exercise and yet remain lean. They may be unobtrusive fidgets who carry out sufficient small movements each day to use up any excess kilojoules they take in from what they eat and drink.

7

The best of the diets

THERE ARE HUNDREDS OF DIFFERENT DIETS published in magazines and books. Most of them are not worth the paper on which they are printed, although many make money for their authors. Few will bring about any permanent loss of body fat. Fewer still have been subjected to properly controlled trials, and even fewer teach the overweight person how to eat in such a way as to maintain any fat loss which does occur. Some of the more recent diets are better in this respect than the older diets and do at least promote a way of eating that is reasonably healthy. But there are still many that promote unbalanced ways of eating. Many diet books are written by people with no qualifications in nutrition other than those they have given themselves or acquired from questionable sources. A few are written by doctors or psychologists who ought to know better, but then neither of these groups has had much training in human nutrition.

Most diet books and diet programs only sell well if they have a gimmick. Mixing fact and fiction seems to ensure top sales but adds to the confusion about food and fat loss. One of the best-selling diet books of all time in both Australia and New Zealand has some useful nutritional information and promotes eating fruit and vegetables—a sound nutritional principle. The same book has dozens of nutritional absurdities, yet many otherwise intelligent people buy it and devour its contents with great fervour because they find it contains some statements that they know to be true and reasonable. Unfortunately, after some months on this and other diets based on false premises, the effects of nutritional deficiencies can occur.

After explaining the useless—and sometimes potentially dangerous—myths in many diet books and weight loss programs, I am often asked why such incorrect ideas are allowed to be sold. The answer is that a gullible diet market will buy anything written by anyone who claims to be able to solve their problems. Clever advertising for diet programs, diet products, weight loss wraps and diet pills can convince people that this might just be the easy answer they have been waiting for.

Not all diet programs or diets in books and magazines are bad. Some are well-balanced and extremely useful. I have no hesitation in recommending quite a few. However, with only a few exceptions, those which are sensible and based on sound medical principles tend to attract a smaller market than those which promise a little magic. When it comes to weight loss, there is no magic.

The following reviews are offered to help readers make up their minds about the worth of particular books and programs. Obviously what is good for one person may not suit another. If in doubt whether a program or diet book is based on sound nutrition principles, contact a dietitian or qualified nutritionist through the Dietitians' Associations in Australia or New Zealand or the Australian Nutrition Foundation or its New Zealand equivalent.

THE GOODIES

The books listed in this section are not diets, but describe ways of tackling the problem of excess weight that seem sound and sensible.

If Not Dieting, Then What?

Many diet books are worse than useless, often trivialising an important topic with lots of hype or pseudo-scientific reasoning about weight loss that is almost invariably wrong. This book, written by Dr Rick Kausman, is like a breath of fresh air. He treats obese people as normal, encouraging them to stop trying new diets and start liking themselves—whatever their size and shape. Instead of advice, Kausman gives understanding. He obviously likes his patients, irrespective of their size, and his empathy will shine like a beacon for those women who feel they are being constantly judged.

The book is not just a series of feel-good chapters. It contains a structured program that deals with issues such as appropriate sustainable goals for each individual; new and enjoyable ways to approach food, eating and hunger; and how to nurture and treat yourself well. It does not abandon issues such as exercise and fat in foods, but discusses them with understanding and in a context where you can discover their importance. The chapter on activity is especially useful for its gentle and positive approach.

I wrote the foreword for this book and was happy to do so, because it is probably the best approach to the problems of excess weight that I have read. It gives enough insight to allow the reader to find ways to enjoy food without feeling guilty, yet at the same time increases your awareness of what you are eating with discussions about non-hungry eating. Kausman looks after people by helping them to look after themselves. He does not preach—he helps. He does not ram rigid advice at readers and he gives no prescriptive advice. It is a book of self-discovery for those who are concerned about their weight or their attitude to their bodies and food. Readers are encouraged to take an individual approach to finding goals that are appropriate, helped when they think everything has gone wrong and gently led to a positive state of mind.

I recommend *If Not Dieting, Then What?* not only for the genuinely overweight, but also for those who constantly diet in an effort to lose excess weight they don't have, at least by rational medical standards. I also recommend the book for anyone involved in helping others lose weight. If I had the right, I would make it a compulsory text for those who work in the fitness industry.

Rating: the advice 10

GutBuster Waist Loss Guide (2nd edition)

As co-author of this book (with Dr Garry Egger), I obviously like its approach. The GutBuster program was set up in Newcastle in Australia for a group of obese men. They decided they should have a name and christened themselves GutBusters. The name became popular and GutBuster groups sprang up all over Australia. The program has now spread to other countries and has an international advisory board of world-renowned experts in obesity.

Having worked with men for many years, Garry Egger realised they needed a different approach to weight loss. Most programs and books were written for women, although in Australia there are many more overweight men than women. Men look at food and their bodies in a different light, yet most diet books and slimming programs are directed at and attended by women.

The GutBuster program is not a diet and does not focus on body weight. Instead it looks at how to change habits, how to move more (not necessarily the same as the usual concept of exercise), how to eat differently and how to trade off food (or alcohol) and exercise. The book also includes some information about the physiology of body fat and the way the body uses alcohol.

As well as giving an explanation of body fat, the 'beer gut', and the problems associated with lack of physical activity, the *GutBuster Waist Loss Guide* goes through the health risks associated with particular body shapes, the problems of 'off again, on again' weight and gives plenty of information to help men (and women) understand why they gain excess body fat.

There is no diet included, and participants are encouraged to throw away their bathroom scales. There is plenty of practical information about how to change eating habits in ways that can become permanent. Much of the emphasis is on cutting back on fat, especially saturated fat, although, strict no-fat eating is not encouraged. This program advises followers not to make any extreme changes or do anything that won't be permanent. The advice is practical and, not surprisingly, I give it a high rating. There is also a companion volume of GutBuster recipes, which I wrote. These are all filling dishes and all are easy to make—deliberately designed to be easy enough for men who have little cooking experience to give them a go.

Rating: the advice and information 10

Trim for Life

Dr Garry Egger is well-known for his work in clearly communicating the benefits of physical fitness, explaining many aspects of health and de-bunking myths. I must admit to a certain bias in discussing Garry's work, as I have worked with him for many years, and co-authored several books.

Trim for Life was put together with help from dietitian Matthew O'Neill and includes sensible advice in the form of 201 tips to help with effective weight control. These are divided into categories: nutrition tips, exercise tips, information to help maintain weight loss, tips on ways to cope with the fat society in which we live, and information tips related to some of the biological and behavioural influences on eating and exercise. Garry Egger also looks at some of the weight loss fads and points out why they don't work.

The book is easy to read and would make a suitable present or sound information base on which to begin a change in eating and exercise habits. Some of its hints could form the basis of a game of 'Did you know that?'

Rating: the hints 10

Licence to Eat

Written by Kerith Duncanson, a qualified and experienced dietitian, *Licence to Eat* abandons the approach of 'blame the victim' and avoids long lists of dos and don'ts. Instead it points out the flaws inherent in most dietary approaches and takes a more kindly approach, encouraging the overweight to accept themselves as worthwhile people who need to make peace with food rather than seeing it as an enemy.

To cope with the stresses of life without turning to the refrigerator or pantry, Kerith Duncanson outlines a series of strategies, drawing on her own experiences of having to battle alternate bingeing and starving. She also includes many useful case studies, describing each in a dignified and helpful manner.

The book's initial chapters may appeal more to women than men, although the low-key approach and encouragement to eat filling foods rather than 'diet' foods should also appeal to men.

There is extensive accurate information to help people break the dieting cycle and change their attitudes to food, ultimately making better food choices. Many people are nutritionally illiterate, so *Licence to Eat* gives some basic facts about foods, answering many common questions about snacks, sweet foods, exercise, different types of fats and diet products as well as explaining the healthy eating pyramid. As you would expect from a dietitian, the information is sound and mercifully free of inaccuracies and gimmicks. The book is never boring and, without the hype of so many diet books, is easy reading.

The basic message from *Licence to Eat* revolves around low-fat eating, but not no-fat food. Occasional indulgences have a place in everyone's life and this book encourages you to enjoy these, explaining that 'occasional' probably means about once a week. Rather than giving menus, Duncanson gives suggestions for the types of foods you might include at each meal. These are quite specific, including, for example, suitable sandwich fillings, alternatives to butter or margarine, different types of salads and a list of suitable dressings, soup suggestions and even different ways you may select fruits. The information is practical and a short fat-counter chart gives information about the fat level (in grams) in typical servings of various foods. The list is only a starting point and some of the serving sizes are rather low. Shopping skills are also covered.

Like many diet books, *Licence to Eat* includes recipes, giving each a fat rating. Not surprisingly, most recipes rate as negligible, very low in fat (1–3 grams/serving), or low in fat (3–5 grams/serving).

Rating: the eating plan 10; the theory behind it 10

A Weight Off Your Mind

The author of this book, Hilary Tupling, is a psychologist. She has worked for many years with overweight people and understands the problems they have in our slim society. She also works with women with eating disorders, many of whom are unable to come to terms with their body size.

This book is one I am happy to recommend. It explains important principles central to successful weight loss. These include a readiness to change. As Tupling correctly points out, going on a diet is often a soft option and avoids altering old beliefs, feelings and behaviours. She also understands that many people experience a deeply personal struggle with their weight and traces some of the psychological problems associated with losing weight.

While sympathising with the overweight, Tupling does not believe we should leave people fat and at risk of health problems. She points out that people who are very fat were once only a little fat and before that, not fat at all. By the time the person has a real medical problem, it is difficult to make the many and complex changes necessary. She then explores the way to help overweight people make such changes. At all times her approach is soft and non-demanding. Tupling wants the overweight person to feel good about making changes, to accept that she is an individual and must find her own way through the maze of complications. Above all, this book proposes that you take change at a pace which you can enjoy.

A Weight Off Your Mind has a refreshingly different approach. It looks at the psychological aspects of eating and being fat, how fatness starts and the way to prepare yourself for making changes. Throughout the book, the overweight person is treated with dignity and understanding and is gently guided into making changes. Having worked with overweight people for many years, I think this book would really help most women to lose excess fat and learn to accept their bodies as they are now, as well as developing a realistic expectation of what they might become. It is in total contrast to many of the other diet books available in that it does not blame the victim but takes a positive path to changing behaviour. Sections on willpower, coping with families, shopping, planning and managing stress are all valuable.

Rating: the plan 10

The Diet that Works

Written by Dr Mileham Hayes, a general practitioner from northern New South Wales, this book has 2005 points. Some are tips for losing weight, others are factual statements that the author believes may help readers accept the need for changes in diet and exercise. These presumably fit the criteria of 'better eating' as the title suggests. Many of the points are single-liners; others get a little more room. The tips all look useful, although the huge number may be a case of overkill. No one could be expected to read the entire book through at one hit. Opening it at random, you can easily miss some of the gems, such as Tip 1280 which says that 'Einstein formulated $E=MC^2$ while walking in the woods'—presumably a tip extolling the value of exercise. Some of the tips are recognisable and I picked up several from my own papers. None appear to be from unreliable sources, although I did find one questionable statement claiming that men and women have the same total body fat. Still, out of 1918 statements, the odd one that is open to debate isn't too bad.

It is not too difficult to work out Mileham Hayes' basic philosophy on weight loss. From the information he gives, Hayes is advocating what he calls a 'Genic Hunter-Gatherer Diet' where 20 per cent of the kilojoules come from fat. He has also embraced recent concepts such as the Glycaemic Index of carbohydrate foods. He also discusses problems such as anorexia, although the enormity and complexity of this subject cannot be properly discussed in dot point form.

There are sections within the book discussing such subjects as the side effects of diets, why diets don't work, motivation, goals, weighing and measuring, behaviour modification, how to change foods to fit the Genic diet, physical activity, fat redistribution (no, he doesn't tell you how to lose weight from the thighs, which he rather unkindly refers to as 'jodhpurs thighs'), genetics, body image and drugs. At the back of the book, he gives some figures for the fat content of some foods.

Rating: the tips 10

The Pritikin Program

The late Nathan Pritikin devoutly believed that he could reverse many of the effects on health of poor diet and lack of exercise. His Pritikin Program, with its minimal levels of fat and cholesterol, little protein and no sugar, salt, alcohol or caffeine, was first used at the Pritikin Longevity Centre in Santa Barbara in California. Results were excellent, with huge drops in cholesterol and triglyceride levels and reductions in blood pressure and uric acid. Most people also lost weight.

Pritikin's initial results have been documented in controlled studies and there is no doubt the program works. It promotes fruits, vegetables and carbohydrate foods such as breads, cereals, grains and beans. To these basics are added small amounts of skim milk and very lean meat, fish or chicken. Eggs are forbidden, although such strictness is almost certainly unwarranted. The basic diet claims that around 80 per cent of its kilojoules come from carbohydrate (mostly complex and unrefined), 5–10 per cent from fat and 10–15 per cent from protein. These proportions are more stringent than most current health authorities' recommendations to eat less fat and more carbohydrate. The Pritikin Program also gives great emphasis to regular exercise.

In practice, those following the Pritikin Program do not need to worry about weight because it is difficult to eat enough of the permitted foods to gain weight. For some people, such as small children or endurance athletes, it can be difficult to eat enough to support the needs of growth or physical activity. For example, some elite endurance athletes need 21 000–25 000 kilojoules (5000–6000 Cals) a day. To take in this many kilojoules from the foods on the Pritikin Program is almost impossible, simply because there are not enough hours in the day to engage in so much exercise, sleep and eat the mounds of food required. Young children who are growing rapidly will also find it difficult to eat enough of the Pritikin Program foods to supply their energy needs. Parents who decide to use this program for their own health or weight needs should be mindful that it is too strict for children.

For many adults, however, the Pritikin Program probably presents few difficulties and the newer program promoted by Robert Pritikin, Nathan's son, is more flexible, with more seafood and even small quantities of some 'good' fats.

The Pritikin Program is good for those who like to eat a large volume of food. Most dietitians would argue that a *modified* Pritikin Program might achieve the same aims and be easier to live with, but there is no doubt that many people have found a new, active life after following the Pritikin Program. The major problems with the program include the difficulties of eating out at friends' houses, or at restaurants, although such problems are addressed in the latest versions. There really is no evidence that the body cannot safely handle small quantities of fat or sugar or alcohol and those following the Pritikin Program need not fear that occasional indulgence in some cheese, ice cream or even a small chocolate will cause any damage. There is also plenty of evidence from Mediterranean countries that using some olive oil is not an impediment to longevity, and wine in moderation may even do some good.

There are those who try the Pritikin Program and find it so restrictive that they go back to eating a diet full of junk foods. A less strict program they could stick to would be a better option.

With such good weight loss results provided by the Pritikin Program itself, it is strange to find there is also a Pritikin Maximum Weight Loss Diet. This is a stricter version of the regular program and allows only one serving of grain foods, one serving of low-fat dairy products and only one piece of fruit a day. Vegetables are freely allowed and you are advised to carry around a plastic bag filled with raw vegetables to eat all day. The kilojoule level for the day is around 2500 (600 Cals)—an extremely low level. A 4200 kJ (1000 Cals) version is also given. A variety of recipes is provided to add interest.

The Pritikin Maximum Weight Loss Diet does point out that most people lose excess fat effectively on the regular Pritikin Program. It seems unhelpful, then, to recommend the stricter version from which the average person would be unable to meet the recommended dietary intakes for several nutrients, including protein, iron, calcium, zinc and some of the B-complex vitamins. From my experience, most devotees of the Pritikin Program stick to the regular version and achieve good results from it.

Rating: the Pritikin Program diet 8; the theory behind the diet 9.
Rating: the Pritikin Maximum Weight Loss Program diet 4.

Eat More, Weigh Less

Dr Dean Ornish, Head of the Preventive Medicine Research Institute in California (an organisation which he founded) made his name on the world medical stage by comparing the arteries of patients who followed his dietary recommendations with those of a group following a more conventional cardiovascular diet. With the Ornish diet, after even one year, his patients had greater reduction in LDL cholesterol, less frequent angina, and narrowing in their arteries from fatty deposits had regressed. The control group had become worse. From the 48 patients in the original study, 35 agreed to continue with the stringent diet and lifestyle changes for five years. At the end of that period, their improvements had continued, although studies have not yet shown that the patients actually live longer.

Weight loss on the Ornish diet is not surprising. The diet has only 10 per cent of its kilojoules as fat and recommendations also include moderate exercise. Ornish's cardiovascular patients also undergo stress management training, must stop smoking and get group support. They do not take any drugs.

Ornish's diet is similar to the Pritikin Diet—perhaps even slightly more strict. You can eat as much low-fat vegetarian food as you wish, although *Eat More, Weigh Less* warns that sugar, alcohol and even white flour may lead to swings in insulin production and prevent weight loss. Complex carbohydrates such as those found in wholegrain foods are encouraged.

The total fat content in the diet works out at 15 to 25 grams a day. Ornish does accept the importance of essential fatty acids and recommends two 1-gram capsules of flax seed (linseed) oil/day and also two 1-gram fish oil capsules/day. A better solution, especially in Australia, would be to eat some linseeds (they are available in breads and cereals) and to eat fish once or twice a week. Linseed oil—even in capsules—can easily oxidise and its fats then become highly undesirable. Keeping them refrigerated can decrease oxidation, but getting them from shop to home in an Australian summer would not be advisable. So-called fatty fish has much less fat than most people imagine. For example, a salmon steak weighing 125 grams has only 3 grams of fat. There is evidence that these fish fats are not converted to body fat but used for essential functions in nerve and brain cells and in cell membranes.

Eat More, Weigh Less recommends that you choose enough of the following foods until you feel satisfied (but not stuffed):

- all legumes (lentils, kidney beans, peas, black beans, red Mexican beans, split peas, soybeans, black-eyed peas, chick peas, navy beans), and so on)
- fruits of any type
- whole grains (corn, brown rice, oats, wheat, millet, barley, buckwheat)
- vegetables of any kind, including potatoes

You can also eat in moderation:

- non-fat dairy products (skim milk, non-fat yoghurt, non-fat cheeses)
- egg whites and fat-free egg substitutes
- non-fat or very low-fat commercially available products, including wholegrain breakfast cereals, non-fat mayonnaise and no-oil salad dressings, baked corn chips
- other fat-free products (many more available in the United States)

Ornish also warns followers to read labels and avoid non-fat or very low-fat products that are high in sugar. Other foods to avoid as much as possible include:

- meat, chicken and fish
- all oils, and oil-containing products, including margarines and most salad dressings
- avocados
- olives
- nuts and seeds
- regular or fat-reduced dairy products (Ornish recommends fat-reduced soy instead)
- egg yolks
- sugar, honey, molasses, corn syrup and other sugars
- alcohol
- and any commercially available product with more than 2 grams of fat per serving

This is where the diet becomes highly restrictive and the possibilities of too-low an intake of iron, calcium, vitamin E and essential fatty acids becomes a possibility. While these may seem like minor problems for those faced with severe cardiovascular disease, they are important for younger people. For example, iron-deficiency anaemia is relatively common in young women and a lack of calcium can prevent optimal bone density in younger people.

To counter the problems of nutrient deficiencies, Ornish recommends a barrage of supplements, including beta carotene, large doses of vitamin C (2000–3000 mg/day), vitamin E (400 IU/day), folate (1000 micrograms/day), selenium (100–200 micrograms/day), as well as a multivitamin and the oil supplements referred to earlier.

There is evidence that large doses of beta carotene are undesirable, with two major clinical trials involving 29 000 and 18 300 smokers showing that beta carotene increased their incidence of lung cancer (especially in those who continued to smoke and drink alcohol); three trials of people who had bowel polyps developed a greater incidence of further polyps with beta carotene. There is also evidence that large doses of vitamin C can act undesirably as a pro-oxidant, even though smaller doses (500 mg/day) have antioxidant functions. Selenium also functions as an antioxidant at moderate doses and as a carcinogenic compound at high intakes. For these reasons, it seems a backward step to make the diet so strict that you need to add supplements, some of which may be undesirable if taken over a prolonged period.

Eat More, Weigh Less, like other books of its type, is about half information and half recipes. The latter are listed as 'gourmet' and while many would argue that they fit that category, they are useful to counter the high-fat recipes so commonly seen in regular recipe books.

The total package of Ornish's diet, exercise and stress reduction takes a complete life change. For those with established coronary heart disease, it may be worthwhile, although other studies using a Mediterranean diet with plenty of 'good' fats in the form of olive oil and nuts, show a dramatic reduction in deaths and are much easier to accept. Ornish maintains that a total lifestyle change and commitment is easier *because* it is total. But the fact remains that many cannot follow such a strict protocol.

Rating: the diet 7; the theory behind the diet 8.

THE ALMOST-MAKE-ITS

The diets discussed in this section have many good points and may suit some people. However, all suffer from a slight degree of obsession, a criticism that some would also make of the Pritikin Program, listed above. Categories are always difficult. The first diet discussed is similar in many ways to the Pritikin Program, but as it is even stricter, it didn't quite make it into the 'goodies' category.

Eat More, Weigh Less

This book, with the same title as Ornish's book, was written by Dr Terry Shintani, Director of Preventive Medicine at the Waianae Coast Comprehensive Health Centre in Hawaii, a former lawyer who went on to become a medical doctor and then to study nutrition at Harvard University. Shintani's diet is almost the same as Dean Ornish's approach, but Shintani uses a somewhat enthusiastic writing style that includes some dubious headlines such as 'how to lose weight while eating 200% more food', 'how to lose weight while you sleep' and 'six steps to lower your cholesterol in just 30 days'. Dr Shintani may have considered such hype necessary to be noticed among the plethora of diet books. Indeed, he says he chose the title to get attention, but at least he puts some facts behind his claims and each chapter includes references from genuine sources, unlike many faddish diet books. This diet has no fads and Shintani correctly points out the futility of looking for magic bullets.

The book starts with an explanation of Shintani's Eat More Index (EMI), in which he claims to grade foods on a system based on how filling they are and their nutrient content. The EMI values given as an Appendix are actually based on the number of pounds (1 pound is approximately equal to 450 grams) of the food that provide 2500 Calories (10 500 kJ). The lower the caloric value of the food, the higher its EMI value. This is a sound principle and encourages people to eat more of the most bulky foods. For example, a comparison between a fast-food burger, fries and milkshake and a plate absolutely laden with vegetables and grains—each meal contains almost the same number of kilojoules, but the fast-food meal weighs 636 grams whereas the more bulky (and nutritious) grains and vegetables meal weighs 1883 grams—almost three times as much by weight. This approach continues throughout. The foods that score well would also score well with the Pritikin Program.

Fats have the lowest EMI value. *Eat More, Weigh Less* does not like fats of any sort. The book also favours calculating fat as a percentage of energy in a food, the method preferred by the Pritikin Program. While this has some virtues, it can also give some misleading results, especially where any food is consumed in a small portion. For example, the amount of milk added to a cup of tea would contribute only 0.7 grams of fat—not really worth fussing about one way or the other. However, if you calculate the percentage of the energy coming from fat in your slurp of milk, it works out as 50 per cent—which looks alarmingly high, even though the absolute figures are low. Working out percentage of energy from fat may be valid for high-fat foods or for foods consumed in large quantities, but is irrelevant when the overall amount of fat being consumed is low.

It is true that overfeeding with carbohydrate causes very little increase in body fat whereas overfeeding with fat rapidly increases body fat. Good references from world experts are used to support this theory. However, equally good references which support the essential nature of some types of fat are missing.

Dr Shintani has devised his own inverted food pyramid which recommends daily consumption of 8–13 servings of wholegrains, 3–5 servings of vegetables, 2–4 servings of fruit, 2–3 servings each of non-dairy calcium foods and non-cholesterol protein/iron-rich foods. The recommendations are almost totally vegan, although there is a small optional or occasional inclusion of low-fat fish, poultry, meat and non-fat dairy foods. According to Shintani, Mediterranean and Asian populations did not eat animal foods on a daily basis and rarely suffered from the diseases that now plague us. He omits to mention that Mediterranean populations consumed large quantities of olive oil, goat's cheese and yoghurt and felt no guilt about eating eggs or fish.

Calcium and iron-rich foods are listed according to the milligrams of the mineral they contain per 100 Calories (4200 kJ). While the figures are correct, few people could eat enough of the most calcium-dense foods such as watercress, collard greens, mustard greens, and other greens listed, to get sufficient calcium. In terms of likely consumption, most of these foods will contribute only a small percentage of calcium. There is no valid reason given for omitting low-fat dairy products, which would make it much easier to reach an adequate calcium intake.

A similar criticism can be made of the lists of iron-rich foods. Two types of seaweed are listed among the top three foods, but few people would eat enough to contribute the quantities of iron needed, especially by women. Mushrooms, listed as the fourth best source of iron, may be rich in their quantity of iron per calorie, but a reasonably large serving of 100 grams of mushrooms contributes only 0.2 grams of iron, which is less than 2 per cent of even the lower level of the 12 to 16 milligrams women need each day.

To help the reader get started, *Eat More, Weigh Less* gives some typical menus; while there are no set quantities, you would need to eat very large portions to keep hunger pangs at bay. Some fairly basic recipes follow, all with virtually no fat, except for a few drops of sesame oil occasionally. Some of these recipes would be useful, however, especially those that use various types of seaweed.

Rating: the eating plan 7; the theory behind the diet 7

The Hip and Thigh Diet

The name of this diet has ensured its position high on the charts for several years. The name is a pity because this is not a bad diet. Its major flaw is the title.

There is no way you can direct the body to reduce fat only on certain parts. When fat is burned to supply kilojoules of energy, it is taken from cells throughout the body. Just as you cannot tell your car that it is only to burn the petrol in the bottom half of the petrol tank, neither can you direct your body to leave fat on the breasts and remove it only from the hips. In fact, the fat on thighs and buttocks is present in very small fat cells and only small quantities are lost, even with a sensible diet and exercise.

If you are fat all over, a sensible diet plus exercise can cause fat loss from the whole body. Your hips and thighs will lose some of their fat but so will your shoulders, arms and breasts—even the rings on your fingers will become loose as your fingers become slimmer. There is no way you can lose fat only from the lower portion of the body, however strong your desire to do so. Fat loss is generalised and in accordance with your basic body shape. If you are an overweight pear, you will become a smaller pear.

There is one possible explanation for the title of this diet. At the time of menopause, the shape of a woman's body often changes. More fat is deposited on the upper body and less on the lower. From the health point of view, this is undesirable as upper-body fat is such a health hazard (see Chapter 4). It is feasible that a woman approaching or just past menopause will be experiencing some change in body shape. If she follows the Hip and Thigh Diet, she may well think her change in shape is due to the diet rather than her hormonal changes.

The Hip and Thigh Diet itself is not a bad diet and the author, Rosemary Conley, has taken the trouble to find some nutritional information. The first part of the book talks about the need to eat less fat, a point now emphasised by dietary guidelines in all western nations. This is followed by some rather dubious 'proof' of the diet's effectiveness in the form of testimonials from grateful followers, detailing the results of 17 people's weight loss in different areas of the body.

No medical study would accept such results as 'proof'. A properly conducted study would look at an entire sample of users (not just the satisfied ones who responded) and compare their weight loss measurements with those of a similar group following a different diet, and those of a group not dieting. Rather than having people taking their own measurements, the same person(s) would take standardised measurements. Where, for example, do you take a hip or an arm measurement? Such finer points are essential to test the claims made.

The diet itself is very similar to the sensible eating patterns recommended by most dietitians and health departments. The day's foods are divided into three meals with sensible suggestions to allow plenty of variety. Two alcoholic drinks are allowed daily, some skim milk is included and advice about suitable drinks is given. The daily totals of protein foods, vegetables, fruit, breads and low-fat dairy foods are similar to other balanced diets.

All sources of fat are forbidden. This is unnecessarily strict and contains a few anomalies. For example, so-called fatty fish is excluded

THE DIET DILEMMA

yet meats are allowed. Even a fatty fish such as mullet contains less than 6 per cent fat and the type of fat is extremely valuable. A little leeway on other nutritious foods such as eggs, avocado, cheese, sunflower seeds and a little olive oil would make the diet perfectly suitable to follow as a permanent eating pattern. Perhaps a small portion of some of these useful foods could be swapped for one of the glasses of wine.

Carbohydrates are included in reasonable quantity and the balance of the diet is fine. Supplements would not be necessary. Women are also encouraged to exercise.

My major criticism of the book concerns the name and the fact that it reinforces women's concern over hips and thighs. For fat women, generalised fat loss with a balanced diet and exercise is a good idea. However, many women of perfectly normal weight have a fetish about fat on their hips and thighs. Fear of the dreaded cellulite (which the Hip and Thigh Diet describes as 'very unattractive') is responsible for many normal-weight women going on diets and adopting bizarre and unhealthy eating habits. We need to de-emphasise hips and thighs and encourage women to like their bodies, keep them fit and healthy with good food and exercise, and stop dieting. My fear is that the Hip and Thigh Diet will do nothing to improve women's mental attitude to their bodies.

Conley's idea that 'toxic waste products' are stored in cellulite so 'they don't pollute the bloodstream' and that cellulite is the result of 'faulty circulation' are not correct. Nor is it correct that 'sugar, salt, spices, fat and alcohol can aggravate a cellulite condition by cluttering up the system with additional waste matter that is poorly eliminated' or that constipation encourages cellulite. Also incorrect is the idea that massage and special creams will help cellulite. Some creams may cause a temporary tightening effect on the skin, just as your skin would feel tighter if you painted it with some dissolved gelatine or certain types of glue. Any such 'benefits' are temporary. It is a pity that the chapter on cellulite contains so many inaccuracies.

The remaining 25 per cent of this slim little book is taken up with a food index which shows graphically the amount of fat in various foods. Unfortunately, all foods are given in 25-gram portions which will give a false idea of the fat in foods such as cheesecake, pizza, quiche and meat—which are eaten in much larger quantities—while giving an overestimate of foods such as olives or some nuts.

Rating: the diet 7; the theory behind the diet 6

The Complete F-Plan Diet

An immensely popular diet, the Complete F-Plan is a later edition of the original F-Plan Diet. This diet book was one of the first best-sellers which promoted a healthy way of eating. Its author, Audrey Eyton, is no stranger to the slimming business, having started and edited *Slimming Magazine* in the UK.

Unfortunately, Eyton's major premise—that eating fibre will make you slim—is not correct. She has misinterpreted a report from the Royal College of Physicians on dietary fibre. Part of this report discussed the fact that a diet high in dietary fibre will usually induce a significant weight loss. Eyton has taken this to mean that fibre is not digested and, by extrapolation, that eating more fibre will lead to a loss of kilojoules along with the excretion of the fibre. Eyton has the right message for the wrong reasons.

We now know that dietary fibre which is digested by helpful bacteria in the large intestine does contribute some kilojoules and that these are valuable in supplying energy directly to the cells in the large bowel. We also know that foods which are high in dietary fibre are filling and most are low in fat. A high-fibre diet is unlikely to lead to excess weight and switching from the usual high-fat/low-fibre western diet to one which is low in fat and high in fibre will assist weight loss and weight maintenance.

In spite of its shortcomings in explaining some of the finer points about why dietary fibre is good for you, the Complete F-Plan presents several well balanced eating plans, all high in dietary fibre and moderately low in fat. Recipes and menus accompany the diets. This version of the book gives plans for women who have little time to cook, for those who do have time to prepare foods, for those who like to snack or eat during the evening hours. There are also versions for men and children.

Anyone following this diet would do well to like canned baked beans, frozen peas, canned corn and canned kidney beans. Baked beans and canned corn are each included in more than 30 recipes! Beans, corn and peas are all wonderful sources of dietary fibre. It is a pity that the recipes use canned baked beans and do not provide much-needed information on how to cook dried beans and peas.

Eyton's breakfasts are a little on the meagre side—often only her special fibre-filler breakfast cereal. On the whole, however, the book presents healthy meals and snacks. The basic daily eating plans provide 4200 and 6300 kJ (1000 and 1500 Cals) and some advice is also given for a 3500 kJ (850 Cals) menu. Apart from this last plan (which, to be fair, is not emphasised), the diet plans are high in complex carbohydrate, low in fat, high in fibre, and would provide the recommended quantities of essential nutrients.

Rating: the diet 8; the theory behind the diet 6

8

The rest of the diets

CURRENT TRENDIES

Many of the craziest diets of the past have thankfully disappeared. Some of their replacements promote good foods and eating habits, but often for reasons which are incorrect. I have given each diet a rating in terms of its nutritional accuracy and its likely effectiveness.

The Liver Cleansing Diet: love your liver and live longer

One of the most popular diets to hit the Australian market, this one is designed to appeal to all—overweight or not. According to its author, it 'balances your metabolism' and only leads to weight loss if you are overweight, hence the second part of the title, 'Love your liver and live longer'. Along with the diet, the reader is also encouraged to take liver tonic capsules and a variety of supplements, all of which are available—at a price—from the author. Her web site address makes purchasing easy. The whole package is supposed to strengthen the body's immune system, which sounds admirable, although the proof for many of the components is lacking.

To her credit, the author, Dr Sandra Cabot, a general practitioner who specialises in women's health problems, does advise followers to make permanent changes to their diet, although she appeals to the diet mentality by including an eight-week menu plan. Full marks, however, for speaking out against the quick and easy approach. Full marks, too, for promoting fruits and vegetables, and for including information on the importance of essential fatty acids. The healthy, low-fat recipes are also good.

The diet includes 12 vital principles to improve your liver function.

In themselves, there is nothing wrong with these principles. They include advice to listen to your body so that you eat when you are hungry and stop when you are satisfied, drink lots of water, avoid large amounts of sugar, don't become obsessed with measuring calories, avoid foods to which you are allergic, be aware of good intestinal hygiene, don't eat if you are stressed or anxious, look for organically grown fruits and vegetables, take protein from a wide range of sources, choose breads and spreads wisely, avoid constipation and steer clear of excessive saturated or damaged fats.

Some of the reasoning behind these excellent rules, however, is faulty. For example, the water is supposed to 'cleanse the liver and kidneys and aid with weight loss'. Water certainly cleanses the kidneys, but it has no effect on body fat. Sugar is basically a junk food but it is not, as Dr Cabot asserts, 'converted into cholesterol'. Nor is sugar 'transported to the thighs, buttocks and abdomen for storage . . . increasing risk of cardiovascular disease'. In fact, sugar and other carbohydrates are converted to body fat only with an exceptionally high intake, and fat on the thighs and buttocks is not a risk for cardiovascular disease.

Dr Cabot's advice that you should eat raw fruits and vegetables is good but her reasoning that raw produce contains living enzymes to enhance digestion ignores the fact that any enzymes present in fresh produce would be killed in the normal acidity of the stomach, providing a minute amount of extra protein. Her assertion that brown breads are just coloured white breads is inaccurate in Australia and the notion that 'a healthy liver pumps fat out of your body and keeps you slim' is not correct. Even though some fats are much better for you than others, the only types of fat that pass through the body are mineral oils and some fake fats. All other fats are almost totally absorbed and are a major cause of excess weight in those who are not active enough to burn them for energy.

Dr Cabot also advises a mixture of two parts each of linseeds and sunflower seeds and one part almonds (called the LSA mixture). This mixture has no ability to cause weight loss, but it is nutritious and introduces the important concept that there are 'good' fats. She also advises grinding the mixture, although there is no real reason to do so. Linseeds contain omega-3 fatty acids which undergo rapid and undesirable oxidation once the seed is ground. If consumed whole, linseeds attach to the wall of the large intestine where helpful bacteria gradually break them down, releasing their valuable contents directly into the bowel. For the total fat content of the linseed-sunflower-almond mixture, I calculate that every 10 grams (approximately 1 tablespoon) has 4.7 grams of fat, of which only 0.4 grams is saturated fat, 1.3 grams is monounsaturated and 2.9 grams is polyunsaturated, including both omega-3 and omega-6 types. This makes the fat in the LSA mixture well balanced. However, more would not be better and anyone who consumed large quantities could gain weight.

The major problems with the Liver Cleansing Diet lie in the inaccuracies mixed in with its good recommendations, and the lack of proof for many of the author's statements. For example, the idea that 'excessive weight is a symptom of liver dysfunction and not solely due to the number of calories you eat' is not supported by even one scientific study. There is not a shred of evidence to support the idea that the massive number of overweight people throughout the world all have malfunctioning livers, and the author offers no supporting studies or evidence.

The only evidence for the usefulness of the Liver Cleansing Diet is the author's claim of successful treatment of 1540 patients' livers with 100 per cent success, as measured by parameters of weight loss and well-being in those patients she has been able to see regularly. We are not told how many patients this includes, but anyone with a 100 per cent success rate would usually want to share the success with the thousands of researchers spending their lives in obesity research.

Dr Cabot's web site page (which was not updated between 1997 and 1999) claims that 180 000 people are following her diet. This makes it even more amazing that she has not published a single paper on her spectacular results. However, time may well be a problem, as Dr Cabot says she discovered the role of the liver in weight gain in 1994. She must therefore either have seen or had contact with an extraordinary number of people—about 1000 a week. One would also assume that each person would generate more than one contact, as normally occurs with patients under medical care for weight loss.

The Liver Cleansing Diet does correctly list many causes of liver disease, and there are plenty of scientific papers to back the valid information that the liver is infiltrated with fat in those who drink a lot of alcohol, have diabetes, are severely obese, suffer from malnutrition, have been exposed to organic solvents or iron overload, or have had severe hepatitis. But there is no evidence that the major cause of excess weight is a malfunctioning liver.

Dr Cabot has a liver quiz on her web site, asking if you have symptoms such as nausea and/or bad breath, foggy brain syndrome (no good explanation is given as to what this is), mood swings and depression, allergies, respiratory infections, skin rashes, acne rosacea, auto-immune diseases such as connective tissue diseases or vasculitis, frequent fatigue, frequent headaches, inability to lose weight, excessive weight gain, abdominal bloating, abdominal obesity, poor digestion and bowel problems, constipation, an intolerance to alcohol and/or fatty foods, unstable blood sugar levels and cravings for sugary things, fluid retention, high blood pressure, hardening and blockage of the arteries, high cholesterol and/or triglycerides, excessive body heat or body odour, viral infections of the liver or other liver diseases, gall bladder disease (or had it removed), excessive intake of alcohol, recreational drugs or analgesics, or if you simply enjoy the good life too much.

If you answer 'yes' to three or more of these questions, Dr Cabot says your liver needs help. In fact, there is no evidence that most of these problems have anything to do with a faulty liver, and some represent serious medical problems that require other treatment. An intolerance to alcohol and fatty foods may indicate some liver problem, but somewhat ironically, many overweight people not only tolerate these foods, but manage to eat them in abundance without signs of intolerance.

The Liver Cleansing Diet should lead to weight loss since the menus and recipes are low in kilojoules and fat and many of the 12 rules emphasise habits that would keep kilojoule intake low. There is nothing wrong with the diet itself and my quibbles lie with the reasoning behind it. Apart from a total lack of proof that a malfunctioning liver causes obesity, there is no valid reason for the omission of all dairy products (including low-fat varieties) and red meat (although the latter is allowed in limited quantity after the eight-week period of the diet). Soy drink, fish and skinless chicken are permitted and, providing the soy drink is calcium-enriched, there is no nutritional problem with omitting meat and dairy products, but neither is there a valid reason to do so. Researchers at Flinders Medical Centre in Adelaide have shown that milk does not cause mucus, as is claimed. (The thickish substance that some people get in the mouth after drinking milk is chemically as different from mucus as shaving cream is from whipped cream.) Non-fat dairy products and lean meat are not essential foods, but they do not need to be omitted for weight loss or liver health.

The Liver Cleansing Diet is not marketed as a low-fat diet, and high-fat foods such as avocadoes, nuts and seeds are, wisely, permitted. However, about 80 per cent of the recipes given fit the usual definition of low fat, and only some salad dressings, dips and spreads contain fat, as you would expect. In all cases, the fat included in the recipes fits the category of 'good' fat and is not a problem. Indeed, this section of the book would be useful for those who are overweight and want some good-tasting healthy food. The recipes are quite suitable to share with the family or friends wanting healthy meals.

The major problem with the Liver Cleansing Diet is not the diet itself, but the assumption that excess weight and many other physical signs and symptoms are due to a fatty liver. Where is the proof? The anecdotal testimonials from Mrs B of Melbourne or Mrs F of Sydney represent a *belief* that the diet has cured their acne rosacea, aches and pains, auto-immune disease, vasculitis or diabetes. However, time, weight loss itself or a positive attitude could have cured each of these ailments, and anecdotal information from untraceable people is not proof. The testimonial from one woman who claims 'the less I ate, the more I would put on' defies reason, and the note from the owner of a horse whose liver was cured by one of the Livatone products is hardly relevant to human health.

There is no mystery as to why so many people report that they feel better on the Liver Cleansing Diet. It follows the principles of a healthy, moderately-low kilojoule diet with no junk food and plenty of nutrients from fresh wholesome foods. You would expect to feel better with such food, but it is the food you are eating, and what you are not eating (saturated fat, highly processed food and take-away junk meals and snacks) that are responsible, not the notion that your liver is being cleansed. In genuine cases of non-alcoholic fatty liver (detectable by tests of liver enzymes and by ultrasound, and by liver biopsy if levels of liver enzymes are chronically high), the main treatment is weight loss with a low-fat diet. But it is not valid to imply that all overweight people have a fatty liver or need 'liver cleansing'.

The products associated with the Liver Cleansing Diet cannot be ignored. As well as Livatone tonic powder and capsules, Dr Cabot offers for sale Livatone-Plus tonic powder and capsules (ingredients not stated) and a wide range of other supplements, herbs and skin care products. Some may be useful for those who are deficient in certain nutrients. However, there is no evidence that those who can eat regular food need a supplementary amino acid complex, and also no evidence that products such as spirulina work any magic. Indeed, the vitamin B_{12} for which spirulina is famous is not in a form that the human body can use. Without knowing what is in the Livatone products, it is difficult to judge their efficacy. Only a controlled trial comparing the products with a placebo could establish that they are effective. No such trial has been published.

One product which Dr Cabot does not offer, but for which there is some evidence of usefulness in cases of fatty liver, is oolong tea. A Japanese study has shown that mice with a fatty liver induced by a high-fat diet showed benefits from oolong tea. Part of the effect was due to caffeine, but it also seems to have some other component that inhibits fat-splitting enzymes produced by the pancreas.

Rating: the diet 6; the recipes 9; the theory behind the diet 1.

The Zone

Now several years old, The Zone diet was more popular in the United States than it has been in Australia. Nevertheless, it still features prominently in the diet and health section of most book shops and has spawned several books based on similar theories.

Written by American Barry Sears, The Zone espouses the idea that carbohydrates are the root cause of obesity—an idea that dietitians and obesity researchers thought had been put to bed long ago. The Zone blames the policies of groups such as the American Heart Association for the rise in the incidence of obesity in the United States, claiming that more carbohydrate and less fat keep people fat.

Sears maintains that the key to health and slimness is to keep the body's insulin level within a relatively narrow zone: neither too high nor too low. According to Sears, the more carbohydrate you consume, the more insulin you produce and the fatter you will become.

The Zone acknowledges that too many kilojoules at one meal can increase insulin, but rejects the well-proven fact that excess dietary fat or excess total kilojoules allows dietary fats to be converted to body fat. This insistence that dietary fats don't add to body fat flies in the face of studies using highly sophisticated techniques which show that when we eat more carbohydrates, the body increases the quantity of carbohydrate oxidised (that is, it burns more kilojoules), but when we eat more fat, there is no increase in energy production. The facts are that if you are not burning up the energy from dietary fats in metabolism, growth and physical activity, fat is readily deposited on the body. It is also true that if your total kilojoule intake from carbohydrate is very high, then any fats you do consume (and no one can avoid them all) are converted to body fat.

Sears maintains that the increase in obesity can't be caused by fat because fat consumption has decreased by 14 per cent in the United States in the last 15 years. The 'evidence' that fat consumption has decreased is often quoted, but is shaky data. Subjects are given questionnaires asking how often they eat particular foods. The good surveys may ask about 170 foods, although most, including those used until quite recently, included less than half that number. A typical supermarket in Australia stocks 15 000 items and the average American supermarket stocks many times more, so these questionnaires miss a lot.

We also have good evidence that almost everyone underestimates what they eat—and overweight people underestimate the most—by as much as 50 per cent in many cases. This does not mean people lie, but it does mean that many people are not good at estimating and remembering every morsel they have consumed—hardly surprising considering that we rarely weigh or measure foods and many foods these days are made up of multiple ingredients. There is also evidence from Scandinavian studies that people now selectively under-report their fat intake. Again, this is not surprising since fat has had such a bad press that few people will admit to eating a lot of it. Also, many people simply don't know how much fat they are eating. They report eating pasta, for example, but are unaware that pasta served in a restaurant or bought as a take-away will have been well oiled.

Researchers also translate food questionnaires poorly. For example, if you record on a dietary questionnaire that you had chocolate cake, the Australian data base entry will credit you with a piece of chocolate cake that has 10 to 14 grams of fat, whereas a slice of a rich chocolate cake has over 80 grams of fat. There are hundreds of similar discrepancies between what the creators of data bases consider a serving and what is likely to be dished up. A few more examples: a chicken curry will be entered as having 18–25 grams of fat, compared with real life figures of 45–80 grams, lasagne is listed as 24 grams/serving compared with 55 grams in most recipes, and even spaghetti bolognaise comes up with 12 grams of fat instead of the more realistic 40 grams/serving.

Dietitians are better than most at estimating portion sizes, but even they get it wrong. In one report, dietitians in New York were asked to estimate the fat content in portions of food set before them. They were fine at judging the fat content of something as simple as a glass of milk, but rated a New York tuna sandwich as 18 grams of fat when analysis showed it had 43 grams, a serving of lasagne as 35 grams of fat when it had 53 grams and a hamburger with onion rings as having 44 grams of fat when it was analysed as 101 grams! The assumption that Americans (and Australians) are eating less fat should be taken with a grain of salt.

The Zone espouses the theory that carbohydrates boost the body's production of insulin, which then causes you to store carbohydrates as fat. The book also claims that high levels of insulin increase the appetite. To a layperson, these theories and the way they are explained sound reasonable, but experts in the area of insulin are unanimous that Sears' argument is fallacious.

There is evidence that a diet very high in carbohydrate and very low in fat can raise insulin levels in some people. It is also true that high insulin levels increase the risk of heart disease, diabetes and high blood pressure. But that does *not* mean that excess insulin makes people fat.

Endocrinologists are adamant that it is misleading to blame high insulin levels for increasing obesity, and pure speculation to say that insulin increases the appetite. No studies support such claims, and there is ample evidence that eating high-fat foods leads to higher overall kilojoule intake, partly because fats don't turn off the appetite. By contrast, there are studies showing that foods high in carbohydrate and dietary fibre, such as potatoes, bread and pasta, are filling and can result in lower kilojoule intake—although not if they are smothered in fat.

There is no real evidence presented in The Zone to support its claims, although Sears does cite a 43-year-old study showing that hospital patients lost more weight on a diet high in fat or protein and gained weight when given a diet with 90 per cent of the calories coming from carbohydrate. However, the study involved only 14 patients who were on the various diets for only a few days, and most did not cooperate with the restrictions placed upon what they could and could not eat. Later studies have not replicated the findings.

Non-insulin dependent diabetes is increasing rapidly in western societies. In most cases, excess weight is the cause. The person produces enough insulin, but the insulin can't carry out its normal function of taking glucose across the cell membranes into the cells where it can be used for energy. This is because there is a resistance to the action of insulin due to increasing levels of fat within the cells and even within the membranes around cells. When insulin can't get glucose across into the cells, the body responds by producing more insulin—still to no avail. When this situation continues for some time, and glucose cannot get out of the blood into the cells, diabetes eventually results. In such cases, insulin levels are high, but it was obesity that led to the insulin resistance, not the other way around as The Zone alleges.

When people with insulin resistance lose weight, their insulin resistance usually decreases and their diabetes goes into remission. Any method of weight loss is fine, and the greatest success is likely to occur with a balanced intake of protein, 'good' fats and carbohydrate. Some people with diabetes do better with a Mediterranean-style diet based on a moderate quantity of monounsaturated fat (as olive oil) plus a moderate intake of carbohydrate and plenty of fruits and vegetables, rather than adopting a diet with minimal fat and lots of carbohydrate. But this moderate diet does not fit the recommendations of The Zone.

For many years, weight loss success was judged on the basis of how fast you could lose weight. And there is no doubt that you can lose weight faster when you omit carbohydrates. But as countless failed dieters have shown, fast weight loss is accompanied by a return of the lost weight once you go off the diet. There is no mystery to the faster weight loss that occurs with a low-carbohydrate diet; much of it is due to a loss of fluid, some of which is used to get rid of the toxic by-products that result when the body has to convert proteins (from food or lean body tissue) to glucose.

The Zone claims that 25 per cent of the population is genetically lucky enough to have a low insulin response to carbohydrate and will never become fat. The other 75 per cent are seen as an at-risk group if they consume carbohydrates. Endocrinologists, by comparison, think that 20 to 25 per cent of the population may be insulin resistant, although they maintain that this is mostly caused by accumulation of excess body fat. The Zone thinks otherwise. Claiming that there was no overweight before grains became a part of the human diet 10 000 years ago, The Zone diet recommends we return to a diet low in carbohydrate and high in low-fat proteins. We may have evolved on such a diet, but that does not make it any more desirable than the short lifespan that was also part of those times.

In the 10 000 or so years that humans have been growing grains, it is only in the last 30 to 50 years that we have seen large numbers of people becoming overweight. Most of the world's population lived largely on some type of grain (usually rice), with almost no obesity until they were introduced to western high-fat meals and snacks and habits of eating at all hours of the day, whether one is hungry or not. Coupled with a drop in physical activity, these are the causes of excess weight.

Not according to The Zone, which not only claims that insulin makes you fat but says that having more fat in the diet reduces insulin. The authors correctly point out that elevated insulin levels are a risk factor for heart disease, but neglects to note that when people become overweight—depending on genetic factors—their insulin levels rise. Weight loss decreases insulin levels. The error arises in which comes first. They assume that insulin levels increase and weight follows, whereas research points to weight gain being followed by rising insulin levels.

The Zone diet will almost certainly work, at least in the short term, simply because it is a relatively low-kilojoule diet. Followers are allowed three meals a day with each to contain 40 per cent of the kilojoules from carbohydrate and 30 per cent from each of protein and fat. This differs from the usual recommendation to consume 50 to 60 per cent of energy from carbohydrate, 20 to 30 per cent from fat and 15 to 20 per cent from protein throughout the course of the day. The Zone is much more prescriptive and recommends that we treat food as a drug, taking protein or carbohydrate blocks. However, the resulting diet ends up being low in kilojoules and it is this fact, together with the recommendation to exercise, that will bring about weight loss.

Some of the claims made in this book are of concern. For example, there is no evidence to support the claim that eating a low-fat, high-carbohydrate diet will cause an imbalance in the body's production of eicosanoids, producing arthritis, multiple sclerosis, heart disease and cancer. There is published proof that followers of the Pritikin Program and similar low-fat eating regimes avert or avoid these conditions.

By contrast, The Zone claims that staying within the zone of 30:40:30 per cent of kilojoules from protein, carbohydrate and fat will balance eicosanoids and promote health and reverse multiple sclerosis, cancer and even AIDS. (Eicosanoids are hormone-like substances that control many body functions, including the extent to which blood cells stick together, inflammatory reactions and hardening of the arteries.) There are no studies showing any effect on eicosanoid levels in those following The Zone diet and such claims have no scientific backing. The only 'proof' given in the book comes from untraceable satisfied customers who provide their initials and testimonials. Of course, those who are not satisfied are not quoted and since neither Sears nor anyone else is monitoring people on this diet, we have no idea of its true results.

However, we do know from published trials that insulin levels at one point in time have no relation to later obesity. One Italian study measured insulin levels in factory workers in 1981 and also measured their response to an oral glucose challenge. Despite a six-fold difference in these responses, follow-up over the next 14 years failed to find any difference in absolute or percentage weight gain between those with different insulin levels or responses. Other studies from the United States, published in medical journals, report that insulin resistance and high insulin levels do not play a causal role in the development of obesity. Quite the contrary, since longitudinal studies in adults show that low fasting insulin concentrations are associated with increased weight gain. However, in Pima Indians—a group with a strong genetic tendency to obesity—high levels of insulin in children may be a risk factor. Even with this group, however, reduced physical activity and a high-fat/high-kilojoule diet are more responsible for weight gain.

Followers of The Zone diet may find themselves in a 'constipation zone', since the fibre content is well below recommended levels.

In spite of the attack on those who recommend reducing fat, the Zone's recommended fat level sits within the limits usually recommended for good health. However, it is difficult to understand the restriction on vegetables such as carrots, fruits like bananas, and orange juice. These are healthy foods that are extremely unlikely to ever make anyone fat. Sears does not like vegetarian diets and claims they are only one step better than eating nothing but Snickers bars. Here his ignorance shows, because there are many studies showing that vegetarians have lower rates of heart disease, cancer and stroke and are less likely to be overweight.

As is usual for many diets, you can now buy a range of high-protein products via the Internet. Protein bars, for example, are marketed by a Zone-believing chiropractor and supposedly fit the principles of The Zone.

Rating: the diet 6; the theory behind the diet 2

Sugar Busters!

Following on from The Zone, a rash of similar books have promoted more fat and protein and less carbohydrate. *Sugar Busters!* is written by three American doctors (a cardiovascular surgeon, an endocrinologist and a gastroenterologist) and a *Fortune 500* Chief Executive Officer. Inspired by Michel Montignac's *Dine Out and Lose Weight* (see page 120), they have taken his theories a step further, making the diet sound more plausible. According to the authors, other books like theirs, recommending more protein and fat and less carbohydrate, are too technical and confuse the reader. Others might see their book as adding to the confusion, with some of their discussion not in accordance with biochemical facts. The web site that has been established continues the confusion.

Sugar is basically a junk food, with no protein, vitamins, minerals, essential fats or dietary fibre, and it accompanies fat in foods such as chocolates, cakes, pastries, biscuits and desserts. Basic dietary guidelines therefore suggest we avoid eating too much sugar or foods containing sugar. This makes good sense, and most nutritionists (except those who work for sugar or sugar-related industries) advise people to eat less sugar. However, sugar does not deserve the damnation this book gives it.

The authors of *Sugar Busters!* claim that sugar has 'evil effects' and that refined sugar is toxic. *Sugar Busters!* emphasises the idea that certain carbohydrates dramatically increase the body's need for insulin. Their clearest example is sugar, but they are quick to point out that other carbohydrates may be equally guilty and go further by claiming that higher levels of insulin inhibit the mobilisation of fat stores and signal the liver to make cholesterol.

Their diet advises readers not to eat carrots, but they are happy for you to consume 275-gram steaks, and include large quantities of cream and butter in recipes. Their chocolate mousse recipe includes 700 grams of chocolate, 1.6 litres of cream and 5 eggs; even if you divide it between 10 (they recommend 8–10 serves), each serving will have 91 grams of fat and 4310 kJ (1030 Cals)! They do at least draw the line at doughnuts, fried chicken and French fries, where the fat is accompanied by carbohydrate, although they forget the carbohydrate in the chocolate mousse. To back up their diet claims, one of the authors notes that once he began to eat steaks, lamb chops, cheese and eggs, his cholesterol and triglycerides fell. He attributes this remarkable change to lower insulin levels, although no details of before and after insulin levels are given.

The book goes on to note that people with diabetes have high levels of cholesterol and triglycerides, and so the authors assume their theory must be correct. As with *The Zone*, cause and effect have been confused. Lower cholesterol and triglyceride levels of one person cannot be taken as indicative of what occurs with most people, while literally hundreds of research studies show correlations between saturated fats in the diet and high blood fats. *Sugar Busters!* ignores these and offers no scientific research results to support their beliefs. Although references are listed at the back of the book, no credible references relate to this issue.

Sugar Busters! quotes the results of the Seven Countries Study, in which the high-fat Mediterranean diet typical in Crete in the 1950s was protective against coronary heart disease, but fail to note that this diet—although high in total fat—was low in saturated fat.

The Sugar Busters! diet forbids potatoes, corn, white rice, bread made from refined flours, beetroot, carrots, bananas, honey, beer and foods containing sugar. They also add that fruit must be consumed on its own—a borrowing from *Fit For Life* (see page 117). Much attention is also devoted to glucagon, a hormone released from the pancreas when the body needs to convert protein into glucose. This occurs when the diet lacks sufficient carbohydrate to restore blood sugar levels. *Sugar Busters!* correctly points out that glucagon is not released when the diet contains carbohydrate. In fact, glucagon is not needed under such conditions and proteins can be kept for their essential function of repairing body tissues rather than being broken down to provide glucose. The authors' claim that once glucagon is released, the body starts burning its fat stores, is not backed by research findings. And their statement that 'glucagon instructs our metabolism to mobilise and convert fat back to glucose' is a biochemical impossibility. Fat cannot be converted to glucose. The body can get glucose only from carbohydrates in the diet, from proteins from foods, or from lean body tissue.

As does The Zone, *Sugar Busters!* makes much of the importance of the glycaemic index (GI) of different carbohydrates. This refers to the speed with which the carbohydrates in foods are converted into glucose within the bloodstream and is an important concept for people with diabetes. Foods with a high GI release their glucose quickly into the bloodstream, while those with a low GI give a slower and more sustained release. Studies on GI are continuing and are important even though there are problems assigning an exact GI number to many foods. By definition, the GI is defined as the body's glucose response to a quantity of food containing 50 grams of carbohydrate. For a food such as carrots this equates to 10 large carrots, whereas for pasta it is less than a typical serving. Researchers are now looking at the glycaemic *load* of a food, which relates the quantity of carbohydrate in a typical serving to its effect on blood glucose. Under this revised definition, a single carrot has a low GI.

There is no doubt that including more foods with a lower

glycaemic load is valuable for those with non-insulin dependent (Type II) diabetes, as these foods release glucose slowly and make fewer demands on insulin supply. But there is ongoing debate about whether the glycaemic load is related to obesity, and no evidence at this stage to suggest it is a cause. On the contrary, in countries where the diet consists largely of rice (which has a high GI), caloric intake is higher and obesity lower than in countries where less carbohydrate and more fat is consumed. *Sugar Busters!* rates bananas as having a high glycaemic index although this does not fit with published figures. Corn is also not permitted although sweet corn has a relatively low glycaemic index. There are other anomalies, including the fact that sugar does not have a particularly high glycaemic index!

The GI is not the only, nor the most important, criterion for judging a food. For example, the GI may be low because a food is high in fat and therefore takes a long time to be digested. Foods high in saturated fat, such as chocolate, have a low GI. Ice cream has a lower GI than many fruits, but is not a better food because of that. The GI concept is useful as an adjunct for people with diabetes, but it cannot replace the importance of looking at the total nutritional content of any food.

Sugar Busters! states that exercise is important but then downplays its relevance by citing a 20 pound (9 kilogram) weight loss in one of the authors—who does no exercise. Thankfully, they do point out that their diet is not suitable for marathon runners or 'exercise fanatics'. In fact, this diet, like all low-carbohydrate diets, would be a disaster for anyone trying to exercise, as muscle glycogen stores for exercise depend on carbohydrate for replenishment. These stores are important for everyone who exercises, not just for 'fanatics'.

The three doctors do the reader the favour of damning diet pills and the weight loss industry, although they do not appear to see themselves as part of it. Those who follow their diet may lose weight initially, simply because the diet rules mean that you will consume fewer kilojoules. However, as with all low-carbohydrate diets, much of the weight loss will be due to water and loss of glycogen stores from muscles. These losses are neither desirable not permanent.

Much of the theory in this book is based on a graph matching the huge increase in obesity in the United States with increasing sugar consumption. The same graph could be drawn for fat consumption, or for the drop in physical activity that correlates so well with increasing body weight. Such associations are useful, but need more stringent and thorough analysis to determine which is cause and effect and which is coincidence. The rise in consumption of both sugar and fat and the fall in physical activity are all relevant to discussions of weight gain, because people are using fewer kilojoules and eating more.

Sugar Busters! gives a 14-day menu plan. Assuming average

THE REST OF THE DIETS

portions of foods, and taking note that they advise trimming the fat from meats, the menu plan provides a fairly basic, high protein, moderately low carbohydrate diet, adequate in most nutrients with the exception of dietary fibre, calcium and folate. Some antioxidants may also be low as the fruit and vegetable content is only moderate. There are also recipes, many of which could do with less fat, especially the aforementioned chocolate mousse!

Rating: the diet 4; the theory behind the diet 2

Fit For Life

In spite of its popularity, this book would come close to the top of the class for nutrition misinformation. It repeats many of the absurdities of the Beverley Hills Diet (see page 128). However, there are enough facts mixed in with the fiction to make the book seem plausible, and the enthusiastic style of writing would help convert many people to theories which have no basis in nutritional fact.

The book begins well enough, pointing out the futility of diets and dieting (a point with which I heartily agree). It then proceeds to recommend changes in eating habits which amount to an eating regime more strictly structured than many which it criticises. After reading the first sensible-sounding section, the many inaccuracies come as something of a shock. Perhaps one should have been warned by the authors' caveat that if 'you use this information without your doctor's approval, you are prescribing for yourself, which is your right, but the publisher and author assume no responsibility'.

Some of the basic errors in this book include the idea that 'toxic waste is the beginning of a weight problem' and that 'if we can eliminate toxic waste from our bodies on a regular basis, we are going to lose weight on a regular basis'.

According to the authors of *Fit For Life*, faulty digestion 'forces the creation of toxic waste in the system, and squanders a great deal of precious energy'. They expound this idea with statements such as 'if you can eat food and have it go through your stomach in three hours instead of eight, there are five hours of energy right there that you have picked up—five hours to be put toward detoxification and weight loss'.

(Reality is somewhat different from this strange concept, as was described on pages 79–81.)

Most foods contain mixtures of protein, fat and carbohydrate. Breads, all grains and cereal foods, legumes (dried beans and peas), nuts, seeds and milk all contain protein and carbohydrate (and in some cases, fat) within the same food. The body is perfectly equipped to cope with such mixtures.

Once in the small intestine where the environment is alkaline, about 7 litres of digestive juices are produced each day. These juices include pancreatic juice, bile and various other secretions. They supply enzymes to complete the digestion of proteins to their component amino acids and to convert fats to fatty acids and carbohydrates to sugars. These simple molecules, together with minerals and vitamins, are then absorbed into the bloodstream and taken to the liver where they are stored or sent out to tissues requiring them. The residue from the small intestine consists largely of dietary fibre and water. This passes to the large intestine where much of the water is re-absorbed and an army of useful bacteria attacks the fibre. Much of the dietary fibre from foods is broken down by the bacteria, releasing some valuable acids in the process. These give a direct supply of energy to the cells in the bowel, contribute some more energy for the body and stimulate wastes to move along the intestine for excretion. The bacteria themselves multiply by the million in this process and much of the faecal material we excrete consists of their dead bodies.

It is not correct to claim that digesting foods faster will save 'precious energy'. If anything, the overweight person needs to expend energy! Like many diet books, *Fit For Life* seems to take 'energy' to mean something different from the biochemical reality that energy represents 'capacity to work'. Those who want to lose weight need to create an energy deficit, either by taking in fewer kilojoules of energy, expending more energy in exercise, or both.

According to *Fit For Life*, 'flesh foods supply no fuel, no energy'. This may gladden the hearts of farmers trying to prove that meat is low in kilojoules but it is simply not true. Flesh foods do not contain any carbohydrate but they certainly provide plenty of kilojoules of energy from their protein and fat. Traditionally, flesh foods have been balanced with other foods which do supply carbohydrate. In various cuisines, traditional combinations have included meat and potatoes, fish and rice or chicken and noodles. Such combinations are the antithesis of the food combining theory of *Fit For Life*, which states that proteins and carbohydrates should never be combined.

This theory surfaces every few years but is not correct. If it were true, humans would not be able to digest any cereal or grain foods, nuts, seeds, legumes or milk. Each of these foods contains both protein and carbohydrate. They also sustain most of the world's population in Asia, Africa and other parts of the world—without making people suffer digestive disturbances, toxic wastes or excess body fat.

Fit For Life makes many exaggerated claims about fruit. For example, 'all the vitamins, minerals, carbohydrates, amino acids and fatty acids that the human body requires for its existence are to be found in fruit'. At best, such a statement is doubtful. At worst, it fails to acknowledge that it would be impossible to obtain the recommended intake of many nutrients by eating only fruit. Even if you could eat 5 oranges, 5 apples, 5 bananas, 5 apricots, a whole pawpaw, a dozen prunes, 2 punnets of strawberries, 3 kiwi fruit and half a kilo of watermelon in a day, you still would not take in enough protein, essential fatty acids, nicotinic acid (vitamin B_2), sodium, zinc, calcium and some other minerals. To make matters worse, your fibre intake would be so great that you would probably have diarrhoea and be unable to absorb some of the nutrients you had taken in.

The book also states that 'fruit does not digest in the stomach'. In fact, no carbohydrate digestion occurs in the stomach, so this is hardly a startling fact. It goes on to say that 'the energy fruit conserves by not having to be broken down in the stomach is considerable. This energy is automatically redirected to cleanse the body of toxic waste, thereby reducing weight.' Fruit is also said to be 'packed, brimming over, with the vital forces of life'. And cooking fruit is supposed to miraculously turn the acidity of fruit to alkalinity. All these claims are absurd.

Many foods are condemned on spurious grounds. Eggs are said to 'stink'. For proof of this, the reader is advised to 'drop one on the driveway on a hot day and let it sit there for about eight hours'. A similar situation might occur with various fruits if they were to be squashed and left in the sun—but this is hardly proof of their lack of worth. Milk is supposed to squander 'vital energy' and overload the system with mucus, making weight loss two to three times more difficult. It is also supposed to prevent absorption of nutrients and thereby to cause chronic fatigue.

The milk and mucus myth has been debunked with some studies from Adelaide which measured post-nasal drip, night cough and a number of other symptoms of mucus in children given varying amounts of milk. Except for a small percentage of asthmatic children who had an allergic reaction to milk, there was no difference in mucus production with different milk intakes. Some parents, however, perceived mucus production as being greater if they knew their children had drunk milk.

Contrary to the work of skin specialists, *Fit For Life* claims the sun revitalises the body. The authors state that they 'cringe' from 'the unbelievable misconception that the sun is dangerous'. They warn against sunscreens and advise regular time in the sun to provide 'that golden glow that is so much a part of living the *high energy lifestyle*'.

I could go on with many more examples of the misinformation in this book. They would certainly pad out the pages of my book. Instead, let us look at why the *Fit For Life* program appears to work—at least initially.

For those people who are in the habit of skipping breakfast, having something to eat—in the form of fruit—will make them feel better.

Those who usually indulge in a heavy meal of bacon, eggs, sausages and other high-fat foods will also feel better with the healthier, lighter choice of fruit. That part of the program is not in dispute, although the idea that fruit must be eaten alone is not factual.

One of the major premises of *Fit For Life* is that various foods must be eaten apart. For example, if you have eaten anything other than fruit, you must wait 3 hours before eating anything else (4 hours for flesh foods). Since the program also forbids consumption of anything other than fruit before midday and warns that you should not eat after 8 p.m., it is obvious that any 'success' from this diet is simply because the total amount you can eat within such rules is small.

After reading this book, you may wonder what you *can* eat other than fruits and vegetables. Other inclusions are nuts (unroasted, in small quantities) and seeds (neither may be eaten with any other concentrated food). Breads are limited to those which are wholegrain or sprouted and include some products branded as 'flourless', plus certain brands of corn bread and wholewheat pita bread. Barley, cracked wheat, millet, rice and one brand of granola are permitted, as well as some crackers and flours. Chicken, turkey, seafood and Cornish hens are also allowed. Oils must be cold-pressed and some seasonings and condiments are suitable. These include sea salt and some seasoned salts, but not regular salt. The fact that sea salt is sodium chloride is ignored.

Rating: the diet 4; the theory behind the diet: 1

The Montignac method

Unlike many of the popular diets, this one does not hail from the United States, but from Monsieur Michel Montignac, a charming Frenchman. Montignac published *Dine Out & Lose Weight* in 1986, followed a year later by *Eat Yourself Slim*. According to his web site, his books are now published in 18 languages in 25 countries and embraced by movie stars, diplomats, European royalty—and most of all by people who love good food, from all walks of life. There is no mention of support from specialists in the field of obesity, probably because many have criticised Montignac's claims.

Montignac himself has no qualifications in nutrition or medicine, although he mentions that he has worked in the personnel department of a large pharmaceutical company, and developed his 'method' while working there. He now promotes his ideas, writes books and sells product lines that fit his philosophies.

Along with the authors of *The Zone* and *Sugar Busters!*, Montignac distinguishes carbohydrates according to their glycaemic index (GI). Like the others, he bans glucose, sugar, potatoes, refined grains and beer, claiming they raise blood glucose levels. The Montignac method also borrows from *Fit For Life* (and its forebear the Hay diet) and recommends that fats and carbohydrates should never be combined in a meal. After eating fats you are supposed to wait at least 4 hours before eating carbohydrates, although if you choose carbohydrates first, you need wait only 3 hours before eating fats.

Montignac seized on the idea that carbohydrates raise blood glucose level, supposedly causing fats to be stored in your body tissues, before *The Zone* and *Sugar Busters!* were written, and the latter gives him credit for the idea. However, this idea had been mooted many years earlier and none of these authors can claim the credit for it.

Other rules in Montignac's method include no alcohol (although he praises red wine at times), minimal liquid with meals (but plenty of water between meals), plenty of fibre, moderation with coffee, and three regular meals a day, with no snacks. Like the authors of *Fit For Life*, Montignac does not allow fruits to be eaten with other foods—although he makes an exception for strawberries, raspberries and blackberries. He advises fruits should be consumed up to half an hour before a meal, or instead of a meal. He also recommends followers not to eat late in the evening.

Some of Montignac's advice is excellent. For example, he recommends healthy fats, especially those in fish, using olive oil for baking and in salad dressings, eating dairy products and increasing physical activity through using stairs instead of lifts and walking or cycling instead of driving everywhere.

Like so many diets, Montignac's method is a mixture of good advice and unsupportable claims. Many European experts in nutrition and obesity have criticised his statements as being 'scientifically unfounded' (Gerard Pascal, head of nutrition and food hygiene at the French National Institute of Food Research); 'nonsense' (T. Leverink-Krebbers, director of a major Dutch obesity clinic); 'a mixture of obvious truth, accepted knowledge and pure nonsense' (Professor Martijn Katan of the Department of Human Nutrition of Wageningen University).

As well as blaming insulin for excess body fat, Montignac believes surplus fats can be excreted in stools. This can occur, but only in cases of severe illness when the digestive system is not working. As we have noted before, fat storage due to insulin is not of major importance and Montignac's ideas about not mixing proteins and carbohydrates within the intestine is not correct.

Montignac has set up shops selling products that are low in glycaemic index, such as lentils and other legumes and wholegrain products. He also sells good quality chocolate at a high price. I endorse his idea about eating very high quality, very bitter chocolate because it is likely that taste buds will be satisfied with a small quantity. Being so expensive will also limit consumption for most people.

Rating: the diet 5; the theory behind the diet 1

Stop the Insanity

After a few minutes reading this book, you almost feel breathless. It's full of very short sentences, lots of questions, quotations, exclamation marks and upper case type to characterise the excitement the author obviously feels. Although Susan Powter is an Australian, she has adopted much of the hyperbole of her adopted home in the United States. She claims to be 'passionate', although many would describe her writing as hyperactive. It can make you feel tired just reading her fast-paced lines.

Like many diet writers from the first half of the 1990s, Powter hates fats and loves exercise. She also loves models and film stars and writes about her meetings with them as though everyone else would be interested. Perhaps some are, but many readers will wish she would get to the nitty gritty. After going through her experiences, the birth of her babies and problems with her husband, her ups and downs with diets and friends, you eventually get to her success stories and then—the method. Powter's method is to stop dieting and learn to hate fat.

Like many others, *Stop the Insanity* recommends you work out the percentage of energy from fat. This enables you to hate fat more. Powter uses cooking oil sprays as an example. Although these products contribute less than 1 gram of fat per serving, she spends almost a whole page sounding as if she's about to have a fit at the horror of the fact that the products are all fat—450 per cent fat, according to her somewhat crazy calculations. She carries on for many more pages about the problems of recommendations to consume 30 per cent of energy as fat. Many of her arguments are fine, but they are not arranged logically and you can almost feel her blood pressure rising as she types her hype.

If you cut through the hyperactive criticisms of everyone and everything, you find some good information. Rule number 1 is never to skip. Rule number 2 is to eat as much as you want—although you have to want low-fat, high-bulk foods (anything except high-fat junk). She then produces her own Food Pyramid with foods listed from the largest to the smallest categories as grains, legumes, vegetables, processed grains and starches, fruit and very lean protein options. Most of this information is fine, although the very lean protein options include only fish (except salmon, mackerel and bluefish), white chicken and white turkey and egg whites. Although Susan Powter rubbishes advice and information from nutrition experts, it's a pity she is unaware of the fact that fish fats are not converted to body fat because they serve so many essential functions.

Some of the dietary advice is geared towards those who want to eat lots, including those with a food obsession. Powter equates 1 glass of milk with 20 cups of spinach, 10 potato chips with 40 slices of Italian bread, 1 tablespoon of peanut butter with 20 cups of lentils, and knows which of each pair she prefers. The fact that these foods are not equal in anything but their fat content is ignored and she slams those who seek to give nutritional advice. It would certainly take a brave nutritionist to face her barrage of words.

The exercise section of the book follows and once you've waded through the hatred of aerobics classes (probably justified if half her stories are accurate), heard how you shouldn't see a doctor before exercising and been given some more of her life story, you get some sound advice about walking, increasing your range and intensity of movement and adding some resistance to your movements, along with some hints on abdominal breathing, deep breathing and the importance of aerobic activity. The book continues with more information on specific resistance training methods, hints on flexibility and strength training.

Eventually you reach the part of the book titled 'sanity' and go through some more of Susan's life changes. This section may inspire some; others may be tired of reading about Ms Powter's life experiences. Still, each to her own!

Rating: the diet 6; the theory behind the diet: 4 (points deducted for some incorrect material)

Beyond Pritikin

Written by Ann Louise Gittleman, a former director of nutrition at the Pritikin Longevity Center in Santa Monica, *Beyond Pritikin* lives up to its name. After leaving the Longevity Center in 1982, Gittleman became interested in fasting, detoxification and full-spectrum light. She also discovered that some fats were essential and became interested in both omega-3 and omega-6 fatty acids, especially gamma linolenic acid, the major fatty acid in evening primrose oil.

Gittleman correctly notes that essential fatty acids are important in lowering blood cholesterol and acting as anti-inflammatory agents. In fact, it is the omega-6 fatty acids (found in vegetable oils such as safflower, sunflower, corn, sesame and soy bean) that lower blood cholesterol levels, while the omega-3 fats have more anti-inflammatory properties. *Beyond Pritikin* also acknowledges that essential fats are important for the skin. However, Gittleman goes beyond the evidence and credits these fats with an ability to control yeast infections, alleviate 90 per cent of premenstrual problems, inhibit cancer cell growth and burn off excess calories. These extrapolations make it difficult for the layperson to know what is proven, what is being studied and what is conjecture.

Beyond Pritikin also claims that the gluten in wheat causes minor malabsorption problems for many people and is linked with multiple sclerosis, schizophrenia, autism and itching eczema. Wheat is also blamed for vitamin and mineral deficiencies which Gittleman claims are the cause of irregular menstrual cycles, vague aches and pains in the bones and ridged fingernails. There is no scientific backing for these claims. *Beyond Pritikin* then bans wheat, oats, barley and rye grains and all foods that contain them.

Milk is also banned, although cheese and yoghurt are permitted. The association drawn between gluten and milk sugar, or lactose, is partially correct. In undiagnosed coeliac disease, the lining of the intestine is damaged and the enzyme lactase, which breaks down lactose, cannot function properly. However, once gluten is removed from the diet, the intestine recovers and most people with gluten sensitivity can then digest lactose without problems. A few people have gluten insensitivity and permanent lactose intolerance, but assuming that everyone has a problem with gluten and lactose is not valid.

As well as forbidding wheat and milk, Gittleman restricts foods that she believes are fermented, including soy sauce, mushrooms, and tomato sauce (claiming that its processing creates fermentation). Curiously, cheese and yoghurt, both fermented foods, do not earn her disapproval.

The weight loss part of the diet, called the New Nutrition Diet, begins with a 'Two-Week Fat Flush'. This stringent diet is supposed to cleanse accumulated bad fats from the tissues and liver and stimulate the fat-burning abilities of a type of fat called brown fat. For this phase of the diet, each day you are permitted:

- two tablespoons of safflower oil
- up to 250 grams of a high-protein, low-fat food such as fish, lean beef, lamb or veal, skinless chicken or turkey
- unlimited raw or steamed vegetables
- 2 portions of fruit (examples of a portion are a small apple, half a banana, 10 cherries, half a grapefruit or 1 nectarine)
- 1 teaspoon powdered psyllium husk in 250 mL cranberry juice
- 1 cup hot water with the juice of half a lemon, twice a day
- 2 × 90-milligram capsules gamma linolenic acid (GLA) and 4 × 500-milligram capsules evening primrose oil
- a mineral–vitamin supplement
- 6 glasses of pure water at room temperature (extra water is permitted and is supposed to speed up fat flushing as it is metabolised by the liver)

THE REST OF THE DIETS

This diet is low in carbohydrate and deficient in many minerals and vitamins. The vitamin–mineral supplements may help. Much of the rapid weight loss that could be expected would be due to a loss of lean body tissue and water—useless for permanent weight loss.

The gamma linolenic acid is supposed to attract oil-soluble poisons and carry them out of the system for elimination. There is no evidence for this. Once the Fat Flush phase is finished, 2 very small servings of starchy foods are added, although these are not included in the menus that follow the diet. The list of starchy foods includes one-third cup of cooked rice, one-third cup of corn, half a cup of beans or 1 large pretzel! Two servings of non-fat dairy products are also permitted as an optional extra, and two 280-milligram tablets of one of the omega-3 fats found in fish are included. Alcohol is forbidden, except in cooking.

Beyond Pritikin has some good information about trans fats and the problems of margarines and refined fats. In general, this section of the book has more validity than the rest.

Recipes are also included, 11 for dressings or sauces, 3 pates (chick-pea, tuna and salmon), 5 soups, 15 main courses, 4 vegetables and 10 desserts, several of which have flavour variations. Portions are quite small and it is likely that most people following this diet would feel hungry.

On analysis, the long-term phase of the diet has about 5000 kilojoules (1190 Cals), a level that is barely adequate for a woman. The protein content is high (more than 85 grams), the fat is moderate at less than 50 grams and the carbohydrate just scrapes out of the danger zone. Fibre is low. For a diet that purports to give a balanced intake of fat, the omega-6 fatty acids are much too high. The Two-Week Fat Flush diet is inadequate in almost all nutrients.

Rating: the diet 1; the theory behind the diet 3

GOLDEN OLDIES

Some of these old diets are trotted out every few years, often in a new book or more commonly in a magazine. They are mentioned here because many are still available in libraries or are picked up at jumble sales, while occasionally one is re-issued in some guise. Let's take a brief look at a few of them. I have given each a rating in terms of their nutritional adequacy and effectiveness.

Dr Atkins Super Energy Diet

This once popular diet also belongs to the low-carbohydrate, high-protein, high-fat school. Atkins, a medical practitioner who should have known better, went so far as to praise and encourage a biochemically hazardous state known as ketosis. This occurs when the body's carbohydrate stores are depleted and it is trying to burn fat as its sole source of energy. Without carbohydrate, fats are not properly burnt and highly toxic ketones form. These can be detected in urine and on the breath. If untreated in a person with diabetes, ketosis leads to coma and death. In other people, it produces weakness, nausea, headache and halitosis (the odour is similar to nail-polish remover).

Atkins encourages ketosis to prevent hunger (it certainly does that—you feel sick instead!) and claims it shows the body is burning fats. He fails to mention that it also shows the body is not burning fats properly. Thankfully, Atkins does say that his ketogenic diet is not suitable for everyone. He cautions pregnant women, those with gout and people who are slim not to undertake it.

Dietitians would extend that concern to everyone. His claims that people can eat 21 000 kJ (5000 Cals) on his diet and still lose weight are false. Atkins' theories that eating fat stimulates a fat-mobilising hormone are also without proof.

Rating: the diet 0; the theory behind the diet 0

The Complete Scarsdale Medical Diet

Moving on a step from Dr Atkins, the author of this diet, Dr Herman Tarnower, recommends that his followers restrict carbohydrate and also restrict fats. Proteins may be consumed with greater freedom, although only a limited number of foods are high in protein but low in fat and carbohydrate. Skim milk powder, egg white, fish and very lean meat are virtually the only options.

The diet must be followed strictly for 14 days and claims you will lose 0.5 kg a day. So you may, for the diet is very strict with only a limited range of 'permitted' foods. However, as with all low-carbohydrate diets, much of the weight loss will be muscle and water and losing weight fast by reducing these vital components of the body is undesirable.

After the initial strict 14-day diet, you move to the Keep Trim Eating Plan which is expanded and allows more variety. One alcoholic drink a day is included but carbohydrate foods such as potatoes, rice, pasta and sugar, and butter, margarine, cream, oil, avocado, peanut butter and regular milk are still forbidden.

As with most strict diets, you could not expect any long-term success on the Scarsdale diet. It is an unbalanced diet and would make exercise difficult.

Rating: the diet 1; the theory behind the diet 1

THE REST OF THE DIETS

The Israeli Army Diet

This was an 8-day wonder diet, the popularity of which came from its brevity and simplicity. For the first 2 days, you ate nothing but apples, to be followed by 2 days on cheese, 2 days on chicken and 2 on salad. The diet was repeatedly disowned by the Israeli Army but resurfaces in different forms from time to time.

Any diet which severely restricts the foods you eat will ensure a loss of weight, although not necessarily much loss of fat. Such diets are low-kilojoule diets by another name. Even if you adore cheese, you will find your consumption is less robust after 2 days of eating nothing but cheese. There is also a limit to how many apples you can eat. Even if you could crunch your way through 3 apples each meal and an extra one between meals (a doubtful feat by dinner on the second night!), your total kilojoules for the day would be only about 2500 (600 Cals)—a very low level.

Rating: the diet 0; the theory behind the diet 0

The Egg Diet

Also called the Mayo Clinic Diet (but disowned by the famous Mayo Clinic in the United States), this diet required the would-be slimmer to eat copious quantities of eggs. Some versions of the diet specified that the eggs should be hardboiled. The theory behind this was that the body used up more kilojoules in digesting a hardboiled egg than the egg provided. Therefore the more eggs you ate, the greater your kilojoule deficit! The theory was yet another fake. Even had it been correct, you would have needed to eat thousands of eggs to achieve any significant weight loss.

Newer versions of this diet stipulate that you can only eat egg whites. Since raw egg white contains a substance which destroys one of the B vitamins in the intestine, this idea is potentially harmful. Fortunately it is too boring to attract many followers.

Rating: the diet 0; the theory behind the diet 0

The Drinking Man's Diet
(alias the Air Force Diet)

Some version of this diet pops up every few years. The original, written by Tim Hall, was described as 'the diet guide for thirsty Australians'. Beer is restricted (because it contains some carbohydrate) but dry wines and spirits are freely allowed. These drinks can be used to wash down plenty of steak or other meats, poultry, seafoods, cheese, eggs and vegetables. No bread, rice, cereal, grain, pasta, fruit or other carbohydrate foods are allowed. Participants are encouraged to exercise although no mention is made of the difficulty of exercising with such minimal carbohydrate levels.

As with any other diet very low in carbohydrates, any weight loss will come from partial dehydration, loss of muscle glycogen and loss of muscle tissue itself. Problems with raised blood fats (from the high fat levels) and potential liver disorders receive scant attention, apart from the author demonstrating some social conscience by advising those with an alcohol problem to join Alcoholics Anonymous. Hall also cautions business and professional men about the dangers of impotence, although he blames this on eating large meals. He is apparently ignorant of the link between impotence and high cholesterol levels or he might not advocate this foolish diet.

Rating: the diet 0; the theory behind the diet 0

The Beverley Hills Diet

Many diets have a short life when their premises are shown to be false. The Beverley Hills Diet died a natural death when its claims that certain fruits would dissolve fat failed miserably. This diet had many devotees among Hollywood's film stars, which probably gave it a longer run than it deserved. Its author, Judy Mazel, has been described as a 'failed Hollywood actress'. She managed to write an absurd diet book, some of whose crazy theories have given rise to more modern diets in which fruits are supposed to be consumed on their own. Such theories were unfounded then and still have no basis in fact.

Mazel had some ridiculous ideas. She claimed that some foods are not digested and therefore cannot be absorbed and get 'stuck in the body—and turn into fat'. Eating cottage cheese with fruit is supposed to 'trap the fruit in your stomach and cause it to ferment. Instead of getting skinny, you get bloated.' Another crazy idea concerned eating meat and potatoes at the same meal. According to Mazel, this terrible practice means that 'potatoes get locked in your stomach and ferment. What are fermented potatoes? Vodka.' It's an interesting concept, but a little difficult to reconcile with the processes of digestion. The poor old grapefruit is accused by the Beverley Hills Diet of having 'almost no fibre so it sloshes around in your stomach not doing any particular good'.

The book goes on and on with its crazy ideas. With its wild claims and lack of essential nutrients, the Beverley Hills Diet has been described as 'deceitful, deficient and dangerous'. This diet also provides a good example of why you should always read the fine print. The diet claims you can indulge 'your food fantasies—pasta, popcorn, pizza, hamburgers, spare ribs, steak, lobster, cheesecake, ice cream, wine, champagne or vodka—and indulge in them, while losing weight'.

When you read the book you find you can have nothing but fruit for the first 10 days, eaten only in a particular order. Pineapple dominates the line-up and anyone who did not like pineapple would starve even faster than those who could manage to eat large quantities of it. Some days you have only 1 fruit, others include 2 fruits and, occasionally, you can have 3-fruit meals (only 1 fruit at a time).

Day 11 allows some bagels or bread with butter and 3 cobs of corn; day 12 you can have pineapple throughout the day and salad for your evening meal while on day 13 you are allowed some oven-baked potatoes. By day 19, you have your first taste of protein with some steak or lobster, although you have a complicated set of rules which do not allow you to eat one food within three hours of eating another.

On day 22, you are allowed your first 'combined meal' in the form of a hamburger or a tuna and salad sandwich. Next day it is back to pineapple, plus 2 glasses of wine in the evening. Pasta lovers should note that on day 26 you can have pasta—but absolutely no cheese or meat or protein must come near it. The following day it is grapes, just grapes (they are supposed to 'help pry your fat loose by pushing stored sugar residues out of your body'). The diet continues in this stupid vein. It does not take a dietitian to realise that such a diet lacks almost every nutrient except vitamin C, vitamin A and fruit fibre.

Rating: the diet 0; the theory behind the diet 0

The Rotation Diet

This diet swept through some areas of the United States a few years ago. Written by psychologist Martin Katahn, it promotes a diet which rotates from a daily intake of 2500 kJ (600 Cals) to 3800 kJ (900 Cals) to 5000 kJ (1200 Cals) over a 3-week period. The book is directed primarily at women but men are included with intakes of 5000 kJ (1200 Cals) to 6300 kJ (1500 Cals) and on to 7500 kJ (1800 Cals). The Rotation Diet claims the average woman will lose 6 kilograms over the 3 weeks with heavier women losing around 9–10 kilograms. If you have not lost all your excess weight by the end of 3 weeks, you have a rest/maintenance period then start the rotation again.

The Rotation Diet for women consists of 3 days on 2500 kJ, then 4 days on 3800 kJ. In the second week you eat 5000 kJ for the entire week. Week 3 is a repeat of Week 1.

Most weight loss diets result in rebound weight gain. Katahn's theory was that a rotating diet could overcome this. It works like this:

if you cut back on kilojoules too far, the body responds by decreasing its metabolic rate and burning up fewer kilojoules. The Rotation Diet claims its followers avoid this drop in metabolic rate and stresses the importance of women eating their full 5000 kJ in the second week to prevent weight gain after the diet.

Those who find the lower kilojoule levels too difficult can eat extra quantities of certain vegetables (referred to as 'free', although I am not sure the greengrocer would share that point of view!) and a 'safe' fruit. This category includes apple, berries, grapefruit, melon, orange, peach, pineapple and tangerine. Eight glasses of water a day are recommended with the statement that 'water facilitates weight loss'. Artificially sweetened beverages are not permitted on the grounds that they keep up your taste for sweet foods.

The Rotation Diet goes on to give detailed menu plans for 3 weeks and supplies recipes and shopping lists. This diet achieved great publicity in some areas of the United States where supermarkets took part in its promotion. Shoppers picked up their new Rotation Diet menus and shopping lists at the supermarket and the foods featured in each week of the diet were promoted in the supermarket. This made shopping easy and there were competitions between towns to achieve the greatest collective weight loss.

There is also a Rotation Diet Activity Plan which gives some excellent information on exercise and encourages everyone to participate in more physical activity. This section of the book is valuable.

After the diet is over (or before you repeat it), you move on to the diet's maintenance phase. You are given some advice about cutting back on salt intake, increasing food intake slowly by 1200 kJ increments and keeping up physical activity. Katahn seems particularly concerned about the effects of sodium retention and gives a list of natural diuretic foods which he claims will bring about a loss of water. (Pineapple gets a mention—was this why it is was so heavily promoted in the Beverley Hills Diet?) He also gives a one- or two-day water loss diet which includes 450 grams of very lean meat, fish or chicken, two cups of cottage cheese, the ubiquitous pineapple (or melon), asparagus, broccoli and citrus fruits as well as some other low-carbohydrate vegetables and fruits. The only difference between this and some of the earlier high-protein/low-carbohydrate diets is that Katahn limits it to two days. Unfortunately that does not correct the basic flaw which is the idea that overweight people have too much fluid. They have too much *fat*—following a water loss diet does nothing but cause partial dehydration.

The final part of the Rotation Diet looks at the psychology of weight loss and attempts to impart Weight-Management Confidence. This includes a Weight-Mastery Workbook in which you practise various techniques to help you deal with situations which commonly lead to overindulgence. This is another part of the Rotation Diet which could be of value to many people.

The Rotation Diet is a mixed bag. The exercise pattern is good, the idea that people should not stay on severely restricted kilojoule intakes is sound and the maintenance suggestions, recipes and sections dealing with the psychological aspects of getting weight under control could be useful to many people. I wonder why the author did not work the whole program on more reasonable kilojoule levels. The 2500 kJ is unnecessarily low, even if used only for 3-day periods.

Rating: the diet 7; the theory behind the diet 6

Negative Calories

From time to time advertisements appear for a book available by mail order offering to give you the secret of 'negative calories'. For a price (which seems to vary from $29.95 to $39.95) you receive a small book titled *Foods That Make You Lose Weight* by Isabelle Martin. The advertisements promise to let you in on the secret of 19 foods which help you lose weight.

A friend fell for this trick, sent off her money and read the book (it took less than an hour—35 of the 208 pages were blank, another 12 were for chapter headings and the rest had large printing, well spaced, with large margins). She could not find the 19 magic foods. I read it carefully and under a section headed 'Foods to go with meats and vegetables' found the statement, 'Among the herbs, grains, powders and juices that are currently being offered to us, some are more preferable than others because you can experience their "fat removal" effect.' I assumed I had found the secret (it is on page 90, for anyone who was taken in enough to part with their money). To save anyone else the cost of buying this rip-off guide, the 'fat removal' foods were as follows:

- Herbs: parsley, anethum (a type of dill), mint, chervil, tarragon, fennel, basil and chives
- Roots and bulbs: horseradish, onion, garlic
- Dried plants: bay leaves, thyme, sage
- Spices: nutmeg, pepper, cinnamon, ginger, cloves
- Natural juices: lemon juice (on fish and meat), grapefruit juice (in light mayonnaise), tomato juice (uncooked, on white meats), fresh pineapple juice (in fruit salads or on raw vegetables)
- Dressings: cider vinegar, celery salt, carrot oil, non-acid yoghurt
- Foods for special diets: powdered seaweed, propolis (bee glue)

Of these the following were listed as the most powerful:

parsley
fennel
onion
sage
nutmeg

cloves
carrot oil
powdered seaweed
propolis

Where the '19 foods' come in is beyond my detection. The foods listed total 29, of which 9 fit the 'most powerful' category. Perhaps the author's ability to add up is as faulty as her knowledge of nutrition. She does say, 'don't expect me to provide you with an in-depth course in dietetics, or to give you detailed explanations of the complicated process of assimilation of the various sugars and fats'. She goes on to explain that all we need to know are the plants, vegetables, fruits and oils the purpose of which is to burn off fat.

As you can guess, no food has any magic fat-burning property. I would suggest you do not set out searching for carrot oil, anethum or propolis (which the book describes as having a most noticeable effect on the gall bladder). I would also suggest you do not take any notice of Martin's statements on nutrition.

Most mail order slimming products are fakes. I have chased several to the address given in the advertisement only to find myself in front of a large block of units. Knocking on many doors gives no further clues. Some offer a 'money-back' guarantee within 30 days. In most cases you will find that the post office box number given has been rented for 30 days and that the person can no longer be found. Give them a miss. Remember there is no magic, but there *are* people wanting to take your money.

Rating: the diet 0; the theory behind the diet 0

The Grapefruit Diet

This evergreen comes in many forms and resurfaces regularly. Modern-day variations include the Orange Diet and the Citrus Diet. The original grapefruit diet fits the familiar low-carbohydrate (no bread, no potatoes) diet. The meals are Spartan and strict and usually include black coffee and a slice of dry toast for breakfast—along with half a grapefruit. Lunch is a salad with hardboiled egg and a piece of fruit (grapefruit) while dinner begins with yet another half grapefruit and includes lean meat or fish or chicken with vegetables.

The original grapefruit diet claimed that grapefruit contained an enzyme which would break down body fat. Needless to say, this turned out to be false, although it sold a lot of grapefruit! Modern-day versions have tagged the 'miracle' ingredient as 'Factor GF 18'. Presumably the idea originated by assuming that the sourness of grapefruit would somehow counteract the fattiness of food. Grapefruit

—and all citrus fruits—are excellent sources of vitamin C, contain some other vitamins and minerals and are rich in pectin, a valuable form of dietary fibre. However, there is no miracle in grapefruit and, as with all low-carbohydrate diets, the initial weight loss on this diet is useless for permanent fat loss.

Rating: the diet 2; the theory behind the diet 0

The High Sexuality Diet

If ever a name guaranteed readers, this one did. The 'diet' featured so-called aphrodisiac foods such as asparagus, oysters, caviar, all seafoods, truffles, partridge (for men only!), peaches, pumpkin seeds, garlic, ginseng and celery, as well as cider vinegar, brewer's yeast, kelp, molasses, parsley, soy beans and sprouted seeds. It was an amusing diet and almost a food lover's delight (brewer's yeast and molasses put a slight dampener on the otherwise gourmet fare).

The recipes included had little relevance to overweight people but may have delighted their tastebuds (although not their hearts) with dishes such as What the Hell Parfait (a concoction of ice cream, raspberries, whipped cream, coconut, brown sugar and kirsch). Not the usual diet book entry! Recipes for 'intimate dinners', 'lovable lunches', 'overtures', Cupid's Casserole (liver, apples and onions), Elusive Eel, Wonder Broth, Sweet Nothing Prawns and drinks such as Between the Sheets, Tingling Sensation and Cool Virgin Sip were a delight to read but had nothing to do with weight loss.

Rating: the diet 3 (mostly for amusement); the theory behind the diet 0

9

Other weight loss methods

WEIGHT LOSS PROGRAMS

There are a number of weight loss programs, some are run by food companies, some prescribed by doctors and some run by entrepreneurs. Some are high-profit franchises, while others are set up by dietitians or local self-help groups to provide low-cost assistance. There are also those that provide meals at set kilojoule levels.

Weight loss programs have many different features. A few of the better ones provide a cost effective way to help overweight people lose weight. Others are rip-off operations which prey on the gullible, selling them expensive products or services (such as body wraps or passive exercise machines) with no proven benefits despite the claims made by those marketing them.

A quack has been described as 'a person who promotes therapies as being safe and effective when they have not been demonstrated to be either'. The common elements are deception and profit. The quack with a product to sell uses anecdotes and testimonials as 'proof' for the product. The salespeople are often unable or unwilling to separate objectivity and subjectivity. There is no doubt that the area of weight loss is a fertile ground for quacks. It is a case of buyer beware! Unfortunately, buyers often find it hard to separate fact from fiction, especially when confronted with what they perceive as a solution to their problem.

Of course, not all weight loss programs are promoted by quacks. Many are genuine, helpful and useful programs. Let's take a closer look at a few of the programs and products available.

OTHER WEIGHT LOSS METHODS

Weight Watchers

Weight Watchers began in the United States more than 30 years ago and is the longest-running weight reduction program in the world. Classes are held in 26 countries and every week about a million people attend one of the thousands of available Weight Watchers classes. The Weight Watchers branded foods, sold alongside other products in supermarkets, are owned by H.J. Heinz, although many are made under licence by other major food companies. The foods are designed to help members and others trying to eat less fat, sugar and kilojoules, but they are not an essential part of the program.

The Weight Watchers program takes a four-pronged approach to weight loss and maintenance of weight loss. The program includes an eating plan, an exercise program, techniques to help members change their eating habits (including provision of recipes) and group support. Members pay a joining fee and then pay weekly to attend the meetings. No up-front payment is required, apart from the initial joining fee. Each group meeting is run by a leader who has successfully lost weight with the program and maintained the weight loss. Almost everyone connected with the organisation is a past member.

In an area where so many fad diets and gimmicks prevail, it is a wonder that an organisation with such moderate ideas has lasted the distance. The Weight Watchers organisation itself puts its success down to the fact that they use qualified people to formulate and check every aspect of their programs, and people with personal experience and understanding of the problems of excess weight to run their meetings. They promote a gradual weight loss of 0.5 to 1 kg a week. Members are praised for success and those who do not lose weight can talk privately to the leader running the group about possible reasons. Revised eating plans are produced every few years, designed to make the program more useful to members. Australia and New Zealand have their own locally designed programs which incorporate local foods and eating customs. The current programs are much more flexible than in the past to allow for members who eat out, take lunch to work, or need to buy prepared foods from time to time.

The basic eating plan takes a balanced and flexible approach. Members are encouraged to eat three meals and snacks to provide all the nutrients the body requires for good health, but foods can be arranged any way the member desires. Fats, sugars and alcohol are cut back in the diet, although they are not omitted. The quantities of all foods eaten are monitored through a Points Plan. Based on basic body weight, members are given a number of Points for each day, with each Point representing a quantity of food. Points are allotted to foods on the basis of their kilojoule and fat level. The higher the kilojoules and saturated fats, the greater the number of Points you will use by eating that particular food.

To ensure members choose a nutritionally adequate diet, foods are divided into various categories: fruits; vegetables; starchy carbohydrates (breads, cereals and starchy vegetables); protein foods (including vegetarian alternatives); and dairy. Members must select a certain number of Points from each of these categories and may then use their remaining Points on whatever they choose. Even small portions of foods such as chocolate, chips, biscuits, fast foods and other high-fat foods will cost a large number of Points, and the limit on a member's Points ensures that no one consumes too much of the less nutritious foods. To ensure a balance of essential fatty acids, Points are not added on for valuable unsaturated fats. For example, the kilojoules in products such as fish, vegetable oils and nuts are taken into account when determining Points, but there are no penalty Points for their fat, as there are for foods containing saturated fats. To simplify the eating plan, members are given a booklet listing the Points cost for various foods and there is also information on Weight Watchers' recipes about the Points for each serving.

Weekly menus are provided and members can easily swap one item for another on the same list. This gives the eating plan flexibility. Most vegetables attract no Points and can therefore be eaten in unlimited quantities, although leaders usually encourage members not to 'binge' on any food.

The basic eating plan provides a minimum of 5400 kJ (1300 Cals) and a maximum of 7800 kJ (1850 Cals) for women and a minimum of 6000 kJ (1450 Cals) to a maximum of 8400 kJ (2000 Cals) for men, with the higher levels only relevant for those who are heavier to begin with. This makes the program attractive to those who are very overweight, as they can eat more—as is reasonable. Adolescents must have a doctor's written permission to join. They are given extra Points and must use more of these on foods such as dairy products to provide for growth of bones. An analysis of the diet shows that it meets the Recommended Dietary Intakes for all nutrients.

Exercise is encouraged and the Points program makes this attractive as members can earn up to 12 Bonus Points each week with extra exercise. The extra food this allows is important to provide for the needs of exercise. Members can also save up to 4 Points a day to use later, for example, when eating out. This flexibility makes the program easier to live with and helps avoid the idea that if you have eaten a food that doesn't fit the diet, you've 'blown' it and may as well eat like a pig. The Points program is intended for permanent use, so all foods can be included—although quantities are limited by the Points they use.

Once a member reaches his or her goal weight (set within the

OTHER WEIGHT LOSS METHODS

healthy weight range guidelines), a maintenance program begins. This is designed to keep the member at goal weight. Recent changes in the basic program encourage members to take responsibility for making selections from a range of foods so that the change to the maintenance diet becomes more of a gentle slide. The Weight Watchers program rests on the premise of a lifelong approach.

Members are encouraged to choose what they eat from ordinary foods. However, they may also use Weight Watchers branded foods, including low-kilojoule jams, jellies, soft drinks, cordials, toppings and canned fruits, and some foods with less fat than their conventional counterparts, such as cottage cheese, cheddar cheese slices, whipped margarine, skim milk, yoghurt and low-fat ice confections. Muffins and breads with lighter weight slices, low-sugar/low-salt breakfast cereals, low-fat/low-salt spaghetti sauces and low-kilojoule soups are also available. Some of these foods are made only by Weight Watchers. Some members, and others who are trying to eat less sugar or fat, find them useful.

Weight Watchers also sell recipe books written by their own home economists so that each recipe fits the program. These books are available to the general public. They also have a magazine with stories from members, regular news articles, information on foods and nutrition, and recipes.

Weight Watchers can be commended for trying to change the eating and exercise behaviours that generally make people fat in the first place. Through a series of weekly lessons, members are encouraged to learn appropriate ways to shop, prepare food, cope with eating out and a variety of other aspects of food and eating behaviour. Leaders and members provide many practical hints to help fellow members develop personal skills. Exercise and general increased movement, especially walking, is also encouraged, and members are given hints on how to incorporate more physical activity through extra movement in their daily activities.

The group support offered by Weight Watchers may be their greatest advantage. Whether we like it or not, overweight people are often discriminated against in our society. A group of overweight people can offer each other encouragement and a feeling that no one is alone in his or her struggle against excess weight. Members can sit quietly listening or they can swap ideas to help each other. They share recipes, shopping tips, cooking methods, and ways of coping with obstacles in the home or work environment. The aim of the group is to provide a means for overweight people to learn self-management so that each can solve his or her own problems.

Those who do not lose weight are encouraged to keep a diary of their food intake and are often given some extra recipes or ideas about food preparation. Other group members often share some experience which they found useful. Contrary to some people's belief, Weight Watchers meetings do not include any punishments or rewards. No one is ever made to feel foolish and members are encouraged to feel a sense of achievement.

Within a group of people who know what it is like to be overweight, members do not feel threatened. They can also identify with the leader and other group members and feel the leader understands their problems, which is not always the case when people are being counselled by a doctor or dietitian.

The eating plan can be adapted for use by the whole family. Weight Watchers is recommended by many dietitians and health professionals and is more cost effective than one-to-one consultations. You cannot join Weight Watchers unless you are at least 5 kilograms above the bottom of the healthy weight range, as shown on page 15. This is in stark contrast to some programs where anyone's money is taken, regardless of whether they are genuinely overweight or not.

GutBusters

Started by Dr Garry Egger in Australia in 1991, in conjunction with the New South Wales Health Department and a program for obese men in the Newcastle region of Australia, GutBusters specifically targets men. Having worked in the area of men's health, Garry Egger realised that men view their bodies differently from women and also respond differently to weight loss programs. At the time GutBusters began, most programs were designed for women.

In an effort to put more emphasis on abdominal fat—the place where men store their excess fat—and direct efforts toward losing this fat, the GutBusters program uses waist measurements rather than scales to gauge success. Men are encouraged to reduce their waist measurement if it is over 100 centimetres, the level at which there is a significantly increased risk of health problems such as coronary heart disease, high blood pressure, diabetes, gallstones and certain cancers. The program also emphasises sleep apnoea, a common problem amongst overweight men, and often undiagnosed.

GutBusters can be purchased as a kit, comprising at-home lessons, a manual, Rosemary Stanton's *Fat & Fibre Counter* and other material, plus free access to qualified personnel by phone, or you can purchase a package which includes a series of GutBusters lectures run by a leader with qualifications in the area of human nutrition and/or physical activity or psychology. All leaders will have attended and passed a Fat Loss Leaders course before running classes. In contrast to Weight Watchers, where leaders are people who have successfully lost weight on the Weight Watchers' program and maintained their loss, those involved in GutBusters have professional training in one or more aspects of weight loss. GutBusters classes run in a lecture format with the leader providing information and answering questions rather than seeking to involve participants, as occurs with Weight Watchers groups. This style of meeting sits more comfortably with most men.

The program is designed for men, but there is no reason why women who are overweight cannot also follow it. There are no gimmicks in the program and it has been designed as a permanent change in eating and physical activity. The program discourages people from making any changes that will not be permanent. For example, men are not encouraged to give up alcohol, as this is unlikely to be a permanent change. Instead, they are encouraged to 'trade off' drinks with extra physical activity, especially walking. There are also many clues given as to how to increase movement throughout the day. The program aims to reduce fat, but only to an extent that can easily be maintained.

In 1996, GutBusters was bought by Weight Watchers, although Garry Egger retains a day-to-day and some financial interest in the business. The program has now spread to other countries and is overseen by an International Scientific Advisory Board (of which I am a member), along with many of the world's top obesity experts. Special snorer's kits, diabetes kits and cardiac rehabilitation kits are also available from GutBusters.

By 1999, more than 70 000 men had completed the program in Australia and the results have been published in a number of scientific reviews. They are better than for other programs; one major study reported that 70 per cent of men who had been through the GutBusters program had reduced their waist size by at least 7 per cent and maintained or increased the loss over a one-year period.

As might be expected from my involvement in the GutBusters program, I consider it excellent.

Jenny Craig Weight Loss Centres

Generally much slicker than Weight Watchers, the Jenny Craig Weight Loss Centres have proliferated in Australia since the first centre opened its doors in 1983. They have also expanded to New Zealand and to the United States, apparently with great success. Overweight people walking into the plushly decorated premises are invited to fill in a questionnaire providing details of their eating habits, any previous attempts at dieting, and relevant medical information. A video display fills people in on the program and the foods which will be part of the program. A personal computer plan is then worked out from height, weight and other factors. This tells clients their ideal weight, how long it will take to reach this and how much the program will cost. The amount you pay depends on how much weight you need to lose. The costs rise according to how much weight you need to lose, but this applies only up to a certain level. After that there is a flat rate.

Should you decide to try this program, do not forget to add on the costs of the weekly Jenny Craig foods. These products are not cheap and add substantially to the overall cost. Take note, too, that at some centres, the costs sound quite moderate when they are quoted in dollars per visit by an enthusiastic salesperson. Prospective clients should be sure they know how many visits they have signed up for—and will be expected to pay for—plus the total cost of the weekly foods. A single person may not find the cost of the weekly foods to be higher than they would pay to eat out or buy takeaway foods. For those who must buy the special Jenny Craig foods in addition to buying regular foods for other members of the family, the extra cost will be substantial.

Jenny Craig is herself a formerly overweight American. She began her program of a combination of diet, behaviour modification, exercise and pre-packaged foods (including a vitamin/mineral supplement) in Australia but has now taken it to the United States. Clients are able to see a weight loss counsellor on a one-to-one basis and also take part in small classes (8–10 people) for 'behaviour education'. Lecturers come from a variety of backgrounds, but those with an ability to sell and communicate with clients are preferred.

The Jenny Craig diet is quite strict, but includes a variety of foods. It certainly helps if you like 'packaged' foods—the menus include packets or cans of soups, frozen lasagne and other packaged pasta meals, instant and canned soups, instant noodles, frozen burritos, packaged salad dressings and four types of pre-packaged breakfast cereal, packeted cakes and snack bars, various pre-prepared desserts such as Frozen Delight and chocolate mousse, drink mixes (banana smoothie and chocolate mocha drink)—even frozen salads. The client adds his or her own fresh fruit (a variety is suggested with the quantities equating to about 2 pieces a day), vegetables (the selection allows some free choice and suggests 2 servings a day, including a cup of salad vegetables), skim milk (1 cup/day), low-fat yoghurt (one-third cup/day), peanut butter (1 teaspoon a week or 4 teaspoons on the upper kilojoule level), plus Vegemite and bread (9 to 12 slices plus 4 to 14 pieces of crispbread for the week). Those on the higher kilojoule (5000 kJ/day) level can add 2 tablespoons of low-fat cottage cheese, 20 grams of reduced-fat cheese and an extra half cup of skim milk for the whole week. Not a lot to get excited about.

The diet is claimed to provide 4400 or 5000 kJ/day with 60 per cent of the kilojoules from carbohydrate, 20 per cent from fat and 20 per cent from protein. There is no way of checking these values since so much of the food is pre-packaged. At the prescribed kilojoule level, some people, especially men and those who are large or active, will feel hungry.

The idea behind the packaged foods is that they will introduce and/or establish sensible eating and cooking habits by the time the clients are gradually weaned from them. Some clients, however, object to paying for a tiny package of macaroni or white rice, and it is difficult to understand how people will learn appropriate cooking and shopping skills when all their meals are coming out of a ready-prepared package.

It is also a problem when a family member following the Jenny Craig program must eat different foods from the rest of the household. Many overweight people have other family members who are overweight or will become so if they follow the usual family eating pattern. It therefore makes sense for whole families to adopt a sensible eating plan together rather than supply one overweight member with his or her own special foods. For an overweight woman cooking for a family, it may also be a hassle to have to prepare one meal for the family and a separate meal for herself. This does little to teach other family members how to eat and also separates the slimmer from the family.

It is difficult to determine the nutritional adequacy of the Jenny Craig diet when most of the food is pre-packaged. A vitamin/mineral supplement is supplied and a perusal of the menu would indicate that such a supplement might be necessary.

The Jenny Craig Weight Loss Centres are fairly expensive and the use of pre-packaged foods may or may not teach people appropriate ways to eat to maintain any weight loss. One-to-one counselling usually requires trained counsellors. Jenny Craig staff are trained internally, and the company in Australia does employ dietitians, but most of the staff have no qualifications which would be recognised outside the organisation. Prospective clients should carefully weigh up the total costs and decide if they will be getting lifelong value for their money.

Gloria Marshall Figure Shaping Salons (and similar passive exercise programs)

The Gloria Marshall program uses a fairly strict diet plus passive exercise machines which bump, roll and wobble the body in an attempt to break down fatty tissue.

The idea of using passive exercise to reduce body fat sounds appealing. Many overweight people, already flabby, dislike physical activity but realise that they need some exercise to keep their body firm, and like the idea that they can restore muscle tone to the body without exerting more effort than it takes to lie on a bed of rollers. People selling programs which use passive exercise machines extol the virtues of their machines with a great sales pitch. But just how effective are these machines?

There is a range of vibrating belts, rollers, pads and other gadgetry which various people promote as an aid to controlling body weight. You stand, sit or lie down while your fat is supposedly 'mobilised' by the pounding, rubbing or electrical stimulation of the various machines. This is supposed to increase the circulation to particular parts of the body and somehow remove fat deposits.

Research using oxygen analysis equipment has shown that the amount of energy you use while being vibrated by belts or bumped around by various pieces of similar apparatus is roughly equivalent to the amount of energy you burn while standing still! Any minor effects from stimulation of the surface of the body are unlikely to be translated into permanent weight loss. According to the American Medical Association: 'The so-called effortless exercisers have a value limited to the intensity and duration of the movement they demand. They do not provide any hidden benefits or values. Their most serious shortcoming is that most of them do little to improve the fitness of the heart and lungs which are most in need of exercise today.' It is my experience that those who are paying for passive exercise also think they need not bother with 'active' exercise.

Some people report that they feel very relaxed after using passive exercise machines. And many people do lose weight while undergoing passive exercise programs. However, this is due to the diet which accompanies the figure control program. Gloria Marshall's diet claims to contain 4200–5000 kJ (1000–1200 Cals) and to be nutritionally balanced to allow for a weight loss of 1 kilogram a week.

After the initial period, adherents are encouraged to make their own food selections from supplied lists of substitute foods. Some emphasis is placed on the need to maintain the new eating habits. The women (clients are almost all female) are also told that the passive exercise treatments will 'firm and tone' the body.

Unless you like the relaxation effect of passive exercise machines, there is no point in wasting your money on them. They do not mobilise fat deposits; any weight loss will come from the strict diet, not from the machines. As emphasised earlier in this book, weight loss from diets very low in kilojoules is unlikely to be maintained. The diets accompanying some popular passive exercise programs are too low in kilojoules and lack adequate quantities of several important nutrients to qualify as healthy eating regimes. With their false promises for passive exercise and their dietary inadequacies, such programs do not represent good value for money.

OTHER WEIGHT LOSS METHODS

Herbalife®

The Herbalife® program promotes a combination of products, including

- A protein drink mix to replace two meals a day (the other is supposed to be a balanced meal). The company claims the drink is rich in soy proteins, carbohydrates and vitamins and is supposed to help you feel full and satisfied so you won't crave unhealthy foods and snacks. They also claim it 'provides all the essential amino acids your body needs for good health and contains carbohydrates for quick energy'. Each serving claims it provides 9 grams of protein, is low in calories, fat and sodium, a good source of dietary fibre and is rich in vitamins and minerals, including the antioxidant vitamins A, C and E, which can help protect against cell damage. It is also supposed to provide dietary amino acids which the body cannot produce on its own and has 'breakthrough enzyme technology'.
- Multi-vitamin mineral herbal tablets containing '39 vitamins, minerals and important nutrients'. Sales material also states that this product contains natural Chinese herbs that are supposed to work synergistically to create a foundation for long-term good health, betacarotene, vitamin C, vitamin E, selenium and chromium GTF (glucose tolerance factor).
- Cell Activator® to boost absorption of minerals and vitamins, and herbal blends for increased energy.
- Thermobond®, which is supposed to help the body absorb less fat, assist the system and help keep you regular.
- Cell-U-Loss®, which supposedly helps the elimination of fluids that they claim are a factor in cellulite.
- Aminogen®, which is supposed to act to improve assimilation of dietary protein. Used in conjunction with a calorie-reduced, low-fat diet, it is also supposed to help reduce serum cholesterol.

There are many meal replacement drinks on the market, including those used as part of some very low-calorie diets. While these may have some use for urgent fast weight loss (for example, in preparation for surgery), there is no evidence of long-term weight loss with such products. It is difficult to see why any of the other ingredients in the Herbalife® package would be help with loss of body fat. Products which claim they help with fluid elimination may contain diuretic substances, and there is a possibility that these could cause problems. There are also many herbs, including Chinese herbs, with diuretic or laxative functions. As the Herbalife® products do not list their specific ingredients, it is not possible to comment on the theoretical basis for a role in weight loss. However, if these products cause weight loss by increasing fluid loss or by increasing laxation, such losses would be largely due to a loss of fluid and would be temporary. There is no reason why beta carotene, vitamins E and C and selenium would be associated with weight loss. Chromium is discussed on page 57.

Neither the range nor the components of the Herbalife® weight loss packages have been tested in published controlled trials. Support comes from anecdotal testimonials from people identified by their initials and general place of residence only. The presence of Chinese herbs in products is of potential concern. While some Chinese herbs may be harmless, and there is no evidence to incriminate those used in Herbalife® products, there have been reports of serious problems with Chinese herbs used in other slimming regimes. For example, reports from Belgium describe 71 cases of severe kidney problems in young Belgian women who used Chinese herbs for slimming. These cases were due to the herbs *Stephania tetrandra* and *Magnolia officinalis* being contaminated by a herb containing aristolochic acid, a known carcinogen and kidney toxin. While there are no reports to date of similar cases, there have been warnings about the potential dangers of unknown Chinese herbs and there is no evidence that they have any role in promoting loss of body fat.

The Herbalife® program claims it is designed to burn off kilojoules and eliminate hunger pangs. The herbs are supposed to curb your appetite and 'cleanse the system'. If this means they have either laxative or diuretic properties, they are undesirable.

The total vitamin intake from the program is high. The balance of amino acids is no better or worse than one normally obtains from regular protein foods.

The program makes a series of claims including the following:

- inch [sic] loss at waist and other fat accumulation areas;
- excellent condition of the hair and fingernails;
- tightening of the skin;
- vitality and energy throughout the program; no mid-morning or mid-afternoon let-down;
- savings in food cost.

They do acknowledge that 'whether or not one receives any of the above benefits is an individual matter. You can only find out by trying the program. The products are sold on a money-back guarantee by nutritional consultants . . .' In fact, their nutritional consultants do not have any recognised qualifications in nutrition or dietetics. They sell the program enthusiastically and many are past users.

The Herbalife® program is well organised and the company's magazine and web site contain articles on the benefits (and profits) to be made by becoming a distributor (or 'consultant'). Case histories of big earners are also distributed.

Like many other diet programs, this one comes from the United States. Like many others, it also talks of the need to detoxify the body. In fact, some Herbalife® literature claims that the program is not a diet but a 'detoxification program to cleanse the body of acids, toxins and poisons that have been deposited in the body from pollution, processed foods, excess protein, white flour products, sugars, soda pop, alcoholic beverages and smoking'. One wonders why they then use a protein powder drink which will increase protein intake further.

The Cell-U-Loss® product, which is supposed to 'beat the cellulite bulge through the magic of natural herbs' includes herbs, vitamin C and minerals and claims to increase circulation, break up and liquefy fatty tissues, and through the natural diuretic action of herbs, eliminate the excess fluids and waste build-ups from the system. Potential customers should be warned not to fall for such a product!

There is no doubt that some people can and do lose weight with Herbalife®, as they do with many formula diets. However, it is an expensive method of weight loss and does not teach you how to eat in a way that will enable you to avoid regaining the lost weight. Herbalife®'s answer to the problem of regaining weight is to continue to replace one meal a day with a formula meal. This may be great for future business but is hardly teaching people how to choose well from the range of highly nutritious food products available.

There is also a range of other products sold at high prices, often using persuasive selling techniques. If approached by a Herbalife® salesperson, try to resist the sales talk. In spite of their persuasive sales pitch, none of the products has been subjected to properly controlled tests. In spite of the white-coated doctor on the front of one of Herbalife®'s promotional brochures, reputable dietitians or health professionals who understand the principles of losing weight and keeping it off do not recommend this program.

Local or state government programs

In many areas, community dietitians, hospital dietetics departments or health education departments have set up weight loss groups or programs. There are also small groups of people within some communities who have a common interest in losing weight and so begin a weight loss group.

Groups can offer valuable support to overweight people and are a cost-efficient way to help solve genuine weight problems. Many overweight people are discriminated against, some find little help with their weight loss efforts at home and others are depressed by the number of times they have failed to lose weight in the past. Regular meetings with others with similar problems can be helpful. These groups often help solve practical problems and provide a place where members can swap recipes or simply meet for a chat.

The usefulness of any weight control group depends on the accuracy of the information they disseminate. Those with the expertise of an Accredited Practising Dietitian (APD) usually have balanced diets and offer sound dietary advice. Some encourage members to exercise and also run cooking demonstrations to teach members how to prepare healthy foods.

Anyone thinking of joining a weight loss organisation should check that there are people with qualifications and experience backing it, and that these people are available for consultation if required. Use the information in Chapters 3 and 6 to check the validity of the diet being promoted. Remember that a soundly-based program will not offer dramatic results but will be realistic, practical and give guidelines for the whole family to enjoy a healthier way of eating.

Exercise groups

Groups which hold exercise classes or organise members to walk, jog, dance or do aerobics, aquarobics or Tai-chi routines can be valuable. However, exercise groups can create more problems than they solve if they promote ideals of extreme slimness, as some gyms and fitness centres do. Some promise 'thin thighs', 'new bodies' and a range of similar hopes which are unobtainable and not necessarily even healthy. Sometimes women feel so inadequate about their abilities to ever achieve the promised perfection that they go off and wallow in cream cakes or some other indulgence.

Not all exercise groups fit this mould and many provide a great way for people to learn to enjoy walking or some other exercise in a group setting. Exercise or weight loss groups can be useful if they are backed by people who can give accurate advice on diet and exercise. Check the instructors have had recognised tuition in exercise.

Prepared meals
(Diet Factory, Diet Kitchen, Diet Lite and others)

Various companies prepare meals for slimmers. Some deliver the week's prepared meals, while others ask the client to call in and collect the food. The quality of the meals from these outlets varies. Some provide everything you need while others expect you to add your own bread, fruit and vegetables. Meals may be prepared and frozen, or come in packets.

The idea behind these schemes is that the slimmer can buy a week's meals at a particular kilojoule level and need only pop them in the oven or open the packet at the prescribed time. Using the pre-packaged system, the slimmer can forget everything about counting kilojoules, buying special foods, or learning different cooking techniques. These programs also claim that slimmers will learn how much they should eat to fit into a particular kilojoule level. This has some validity, especially since what one person may describe as an 'average' serve may be very small or very large to others. Overweight people often underestimate how much they eat so prepared meals could be helpful. However, good nutrition does not always mean eating less. The volume of food you can eat depends on what you choose. Vegetables, for example, can be eaten in very large quantities whereas a concentrated food such as chocolate needs to be served in very small pieces.

Prepared and delivered meals remove from the slimmer any need to learn how to live in the real world of free-choice foods. In some cases, these meals will not supply everything the slimmer needs. Dietary fibre, for example, is almost always low with pre-cooked and packaged foods, although some companies do advise people to add their own fruits and vegetables. Nutrients such as calcium, found mainly in milk and cheese, will also be low unless the client remembers to drink the appropriate quantities of milk or to include some form of calcium. While almost anyone can include the occasional pre-cooked and reheated meal without suffering any nutritional ill-effects, a steady diet of these foods may lack some of the B complex vitamins.

Some prepared meal packages are also too low in kilojoules—most seem to include daily menus from 3300–6300 kJ (800–1500 Cals). The menus with fewer kilojoules are often popular with those who want to lose weight quickly. These meals are usually cheaper too, although you are still paying dearly for someone else to do your cooking. Also, as stated previously, 3300 kJ (800 Cal) does not provide an adequate diet, especially for anyone who is exercising.

Pre-prepared meal plans vary a great deal in their nutritional balance and quality. Some may be useful for those who have no idea of appropriate servings for some foods. Before buying them, consider their cost. If you are one member of a family, the extra cost of buying these prepared meals for yourself is unlikely to be matched by a similar reduction in the weekly housekeeping budget when you are not eating the regular family food. Also, do you really want to eat a different meal from the rest of the family?

MEAL REPLACEMENT PRODUCTS

These products may be in the form of a drink, a biscuit or some type of powdered product. They are designed to replace a regular meal, usually breakfast or lunch—or both. Most of the products have added minerals and vitamins. Some have added collagen, branched chain amino acids or L-carnitine, essential fatty acids, antioxidants and so-called fat metabolisers. These ingredients are discussed in Chapter 5. Most products are low in kilojoules. The promoters of meal replacement products claim that their products remove the temptations of having to think about or select foods.

Some meal replacement products claim that they will do away with hunger pangs, help you lose weight effortlessly (without exercise), bring about substantial weight loss, provide few kilojoules—and still provide energy. Beware of claims that foods with few kilojoules will provide lots of energy. Kilojoules are a measure of energy and you cannot have one without the other.

Meal replacement products aim to convince you that the product will make slimming simple. Most of the associated literature also promises fast weight loss, emphasises the ease of using the product and is accompanied by glowing testimonials from supposedly satisfied customers. Some of these products are sold in supermarkets, health food shops and pharmacies; others are available only from doctors; some are sold through direct marketing schemes using high-powered salespeople, and many sell through the Internet.

With their powerful selling messages and promise of fast, easy results, it is little wonder that meal replacement products sell so well. However, most of these products will part you from more of your money than your fat. Let us examine a few products.

Meal replacement formula drinks

During the 1970s, meal replacement formula drinks were developed in the United States and sold to millions of hopeful people who were led to believe that these 'magic potions' would miraculously and painlessly make their excess fat disappear.

The original products were developed under medical supervision and were intended for obese people who needed to lose weight quickly, for example, before surgery. Since any rapid weight loss is always accompanied by the body breaking down its own tissue, the products were supposed to provide just enough protein to 'spare' the loss of the body's own tissues while allowing for maximum weight loss. This was the rationale behind the first 'protein-sparing modified fasts'.

One of the best known of the American promoters of liquid protein diets was Robert Linn, an osteopath who developed a formula consisting of amino acids extracted from the collagen in beef hides. He promoted the wonders of his idea in a book called *The Last Chance Diet* which various cynics quipped was the 'last chance' to diet before death! Some of the early protein-sparing products did prove fatal—for 60 people.

Meal replacement products were originally intended only for use by people under strict medical supervision. The potential for yet another weight reduction scheme, however, proved too much for the entrepreneurs of the slimming world.

The original formula products gave birth to many commercial high-protein formula products in which the protein came from sources such as soy beans, skim milk, egg albumen, casein and wheat. In some cases, these other foods were used in an attempt to achieve a better balance of amino acids than the early, much criticised formulas. However, even if the newer products have a better balance of amino acids, this does not make them any more desirable for most overweight people. Any low-carbohydrate, very low kilojoule diet will cause a loss of water and muscle protein with little permanent fat loss.

Meal replacement drinks have proliferated largely because they are fairly cheap to make and can be marketed at a price which brings in a high profit. One product, for example, consists of skim milk with added vitamins and minerals and sells for seven times the cost of ordinary skim milk powder. That's a hefty premium for having your skim milk pre-weighed with a few vitamins added. In the late 1990s, another collagen product was being sold through a multi-level marketing company which claimed that it would build muscle and help you lose weight while you sleep! This company, like many others, combined some relevant and accurate material with many outrageous claims. A combination of truth and rubbish makes it hard for the lay person to judge validity. The high-powered marketing hype inevitably sucks people into these programs, many of which encourage participants to 'research' their products and program, supplying 'references' to supposed scientific information. It sounds convincing, but is usually spurious. If you have doubts and wish to do some genuine research, ask an Accredited Practising

MEAL REPLACEMENT PRODUCTS—SIDE EFFECTS

Side effects of some meal replacement products include fatigue, irritability, nausea, constipation, headaches, dizziness, hair loss, dry skin and bad breath. In the state of near-starvation, which occurs with some meal replacement products, the body is enduring a significant degree of stress. To withstand such stress, the slimmer needs healthy kidneys and liver. Yet a number of people have suffered kidney damage with these products and reports of gallstones developing or getting worse have been published in medical journals.

Dietitian (contactable through the Dietitians Association of Australia) or, if you have scientific training look for research results through Medline. A good Internet site to find out if information is genuine is www.quackwatch.com.

There are also meal replacement products available from doctors. Doctors often feel powerless to help their overweight clients (perhaps because of a lack of sufficient training in nutrition). Even if medical supervision makes the use of these products safer, it does not necessarily make them more effective.

Some meal replacement products advise users to eat one regular meal a day and substitute the product for the other two meals. However, some include statements such as 'it can replace all your meals for as long as five days at a time. 330 Calories a day for five days must result in dramatic weight loss'. Such a low level of energy intake is little more than starvation and cannot meet the body's total nutritional needs.

Another product has tried to counter criticism by recommending two meals of their drink (at 630 kJ or 150 Cals a meal) and a regular evening meal of 2900 kJ (700 Cals). The main meal will certainly help balance the other meals, but it goes against nutrition education efforts which encourage people to eat more at breakfast and lunch and less at dinner.

Some of the promotional material for meal replacement products extols the wonders of ketosis. One pamphlet tries to claim that the ketosis which accompanies its diet should be distinguished from 'hazardous diabetic ketosis'. That may sound reassuring to someone who knows nothing of biochemistry but it is rubbish. The same program restricts daily carbohydrate to 35 grams—a hopelessly inadequate quantity. In practice, all these products are simply a way to reduce kilojoule intake. Their lack of carbohydrate means that most of the weight lost will be water—just as we have seen with any low-carbohydrate/extra low kilojoule diet.

A FANTASY WORLD OF EXTRAS

There is a fantasy world of extras to accompany meal replacement products. These include products such as

- spirulina (a type of plankton which is claimed to act as an appetite suppressant and 'detoxify' the body—there is no proof it does so)

- aloe vera (one company claims that their 'stabilized juice affords maximum retention of the organic ingredients for which the aloe vera plant is renowned'—but provides no details for the consumer)
- herbal formulae with added vitamin C and minerals (to rid you of cellulite)
- special Chinese substances (no information given as to their virtues)
- herbal sedatives
- fat metaboliser capsules
- chewable tablets of kelp, vitamin B_6, lecithin and cider vinegar (supposedly to eliminate fluid)
- amino acid cakes, made from honey, malt, vanilla, peanut meal, soy and milk protein, egg white, glucose, and—close to the bottom of the ingredient list—amino acids.

It seems there is no end to the imagination of the peddlers of these useless products. And yet gullible people hoping for a miracle pay handsomely for them. See Chapter 5 for more details of 'magic' ingredients.

Meal replacement products also lack dietary fibre, although some manufacturers have added fibre supplements, usually in small and inadequate quantities. In any case, taking fibre supplements is a poor nutritional substitute for eating foods such as wholemeal bread, wholegrain cereals, vegetables and fruits which are rich in dietary fibre and a range of other desirable nutrients.

In the United States, the Food and Drug Administration (FDA) has issued a mandatory warning to be put on any liquid or powdered protein products. This must state:

> WARNING: Very low calorie protein diets may cause serious illness or death. DO NOT USE FOR WEIGHT REDUCTION WITHOUT MEDICAL SUPERVISION. Use with particular care if you are taking medication. Not for use by infants, children, or pregnant or nursing women.

Products which claim to be high-protein formulas, and also have other nutrients supplying energy, and which include a nutritionally balanced plan must carry a warning on the label, stating:

> USE ONLY AS DIRECTED IN THE DIET PLAN DESCRIBED HEREWITH. DO NOT USE AS THE SOLE OR PRIMARY SOURCE OF CALORIES FOR WEIGHT REDUCTION.

In Australia, the National Health and Medical Research Council (NHMRC) has also recommended that the following warning statement appear on the labels of high-protein diet products:

NOT TO BE USED AS THE PRINCIPAL OR SOLE SOURCE OF DIET AND PREFERABLY TO BE TAKEN UNDER MEDICAL GUIDANCE.

Meal replacement biscuits

Meal replacement biscuits are readily available in a variety of flavours in supermarkets. The biscuits are formulated to provide some protein and added minerals and vitamins. A meal (2 or more biscuits as directed on the packs), contributes between 1180 and 1320 kJ (280 to 315 Cals) depending on the flavour. For approximately the same number of kilojoules you could have a chicken and salad sandwich and an apple—and feel like a normal eater.

Meal replacement biscuits are not as nutritionally unbalanced as the protein drink products because they do contribute some carbohydrate (approximately 32 grams/meal). Assuming the dieter eats some regular meals, the total carbohydrate for the day could approach minimum safe levels. However, meal replacement biscuits do not teach the dieter how to make appropriate food choices from the wide range of delicious and nutritious foods available. They may also encourage people to regard biscuits as a meal.

SLIMMING DRUGS

We live in a pill-popping society. Whatever ails us, some pill will fix the problem. Why should excess weight be any different? That is the attitude which leads some companies to try to develop slimming drugs. It is also the attitude which leads doctors to prescribe slimming drugs. Unable to help people lose weight, many doctors turn to their traditional prescriptive approach.

There has been *no* successful slimming drug. Some claim success but no long-term study has yet shown any evidence to support such claims. Some slimming drugs try to suppress appetite to prevent overeating. There is no guarantee that this will work in overweight people as many do not feel hungry in the usual sense of the word and eat whether they are hungry or not.

Other slimming drugs aim to speed up metabolism so that food will be burned faster in the body. The most recent one prevents the absorption of fat. Researchers are also looking for drugs which will stop fats being converted to body fat or cause the body to burn more kilojoules. All slimming drugs developed so far have side effects and some are addictive.

OTHER WEIGHT LOSS METHODS

Fen/phen

Fenfluramine, phentermine and dexfenfluramine are drugs that help suppress the appetite. They were available only by prescription. In the United States, more than 18 million prescriptions for these drugs were provided by doctors. They were also used in many other parts of the world, although very few were taken in Australia.

Fenfluramine was reported to keep suppressing appetite for up to 48 weeks. However, it was also reported to induce sedation and depression and to lead to withdrawal symptoms, including depression and disorientation, when people stopped taking it.

In 1997, a report in one of the world's top medical journals linked fen/phen with valvular heart disease, in which the heart valve is damaged and allows blood to leak backwards. Earlier reports had also linked high doses of either fenfluramine, phentermine or dexfenfluramine with high blood pressure in the lungs (a potentially fatal problem in 45 per cent of its victims within four years) and the makers of the product voluntarily withdrew Redux and Pondimin, two popular diet products containing the drugs. Controversy still surrounds this action, with many referring to the millions of people who have taken the drugs without adverse effects. However, health authorities in the United States are advising everyone who has taken fenfluramine or dexfenfluramine for any period of time to have a thorough medical history and cardiovascular physical examination.

Sibutramine

The United States Food and Drug Administration recently approved a new diet drug containing sibutramine, which has some similar chemical properties to dexfenfluramine and fenfluramine. Sibutramine reduces appetite by interacting with serotonin, a chemical in the brain that makes people feel full.

Side effects can include high blood pressure, which is a serious risk factor for heart attack and stroke. Some people also experience irregular heartbeat and an increased pulse rate. With this, or any drug, it is important to weigh up the likely side effects and compare them with the risks posed by continued obesity. Such drugs are only appropriate for those who are seriously obese, usually at a stage when it is difficult even to walk around.

Xenical™ (Orlistat)

The drug orlistat, marketed by Roche Products Pty Ltd as Xenical™, works on the fat-splitting enzyme in the intestine, allowing it to act partially, but not completely. This means that when you eat fat, Xenical™ prevents the absorption of some of this fat, which is then excreted in the faeces. The maximum inhibitory effect of Xenical™ on fat absorption is approximately 37 per cent of fat ingested. In practice, once you have consumed more than about 25 to 30 grams of fat, any extra fat consumed is not digested and is excreted. Before it leaves the body, the undigested fat acts as a substrate for millions of bacteria which ferment it and produce copious quantities of smelly gas. There is also an urgent need to go to the toilet to pass loose stools. As a result of these somewhat unpleasant occurrences, the overweight person learns not to eat more than 25 to 30 grams of fat a day.

Xenical™ does not act in the same way as chitosan, although, like chitosan, its major aim is to reduce fat absorption (see page 51). Unlike chitosan, however, Xenical™ continues to be trialled in obesity research clinics in major teaching hospitals and universities in centres throughout the world. Controlled clinical trials are now taking place in Australia, where the drug has recently been approved for use. These show that weight loss is greater with Xenical™ than with a placebo; weight loss of around 10 per cent of body weight is being seen. Some do not regard this as an adequate result, but studies have consistently shown that losing 10 per cent of body weight is enough to normalise insulin levels, some blood fats and blood pressure. After a time, the blood pressure tends to revert to a higher level.

The potential problems that have not been adequately addressed relate to whether Xenical™ prevents absorption of carotenoids and the extent to which its effects on loss of fat-soluble vitamins may present problems. Some loss of vitamin E has been confirmed but there is little information on the fate of carotenoids, which normally need fat to be absorbed. Earlier questions about the absorption of essential fatty acids seem to have been resolved positively, these being among the proportion of fat that is absorbed.

Like most drugs, which must be extensively and expensively tested, Xenical™ isn't cheap. Whether it is worth the high financial cost to encourage people to follow a low-fat diet in this way is a debatable point. Some overweight people think it is; many doctors dealing with the massively overweight who find it difficult to reduce their fat consumption are in favour. In Australia, Xenical™ is only recommended to those with a body mass index greater than 25 and many experts in obesity support the drug being used only by those whose BMI is greater than 30. It is neither suitable nor desirable for the person who wants to lose 5 kilograms. In spite of its prescription-only status, however, Xenical™ can be bought via the Internet—a problem not yet adequately addressed.

OTHER WEIGHT LOSS METHODS

Appetite suppressants

Appetite suppressants are commonly prescribed as slimming drugs. Some give a physical feeling of fullness so that one does not feel like eating. Others work on the appetite control centre in the brain. Most affect the central nervous system. Common side effects include a dry mouth, feeling jittery and nervous, insomnia, headache, nausea and gastrointestinal disturbances.

Amphetamines were once widely prescribed as slimming drugs. They have been banned in Australia and many other countries because they produce a psychosis which is similar to schizophrenia. More modern drugs are amphetamine derivatives which are supposed to be less addictive and produce fewer side effects. However, some of the mood-altering effects of these newer drugs may lead to a psychological dependence on them.

Appetite suppressants can only ever act as a crutch. Once you stop taking them, you are soon back where you started. It is also questionable whether excessive appetite is the real reason why many people overeat. There is no evidence that overweight people have greater appetites than others, but many eat whether they are hungry or not.

It is also questionable whether we need to reduce appetite. Overweight people do not need to stop eating—they need to learn which are the appropriate foods to eat when they are hungry. Many of them never actually feel the gut-rumbling hunger pangs which other people get several times a day—their eating is triggered by other factors. Giving overweight people a pill which changes their mood, gives them a dry mouth and a jittery feeling is useless.

It is also hazardous to give appetite suppressants to anyone suffering from depression. In my experience, most people want to try something other than drugs first and it is only when they become depressed because nothing seems to work for them that they turn to drugs. Finding overweight people willing to take drugs, and not already suffering some degree of depression, could be difficult.

Drugs affecting the thyroid gland

Drugs to increase the body's metabolic rate have also been tried. Because the thyroid gland controls the metabolic rate, many people are convinced their excess weight is due to a sluggish thyroid. In fact, it is rare for excess weight to be caused by gland problems.

It is commonly believed that kelp, a potent source of iodine (and also arsenic!), can stimulate the thyroid gland to increase metabolic rate. This is untrue. Even if the thyroid was not functioning normally, taking extra iodine from kelp would not necessarily be the answer. Extra iodine in fact can depress the action of the thyroid gland.

THE DIET DILEMMA

New drugs

Drugs now being researched include some which may turn off the desire to eat by altering certain receptors which seem to regulate food intake. When food accumulates in the stomach, gut peptides such as cholecystokinin are released—their release may be the reason why most people stop eating. By isolating these substances, or similar compounds, and giving them to overweight people, it is possible to give an early signal to terminate a meal. However, in studies in which these substances have been given by infusion, many people have reported a 'sick' feeling. Even if mild, this is not a pleasant note on which to finish a meal. Eating should be a joy. It is possible that some other substances may stimulate a greater natural production of gut peptides and these may work in pill form rather than needing intravenous administration.

Pharmaceutical companies searching for a drug to turn off the craving for carbohydrates have located a substance which seems to be able to do this. However, it may be useless using a drug to reduce carbohydrate cravings if carbohydrates are not responsible for excess weight. The so-called 'sweet tooth' may be a myth. Studies in which the sugar and fat content of foods have been manipulated have shown that those who claim to have a sweet tooth really like sugar only when it accompanies fat. Most of the foods favoured by 'sweet tooths'—desserts, cakes, biscuits, pastries, ice cream, chocolates—are high in fats as well as sugar. When the fat is removed, many of those who claim to love sweets do not like the foods. Fat is the real problem—perhaps drug companies should be looking at ways to turn off the craving for fat. After all, in countries where the diet is predominantly carbohydrate, such as in Asia, there is virtually no obesity. Carbohydrate foods such as bread, grains, cereals and fruits are rarely the cause of excess weight unless they are loaded with fats.

Taking drugs which stop you absorbing carbohydrates or fats means that those unabsorbed substances must find their way through the intestine. In doing so, they may cause problems. Carbohydrates which are not digested ferment in the large intestine and cause flatulence, pain, bloating and diarrhoea. Unabsorbed fats can also cause problems, including diarrhoea and poor absorption of fat-soluble vitamins.

Slimming drugs themselves may be as much of a health hazard as excess weight. There is no point in swapping one health hazard for another. The best way to lose weight is to change the habits which made you fat in the first place.

Laxatives

Many people use and abuse some types of laxatives. There may be a place for laxatives that function as bulking agents or dietary fibre supplements in the treatment of some existing bowel disorders but they have no place in weight control.

It is often believed that taking laxatives will cause food to pass straight through the intestine before it can be absorbed and contribute any kilojoules. Many of the modern diets promote eating large quantities of fruit or bran for a similar purpose. They assume that if food rushes quickly through, it can't make you fat. If this were true, you would also miss out on the nourishment, including the minerals, vitamins, fatty acids and amino acids from the food. The usual bacterial digestion of dietary fibre also produces organic acids which have important roles in health and cancer prevention.

Abuse of laxatives produces diarrhoea, dehydration and loss of potassium and other nutrients. Potassium is important in regulating the action of the heart muscle; its loss is serious and sometimes fatal. Those who take laxatives for slimming become run-down, lack energy, may have problems with skin and hair and are more susceptible to viruses and bacterial infections.

Even if laxatives are not taken to such extremes, they are hazardous. Most of any lost weight is water, not fat. Those who take laxatives also lose muscle tone in the large intestine. Just as it is important to preserve firm muscles in the rest of the body, so we should keep the muscular bowel wall in good condition. Many laxatives make future constipation almost inevitable.

Laxatives are *not* recommended for weight loss. Those who are constipated should eat more high-fibre foods, drink more water and take some exercise. High-fibre foods themselves do not cause a loss of weight but since most high-fibre foods have little fat, replacing fatty foods with fibrous foods leads to a decrease in kilojoule intake. The foods with most fibre are legumes (dried beans or peas, including baked beans); wholegrain cereals and breads; grains such as wheat, oats, brown rice, barley, millet, corn and buckwheat; fruits and vegetables; nuts and seeds. Of these foods, only nuts and seeds are high in fat. Unprocessed wheat bran is also high in dietary fibre but in large doses it may interfere with the absorption of some minerals. Amounts greater than 1–2 tablespoons a day are not recommended.

Diuretics

Many doctors prescribe 'water pills' for overweight people. As discussed previously, overweight people have too much fat; very few weight problems are due to fluid. Diuretics may have a place in the treatment of some conditions such as kidney disorders but they have no place in weight reduction. Herbal diuretics are no safer or more suitable than any others.

ACUPUNCTURE

Some acupuncture practitioners believe acupuncture needles placed in a particular part of the ear can help weight loss. The theory behind this is that one of the nerves ending in this particular spot is connected to the vagus nerve which normally controls the movements of the gastrointestinal tract, and is thought by some to suppress appetite by raising the level of serotonin in the brain and increasing tone in the smooth muscle of the stomach. By stimulating the vagus nerve through the ear, hunger contractions are supposed to cease, making it easier for the person to control his or her appetite. There is also a homeopathic patch which is worn on the wrist over an acupuncture point.

Advocates of acupuncture generally advise a diet to go with the treatment; the acupuncture is only intended to make it easier to keep to the diet. The patch, for example, is sold with the information that it works better if combined with a low-fat, low-kilojoule diet.

Acupuncture has no magic ability to rid the body of fat. No one really knows whether it will help you make better food choices and increase physical activity. At this stage there is no evidence to suggest that acupuncture would benefit most overweight people. Some of the studies quoted in support of products such as AcuSlim are not valid. For example, one South Australian study of 60 patients attached AcuSlim patches to the acupuncture ear points 'shenmen' and 'stomach' twice a day for four weeks, while the control group attached the device to their thumb where there are no acupuncture points. According to this study, those with the device attached to acupuncture points noticed a suppression of appetite which the others did not. However, since every subject and the researcher knew who had the active treatment and who did not, the results could easily have been influenced by expectation. The acupuncture group lost more weight, but weight loss over such a short period in such a study has little meaning, as those using the product may have made more effort to eat sensibly or exercise more. To properly gauge the effects of such devices, we need much more rigorous studies. There are no studies reporting benefits over a long term where the results can be accurately attributed to acupuncture.

SURGERY

Surgical procedures are sometimes performed on people who are massively obese. These include jaw wiring, stomach stapling, gastric banding and intestinal bypass.

In jaw wiring, dental surgeons attach small eyelets to the teeth in the upper and lower jaws and pass a wire through to hold them together. This makes it difficult to eat anything except foods which can be sucked in through a straw. Jaw wiring is a method of enforcing partial starvation. Once the wires are removed, most people regain their weight. This makes it a useless method of controlling body weight. It is also invasive and there is no rational justification for its use.

In stomach stapling (also known as gastric bypass), the surgeon inserts staples into the stomach so that its volume is greatly reduced. After stomach stapling, a very small amount of food will produce a feeling of fullness. Once the stomach has been stapled, the victim is forced to eat less and so weight is gradually lost. However, most people who have had stomach stapling start to regain weight after about a year, often by eating liquid foods such as ice cream or slippery, fatty desserts. The whole procedure is again invasive and many unhappy people wish they had never succumbed to the surgeon's efforts.

Surgery always carries hazards for the obese and stomach stapling is no exception. Surgeons maintain that obesity itself is a health hazard and that those who have tried every other method to lose weight should not be denied the opportunity to have their stomach stapled. On the other hand there have been many reports of people feeling constantly nauseated and unhappy after this operation and it is certainly not recommended for anyone who is not grossly overweight. Even for the massively obese, the benefits must be seen to be greater than the inherent risks associated with the procedure. These include the hazards of the surgery, post-operative complications such as blood clots, wound infections, internal haemorrhage and kidney failure. Future malnutrition is also possible and a lack of fibre may also cause problems.

Gastric banding is now the preferred surgical technique for obesity. A rubber band is placed around the stomach, restricting the amount that can be consumed without discomfort. The band can be loosened or tightened, as required, using laparoscopic surgery.

Intestinal bypass is a procedure in which part of the small intestine is removed. Since food is normally digested and absorbed into the small intestine, the removal of a significant part of this organ means that little of the food that is eaten can be used. With much of the intestine removed, the appetite is also decreased. Intestinal bypass surgery has a comparatively high rate of complication. Apart from the immediate risks of the operation, the victim will need vitamin injections for the rest of his or her life, since some vitamins are absorbed in the portion of the intestine which has been removed. Chronic diarrhoea and an accompanying loss of some minerals are also common after this operation. Vomiting, kidney stones, gallstones, arthritis, hernias, disorders in the blood vessels and a general feeling of misery (possibly clue to malnutrition) have also been reported from those who have undergone this operation. It is not recommended.

FASTING

Fasting has been described as the 'ultimate diet'. Many people recommend fasting one day a week. This may be good for the soul but there is no evidence that it is required by the body. It is certainly not a sensible way to control weight. Fasting can bring about a dramatic weight loss but most of this is due to a loss of water. If the fast continues, severe dehydration can occur. Fasting also causes a loss of lean body tissue.

Many people also claim that fasting 'cleanses the body' or 'removes toxins' or make some similar statement implying that the body is a positive den of impurities. There are many links between food and religion and this is one. Fasting has spiritual significance for some people who regard it as a 'cleansing' period for their soul. The idea that the body must be similarly cleansed by a period of abstinence from food has no medical backing.

The body has one of the most amazing purification schemes ever devised. The liver and the kidneys work for us 24 hours a day, filtering out substances which are superfluous or toxic. These organs keep up this superb task whether we are eating or not, and all we have to do is provide enough basic nutrients and water to keep them healthy. Somewhat ironically, fasting means that the nutrients needed by our automatic cleansing systems will not be supplied. During fasting, the body's metabolic rate decreases so that the kidneys and liver may slow down their usual rate of cleansing. Under such circumstances, fasting will not be much use.

An initially healthy person can fast for a long time, providing water is available. Humans can survive for long periods without food because the body can reduce its rate of metabolism and learn to use less energy for its vital functions. However, fasting, like any very low-kilojoule diet, causes the body to consume its own lean tissue to stay alive. During a fast, the body burns some of its fat stores but only mobilises enough fat to provide energy for minimum physical activity. If the fast continues long enough, the fat stores eventually become so low that the body makes its final, fatal assault on its own protein. Muscles become weak and the lungs cease to operate properly so that eventually pneumonia sets in, to become the usual cause of death. Some people die sooner when protein is withdrawn from the heart muscle and fatal arrhythmias develop in the heart. Others develop kidney failure.

Few people who fast for weight loss take their fasting to this extreme. Most realise that the body cannot survive indefinitely without food. However, some people do recommend fasts of up to a month for weight loss and then regular fasts once a week or for several days each month.

> ### ANCIENT PRACTICE REVIVED!
>
> It is not hard to understand why fasting attracts so many devotees. Every now and then someone promotes fasting as if it were the answer to every dieter's dilemma. *Lose weight faster than ever before! Ancient practice revived!* Such headlines suck in the overweight who want to take the minimum time to lose the weight that took years to accumulate.
>
> The fact that Plato, Socrates and Jesus Christ fasted is often used to convince people that fasting is a desirable habit. I have no quarrel with the idea that fasting may have spiritual advantages. But the idea that people should fast as a means of weight loss is not sound. Similarly, the common belief that fasting is necessary to rid the body of toxins is not correct.

In fact, fasting is one of the quickest ways for those who gain weight easily to assure future fatness. When you begin eating again after a fast, the body will make an extra effort to tuck away some extra fat stores—just in case you decide to fast again.

Fasting and starving are one and the same. The only difference is the intent of the person going without food. The body does not know why no food and nutrients are coming in, it only knows that it must accommodate the change. If the body were to keep using up energy when none was being supplied from food, it would soon collapse. So the body cleverly cuts back on the amount of energy it uses.

If you try to fast, one of the first effects is that you do not feel like any undue physical activity. Sitting or lying soon seem better than running or jumping. Next the body reduces its metabolic rate and uses less energy to keep the muscles and vital organs going.

Fat is withdrawn from fat deposits to use for energy. However, without carbohydrate, the fats are not burned properly and ketones form, producing ketosis. Some medical scientists believe it is the effect of ketones which brings about some of the spiritual feelings associated with fasting. Many people, however, never experience any spiritual benefits and feel only the headaches, nausea, dizziness and weakness that accompany ketosis. At the same time as the body is trying to burn its fat for energy, it also converts some of the protein in muscle tissue to glucose to keep the brain and vital organs functioning. The skin is also adversely affected.

The large quantities of water lost from the body during fasting cause blood pressure to drop. Potassium is also lost and this reduces blood pressure even further. Other minerals may be lost and the nervous system may cease to function normally. Meanwhile the liver and kidneys are working hard trying to convert fat into energy and excrete the products resulting from the breakdown of body protein. Plenty of water is essential for these organs to continue to function.

The effects of fasting impose a considerable stress on the body. A short fast will probably not create problems. However, any fast of more than one day is likely to alter the body's metabolism. Regular fasters can therefore expect that over a period their metabolic rate will be reduced and that when they break their fast more weight will be regained.

Fasting is a most undesirable method of weight control.

10

Changing your eating and exercise habits

THE BEST WAY TO STAY SLIM is not to get fat in the first place! It helps if you chose your parents well, since some people will grow fat more easily than others (see Chapter 3). Prevention is always easier than cure, so it is important to adopt healthy eating habits from as early an age as possible. This does not mean going to extremes and it certainly does not mean subjecting children to 'diets' (see Chapter 12). No one will ever be the same weight all the time while the healthy weight range (see page 15) gives a wide range of weights at any height at which there are no known health risks. Only being above or below the healthy weight range increases the risks of health problems.

If it is too late for prevention, and your weight is above the limits of the healthy weight range, it is possible to lose some excess body fat by changing your eating and exercise habits. There is now ample research showing that a sustained loss of even 10 per cent of body weight reduces health risks associated with excess body fat. It is important to lose body fat, not just weight.

After over 30 years of experience in this field, I have come to the conclusion that those who concentrate on weight—weighing themselves frequently—often fail in their efforts. It makes more sense to concentrate on health, on changing habits by eating healthier foods, on looking for ways to substitute foods with less fat for high-fat items and on looking for ways to move the body more. Some fats are essential, however, so aiming for as low a fat intake as possible doesn't make good health sense either. Because fats carry, and contribute, flavour to many foods, foods with little or no fat may soon become boring.

My recommendations are based on seeking foods with flavour,

abandoning foods where the flavour is not good enough to justify the kilojoules, and trying to move more. Forget about the scales—they are more likely to tell you whether you are at a high or low point in the day's fluid balance and whether or not your muscles have their full complement of glycogen and its associated water. It my be useful to weigh yourself every few months—just for the record—but if your aim is to achieve a particular number on the scales, you are likely to be miserable much of the time. The way your clothes fit and how positive you feel about yourself are more important indicators of how you are going. Most people whose self-esteem depends on the numbers on the scales do not achieve long-term success. Throw away your scales.

To lose body fat, the important factors can be summed up as:

- You need to like yourself as you are. Don't kid yourself that if your life is a mess, it is because of your weight and you will be happy if, and only if, you lose weight. Taking control of your life may well increase your happiness, but of itself, weight loss won't. If your partner's affections depend on your weight, get a new partner. You need someone to love you for yourself, not your weight.
- Not everyone will achieve a thin body. There is no reason why everyone should be equally thin and many genetic reasons why we can't all be the same size. We are not all the same height, our feet are not all the same size, and neither will our bodies all conform to some mythical ideal.
- You cannot lose fat fast. The body takes time to burn fat. Weight lost quickly, as we have seen, is mainly water not fat.
- You need to make only those changes you can live with. If you decide to go on a diet for 3 weeks or even 3 months and then return to your old habits, you will return to your old weight. Similarly, if you decide to go to the gym for a short time and then revert to being a 'couch potato', your new-found muscle will not be retained.
- Give up hoping for a miracle. There is no magic potion to dissolve fat. There are no pills, vitamins, antioxidants, herbal substances, passive exercise machines, creams, garments or other paraphernalia that will get rid of fat, although there are plenty of people willing to sell you phoney products. If it sounds too good to be true, it is. Also be wary of earnest salespeople who claim scientific backing for products they are selling. Their 'evidence' is usually poor or downright shonky, and some of the medical journals they quote are simply sales brochures with names that sound like medical or scientific journals.

- Only make changes because you want to make them for yourself, not to fit someone else's ideas of how you should look or act.
- Not everyone will succeed at weight loss. Some people have a hidden psychological reason for turning to food for comfort. Until you find the reason, trying to lose weight may cause more problems than it could solve. Counselling can often help.

WHAT ARE YOU EATING?

Many people have little idea what they are eating, and it can be difficult to know what is in the 15 000 or so different food items on offer in this country. Products claim to be 'lite' or 'fat-reduced', 'fat-free' or '95 per cent fat-free' without making it obvious what else they contain. When nutritionists put out the message that it would be healthy for the population to eat less saturated fat, they hoped people would stop eating so much junk and consume more fruits and vegetables. Instead, food manufacturers adapted the message as justification to produce a huge range of nutritionally useless products such as fat-reduced chocolate cookies, artificially sweetened foods and products containing fake fats. Many of their products have a high sugar content and almost as many kilojoules as the regular items. There is also an implied claim that you can eat as much of these foods as you desire. Many people who would otherwise curtail their intake feel they can eat much more with fat-reduced products. Some fat-reduced products also fail to satisfy the tastebuds so you keep eating, hoping for the eventual satisfaction that never comes.

Many people also eat junk foods because they don't have the time, effort or skills necessary to prepare something better. This is a major reason for the increased consumption of fast foods, few of which are eaten for flavour.

Some people have little respect for their bodies, and so don't bother to think about what they are eating. They are then amazed when something goes wrong with their bodies or when excess fat begins to accumulate. Brillat-Savarin, the famous gastronome, once said, 'Show me what you eat and I will show you what you are.' Savarin was referring to the more sensual aspects of food and the human personality, but his statement could apply equally well to the physical body.

Everything in the human body is ultimately made from the food we eat. If you eat too much fat, sugar, alcohol, salt and a heap of unnecessary food additives, you cannot hope to end up with as healthy a body as if you had selected good wholefoods. This does not mean you should adopt healthy eating as a religion. The body can easily cope with some junk foods. If you eat well 90 to 95 per cent of the time, it really does not matter what you eat for the rest. Problems are more likely to arise if you eat junk 90 per cent of the time.

Our modern, busy, energy-saving lifestyle has reduced our requirements for kilojoules, but we have not adjusted what we eat and drink to fit. Foods have changed too, with many high-fat items entering the diet as everyday foods where once they were foods to have on special occasions. Chocolates were once a treat, now chocolate and caramel bars have become standard snacks to eat while driving. Crisps were an occasional party indulgence; now almost half of all school children take a packet to school each day.

Many women also try to eat foods which have a small volume. Some think, 'If it's little, it won't make me fat, for example, rejecting a healthy lunch of sandwiches and fruit, then eating chocolate or sweets during the afternoon. They have eaten less in volume, but more in kilojoules. Others skip meals altogether, and later more than make up for what they have missed. When you are very hungry, you may be quite undiscriminating about what you eat.

Proteins, fats, carbohydrates and alcohol all contribute kilojoules of energy. Kilojoules do count. But sensible eating is much more than counting kilojoules. Cutting back too far on kilojoules also leaves you lacking energy. Without food the body finds exercise tiring and reduces the kilojoules it uses for metabolism and activity. For example, if you go to an aerobics class after not eating much during the day, your body will burn fewer kilojoules during the class than if you have eaten.

Until a few years ago, the kilojoules from all foods were regarded as equals. Newer research shows that the body prefers to use kilojoules from certain sources for energy. In general, the kilojoules from alcohol are burned first, followed by those from carbohydrate. Proteins are generally used to repair body tissues, although some can be used for energy. Fat kilojoules are the least likely to be used for energy, with the exception of some of the essential fatty acids, such as those found in fish, which are used for essential purposes and are unlikely to be converted to body fat.

This does not mean that you can eat unlimited amounts of alcohol or carbohydrate, because if your body is busy burning lots of kilojoules from these sources, it won't get around to burning kilojoules from fat. And even foods that we think of as being high-carbohydrate items, such as cereals or bread, have some fat. It is also difficult to eat many high-carbohydrate foods unless you make them more palatable by adding fat. For example, when most people get out the bread, they also get out a spread; most potatoes are now consumed as fatty chips or crisps; pasta is served with cream sauces or with fatty meats and lots of cheese; rice is fried; and sugar accompanies fat in chocolates, cakes, biscuits, pastries and desserts.

It makes sense to cut back on fats, because they contribute the most kilojoules (more than twice as many as carbohydrates), and to fill up on healthy, good-tasting foods that provide nutrients and dietary fibre. Fruits of all kinds, cereals and grain-based foods, including bread, are ideal.

Foods are not 'good' or 'bad' in any moral sense, but some foods are more useful to the body than others. It makes sense to consume more of these foods simply because they help provide vitamins, minerals, dietary fibre, essential fats, proteins and carbohydrates. Plant foods also contain thousands of antioxidants and other food chemicals, many of which decrease the risk of cancer cells growing in the body. Most of the day's kilojoules should come from foods that supply the nutrients the body needs.

Food also serves many emotional needs which should not be denied. Trying to avoid foods that have a strong meaning in your life—or that you love—usually achieves little. Forbidden fruit is sweet and many a binge has arisen because of a rigid ban on some food or other. In a healthy eating plan, nothing need be forbidden, but some foods should be given greater prominence than others.

If you find you do not have time to prepare real foods or eat properly, perhaps your entire lifestyle needs reappraisal. Eating, after all, is one of life's greatest joys. Your body also deserves to be looked after with good food. Go for quality in nutrients and flavour and try to avoid eating vast quantities of mundane foods just because they are easy or convenient or save you thinking about making wiser choices.

It takes a little more effort to seek out fresh wholefoods rather than living on takeaway and ready-prepared foods. The rest of this chapter has a more detailed look at how you can put into practice the principles of healthy eating and exercise.

PRINCIPLES OF HEALTHY EATING

Consider the fats

There are fats which are healthy and many more that are not. The healthy fats are the unsaturated ones found in foods such as fish, nuts, seeds, avocado, olive oil, soy beans and grains such as oats. Fish fats, found in all types of seafood, are especially valuable and play an important part in preventing inflammatory reactions within the body. They also form part of the structure of brain and nerve cells and the membranes that surround every body cell. If you don't eat seafood, the same fats can be made in the body from fats found in seeds such as linseeds (known as flaxseed in some countries), soy and canola. The essential fats in nuts (except coconut), all types of seeds, soy beans, avocado and olive oil are accompanied by important antioxidants.

Saturated fats can cause problems. Once supplied mainly by animal foods such as meat and dairy products, much of our saturated fat now comes from vegetable fats which are turned into saturated fats by processing to make them suitable for processed foods and frying fast foods. Some fast-food chains use beef dripping for frying their chips; others use a mixture of partially hydrogenated cottonseed oil, usually mixed with palm oil. Both types of fat are highly saturated and the vegetable fat has no advantage over beef fat. Some commercial vegetable frying fats and vegetable fats used in biscuits and pastry are worse than saturated fats because they contain trans fats, which not only raise 'bad' LDL cholesterol levels in the blood, but lower the 'good' HDL type of cholesterol.

There is a growing body of evidence that unsaturated fats are more likely to be used for energy, and therefore less likely to end up as body fat, than saturated fats. However, too much of any kind of fat—with the exception of those occurring naturally in fish—can be converted to body fat. So even though some fats are desirable for inclusion in the daily diet, more is not better. It makes good nutritional sense to use a little olive oil, to snack on nuts rather than lollies or chocolate and to spread bread with avocado rather than a yellow spread. But those who gain weight easily should not slurp olive oil over everything, nibble on big bowls of nuts, or eat two avocados a day.

There are also many misconceptions about cholesterol. Most of the excess cholesterol that accumulates in the arteries of the body does not come from the cholesterol in foods such as eggs or prawns, but occurs because some bodies make too much cholesterol. They do this when the diet is high in saturated fat. If your blood cholesterol is high, you need to avoid foods high in saturated fat rather than fuss about whether some food contains a few milligrams of cholesterol.

Only foods of animal origin contain cholesterol, but much of the saturated fat in the modern diet comes from vegetable sources. If you have high blood cholesterol, or are likely to develop high blood cholesterol because it runs in your family, try to avoid foods high in saturated fat. Don't fuss too much about the cholesterol content of foods—its importance is minor.

Few people set out to eat a lot of fat. No one rushes into the kitchen saying, 'I'm hungry, I want some fat!' Nevertheless, most people do eat a lot of fat because so much is present in the foods we buy for meals and snacks. Fast foods and foods prepared in cafés and restaurants usually contain much more fat than the same food cooked at home. Many manufacturers add a lot of fat to foods because it is cheap and reheats well. If a food company takes potatoes and turns them into crisps, they can sell the potato for twenty times the price—without giving the farmer who grew the potato an extra cent. Our food supply is getting fattier because foods high in fat are profitable for manufacturers.

Here are some tips to help you use less—and better—fats:

- When frying foods, use a heavy-based wok or frying pan. When it is very hot, add about a teaspoon of olive oil. By heating the pan first, you can brown foods and bring out their flavour with much less oil than if you start with a cold pan.
- Grill, barbecue, steam, microwave, bake, casserole or wrap foods in foil when cooking to reduce the amount of fat you use.
- Stir-fry using concentrated chicken stock.
- On freshly made sandwiches skip the spread, or use a little avocado if it is appropriate with the filling.
- Try jam or honey on toast instead of butter or margarine.
- Change your snacks to those with healthier fat, less fat or no fat. For example, you could choose nuts for healthier fat or baked corn chips from the health food section of the supermarket for almost no fat (but good flavour). Avoid products like soy crisps, which have as much unhealthy fat as regular crisps. Pretzels are a better choice. Or snack on fresh or dried fruit, fruit loaf, bread, a fresh crunchy bread roll, toast, a crumpet (they won't hold more than a teaspoon of butter) or one of the many varieties of English muffin.

    Use less butter, margarine and cream. Both butter and margarine contain about 80 per cent fat. Most margarines have less saturated fat than butter, but the amount of polyunsaturated margarine most people spread on their breakfast toast has as much saturated fat as two eggs! Reduced-fat spreads have about 60 per cent fat, but are useless if you use more of them trying to get flavour.
- Choose a strongly-flavoured extra virgin olive oil on salads so you get more flavour from each drop. A little olive oil on salad helps your body absorb valuable antioxidants in the salad vegetables.
- Avoid fatty meats. The fat in meat ranges from about 4 to 30 per cent, with low levels in meats trimmed of all visible fat. With an extremely sharp knife and plenty of time, you could reduce the fat even lower, but 4 per cent is quite low. Most sausages and salamis are high in fat and butchers often add fat trimmed from lean fresh meats in sausages.

    Lean cuts of meat include: beef cuts such as fillet, rump or topside; all veal cuts; all new-fashioned or trim pork cuts; trim lamb fillet or leg steaks. Game meats such as kangaroo or venison have less than 2 per cent fat. You can buy low-fat sausages, although they don't have the true taste of a good snag. Among sandwich meats, the lowest fat choices include turkey, lean leg ham, chicken breast or very lean roast meats.

The fat content in minced meat ranges from about 7 to 30 per cent. The more you pay, the less fat you get, although if you cost the meat on the basis of how much you pay for the lean content, the more expensive mince is the best buy. The best way to accommodate the higher prices of lean meats is to buy smaller portions. Fill up the rest of the plate with a healthy selection of vegetables, rice, pasta, couscous or other grain products.

There is no need to avoid meat, although there is no nutritional imperative to include it. Meat is an excellent source of iron, zinc, protein and many vitamins, including vitamin B_{12}. If you decide not to eat meat, choose lentils, chick peas and other legumes plus a range of nuts, grains, seeds and vegetables to supply most of the nutrients found in meat. Vitamin B_{12}—found mainly in animal foods—is also available from yoghurt, milk, cheese or eggs. It is also added to some soy drinks and is present in fermented foods such as tempeh. If you eat no animal foods, you should consider a B_{12} supplement.

- Turkey and chicken are low in fat, as long as you remove the skin and any fatty pads. Take-away chicken is usually fatty as the skin and fat are left on and fat drips from one bird to the next. Fried chicken absorbs a lot of the fat it is cooked in and is a high-fat food. When cooking chicken at home, bake, casserole, grill or barbecue it. A marinade helps prevent chicken becoming dry.
- Fish is a great choice for everyone, including those watching their weight. Even so-called fatty fish have fairly low levels of fat (for example, Atlantic salmon has 2.7 and gemfish 2.6 per cent fat). The highest fat level in commonly available fish is found in swordfish, with 7.7 per cent fat, but most fish have less than 1 per cent. Molluscs and shellfish have even less. The fat in all seafood consists largely of omega-3 fatty acids which are not converted to body fat. Omega-3 fats also form part of the structure of brain and nerve cells, and have anti-clotting and anti-inflammatory properties; they lower blood fats called triglycerides and help prevent irregularities in heart rhythm. Eating fish twice a week significantly reduces deaths from heart attack.

Fish that is battered and fried is high in saturated fat. The vegetable oil used in most fish shops is usually hydrogenated and contains undesirable trans fats. Better to ask shops and restaurants to grill or barbecue your fish, or take it home and cook it yourself. Use a very hot pan and a small quantity of olive oil, or barbecue or grill the fish (use a piece of foil over the griller and you won't

CHANGING YOUR EATING AND EXERCISE HABITS

need to turn the fish or wash a 'fishy' griller). Fish can also be steamed (a bamboo steamer is ideal), baked or cooked in the microwave.

Oysters, mussels, octopus, squid, prawns, bugs, crab and lobster are all very low in fat and are excellent foods, as long as they are not crumbed, battered and fried or served with rich sauces. The cholesterol in prawns is not a problem as seafoods have virtually no saturated fat.

- Choose low-fat dairy products where appropriate. Skim and fortified skim milks have no fat and fat-reduced milk has less than half the fat of regular products. Some fat-reduced milks have more 'body' because their solids content is boosted with concentrated skim milk. Regular milk has 4 per cent fat and while this can add up if you consume larger volumes (a glass of milk has 10 grams of fat), it really does not contribute much fat added to a couple of cups of tea or coffee a day. If you dislike skim milk in these beverages, there is little reason to use it.

The fat content of yoghurt varies from none to over 7 per cent. Products with higher fat levels are usually labelled as 'European' yoghurt. Reduced-fat products are also widely available. Check the total kilojoule level, as some have large amounts of added sugar.

Cheeses have a high fat content, usually ranging from 26 to 40 per cent. Most good cheeses cannot be made with less fat, and the flavour of fat-reduced cheeses usually bears this out. However, technology is improving and some fat-reduced products are better than others. Check the label carefully as some products which people assume to have less fat have the same quantity of fat and kilojoules as other cheeses, but contain less cholesterol. As discussed already, cholesterol itself is not a major problem—saturated fat is. The best way to incorporate cheese into a low-fat eating plan is to use it as part of a meal with low-fat foods such as bread, salad or fruit.

- Try some low-fat choices, for example, fat-reduced ice cream, sour cream, crispbread, cream cheese and many other items. Always check the fat content on the label and calculate it for a realistic serving size. One teaspoon of margarine will not cover a slice of toast and a more realistic quantity, say, 10 grams, of a fat-reduced spread may still contain 6 grams of fat. A smallish 50 mL serving of fat-reduced cream has 9 grams of fat and a 50-gram piece of fat-reduced cheese may have anything from 3 to 13 grams of fat. Most people trying to lose weight need to restrict their total daily fat consumption to 30 to 40 grams. This includes the small amount of fat in foods such as grains, breads and cereals and is not just added fats. There is no point in choosing a fat-reduced product if you don't enjoy it and still crave the real thing. A small portion of a regular product may be more satisfying. Choose fat-reduced products where you do not object to the flavour.

More carbohydrate and dietary fibre

Dietary guidelines in every country recommend that everyone should eat more high-carbohydrate, high-fibre foods such as wholegrains, and products such as pasta, couscous, rice, cracked wheat, oats and barley, wholegrain breakfast cereals, breads, legumes (dried beans and peas) and potatoes. These foods are low in fat and contribute protein, a range of minerals and vitamins, starch and fibre.

Carbohydrates are the ideal fuel for muscles. Eating more carbohydrate will help increase stores of glycogen in muscles, making it easier to exercise for longer without feeling tired. Sugar is also a carbohydrate but has no protein, vitamins, minerals, essential fatty acids or fibre. Small amounts of sugar are not a problem but it is better to get your carbohydrates from foods that also provide nutrients. Honey has a slightly higher content of nutrients than sugar.

Grains are healthy and filling. Some people mistakenly equate 'filling' with 'fattening'. But if a food is filling, you are much more likely to stop eating when your body has had enough. Foods which are not filling, such as sugar, chocolate, crisps, alcoholic drinks, croissants and many lollies are the real culprits in the dissociation between eating and satisfying hunger. By eating non-filling foods, you can inadvertently overdo your kilojoule intake. Choose filling foods whenever possible.

Vegetables and fruits

All vegetables and fruits are highly nutritious, supplying essential vitamins, minerals, dietary fibre, small quantities of essential fatty acids and thousands of plant chemicals that help protect the body against many health problems. A few vegetables, such as potatoes, peas and sweet corn, also supply carbohydrates. No vegetable contains more than very small quantities of fat and all are low in kilojoules. Some antioxidants are more available to the body from cooked vegetables than from raw, but some vitamins—especially folate—are lost in cooking. It therefore is wise to eat some raw vegetables in salads and serve some either steamed, stir-fried (in a little olive oil or in concentrated chicken stock), microwaved, baked, barbecued or made into soups or sauces. Those who are overweight do not need to restrict vegetables in any way. This includes potatoes, one of the most filling foods available. It is only added fat that turns them into high-kilojoule foods.

Legumes such as chick peas, lentils, kidney beans, white beans, black-eyed beans, soy beans, canned baked beans and many others are among the healthiest foods available. They are rich in protein, minerals, vitamins, fibre and antioxidants, and most have little fat. Most people do not use legumes because they are not sure how to prepare them. It is worth getting a good vegetarian recipe book, even if you are not a vegetarian, as legumes are cheap, delicious and highly nutritious.

Fruits provide carbohydrates in the form of fruit sugars, as well as vitamins, minerals, fibre and antioxidants. Everyone should eat about 3 servings or pieces of fruit a day and an extra serving or two will not do any harm. Two fruits, olives and avocados, contain larger quantities of fats, but these are 'good' monounsaturated fats and both items are excellent sources of important antioxidants. Eaten in moderation (one-quarter to one-half a day), avocados will not generally increase body fat.

You can now buy capsules containing a mixture of freeze-dried fruits and vegetables. These are *not* substitutes for fruits and vegetables. Studies from reliable researchers show that each capsule contains the equivalent in antioxidant potential of only 10 grams of fruits or vegetables. This is an insignificant quantity and, despite claims made by some selling these products, there is no valid scientific support for using them. Fresh fruits and vegetables also have the advantage of providing bulk and filling the stomach. Pills are not filling.

There is nothing wrong with enjoying fresh fruit and vegetable juices, but they lack the important dietary fibre of wholefoods. It is easy to overconsume prepared juices and, if you are trying to lose weight, it is better to eat fruit rather than drink juice.

More variety

Many people select only a few foods and endlessly repeat their choice. Australia has the greatest variety of healthy foods of any country in the world, so try some of the wonderful fruits, vegetables, legumes, grains and seafoods available.

One-third of the food dollar now goes on foods prepared outside the home. These usually contain little more than token quantities of vegetables and fruits. When restaurants and cafés charge extra for vegetables, many people skip them, except for chips. I think vegetables should always be served with meals without having to pay extra, but even if there is an extra charge, they are good value.

Within the home, try to learn about new flavours by serving different types of seafood, and buying new vegetables and fruits when in season. There are also many herbs, spices and prepared spice pastes that make foods more interesting. Check the ingredients in these products as many have no added fat or salt and are good buys.

Less sugar

Each gram of sugar has only the same number of kilojoules as a gram of any other kind of carbohydrate. However, sugar slips down so effortlessly that it is easy to consume large quantities. In many foods, sugar is not at all filling. A cup of tea with sugar, for example, is no more filling than one without. Similarly, a can of soft drink may contain 10 teaspoons of sugar but is no more filling than the same quantity of water.

The sugar industry maintains, quite correctly, that we have no evidence that overweight people necessarily eat more sugar than their thinner peers. But with an average consumption of more than 200 teaspoons of sugar a week, Australians are among the world's highest sugar consumers. At the same time, many people fail to consume enough fruit or starchy foods. Fat is worse for weight increase than sugar, but that does not mean sugar has no role in weight increase. We would not eat foods such as sweets, cakes, chocolate, ice cream, biscuits and pastries if sugar did not make their fat taste nice. Claims that studies show people who eat less sugar will eat more fat mainly reflect the fact that the people surveyed had a preference for either chips and savoury snack foods or sweets. Neither are good choices. Most people under-report their sugar consumption, mainly because they do not realise how many foods contain it.

There is no need to avoid all sugar but for those who need to lose body fat, wholefoods such as fruits and bread are better choices. A craving for sweet foods often occurs after you have skipped a meal, or at times when you feel low. As infants, our first food, breast milk, is sweet and is a comfort. Small children are often rewarded or bribed with sweets and sweets are also associated with special occasions and birthdays, so it is not surprising that many people crave them to improve a bad mood or general unhappiness. If this is the case, it may be necessary to find a solution to the problem other than eating. That said, for some people the comfort of sweet food may be important.

Reduce alcohol

Alcohol is never converted to fat, but if your body is getting lots of kilojoules from alcohol, it will not burn kilojoules from fat—either the fat in the foods being consumed with the alcohol, or stored body fat.

Like most things, one alcoholic drink is not a problem for most people. But more is not better. Most people who are trying to lose weight need to restrict their alcoholic drinks to one or two a day.

Health authorities also recommend that everyone has one or two alcohol-free days a week.

All standard alcoholic drinks contain roughly the same quantity of alcohol. Low alcohol beer is an exception and it also has fewer kilojoules than other alcoholic drinks. However, if you drink lots more reduced-alcohol beer, there is little advantage. Before drinking alcohol, always quench your thirst with water or mineral water. Water has no effect on body fat.

Less salt

Salt does not make you fat. In a few people, excess salt can cause a retention of fluid. This may occur in women in the week before menstruation when hormonal changes cause some retention of sodium (from salt) which then holds extra water in the body. The way to get rid of this temporary fluid retention is to drink more water to flush out the sodium. Eating less salt also helps. Almost everyone is better off with less salt. This means avoiding processed foods that are high in salt and using less salt in cooking and at the table.

If you make greater use of fresh vegetables and herbs and spices, and serve foods that are not overcooked, you will find salt less essential. Overcooked, soggy vegetables may need salt to improve their washed-out flavour, but lightly steamed crisp vegetables retain enough flavour to make salt unnecessary.

Much of the salt we eat comes from foods high in fat such as fast foods, processed meats and sausages, crackers and biscuits, sauces and packaged foods. By keeping mainly to fresh wholefoods, you will automatically eat less salt.

EXERCISE

The major reason so many people have too much body fat is a lack of physical activity. Throughout history, humans have been physically active, in hunting and gathering foods. These days we drive to a supermarket, buy foods and load them into the car. Fifty years ago, people scrubbed clothes by hand, now we put them into a washing machine and press a button. Where we once scrubbed and polished, we now spray and wipe. Almost every piece of physical work is done with a machine. We even change the television channel with a remote control device. Another remote control opens garage doors. A button winds down the car window. We use escalators and lifts instead of stairs—many public buildings do not have easily accessible stairs and fire safety standards mean those that do exist are only for emergency use. Most important of all, we drive instead of walk—even for short distances—and expect a parking spot within metres of our destination. People protest they are too busy and do not have time to walk.

In sport, we want the best to win so we train a few sportspeople and the rest of the population become spectators. Children who do not naturally excel at sport prefer not to play at all, for fear of ridicule from their more able classmates. Most adults do not have any regular exercise. Anyone who rides a bicycle is scorned by car drivers.

Many people confuse being busy with being active. Others think that being on their feet all day constitutes exercise. Exercise and physical activity build a strong healthy body that functions well. Inactivity also decreases metabolic rate, so that fewer kilojoules are burned. With so little physical activity in everyday activities, it is little wonder that we are growing fatter.

Most of us are now so physically inactive that we need to make an effort to program more movement. For cardiovascular fitness, you need to work major muscle groups and increase heart rate—by running, brisk walking, aerobics or some other fairly strenuous activity. For reducing fatness, you only need to get the body moving more and more often. But many people don't like programmed exercise. Some have previously tried exercising strenuously and hated it, others have tried to exercise while following a low-carbohydrate diet which depleted muscles of the fuel they needed for activity. Walking across the office, using the stairs, parking a bit further away and walking from the edge of the carpark, or even leaving the car in the next block, taking a longer route, dancing to music, carrying golf clubs instead of using a buggy—these sorts of things will help. Without more movement, few people will lose excess body fat.

Planning more movement

Just as it is important to eat foods you like, so it is important to find physical activities you can enjoy. Walk to the shops if it pleases you, go for a stroll to smell the flowers, fly a kite with the kids, dance, play tennis, ride a bike, swim or surf—but try to find some enjoyable activity you can do regularly.

For fat loss, some type of extra movement is essential and studies now show that it does not have to be done in a single block. You can walk for ten minutes to catch the bus, walk up the stairs at work, go and get your own sandwich at lunchtime instead of having someone else do it for you, get off the bus one stop early on the way home, take the dog for a 10-minute walk or do the garden for half an hour. It all adds up and counts towards increasing the energy you burn.

Here are some tips to increase walking:

- If it is appropriate, walk to work.
- If you drive, park a bit further away and walk a few blocks.

CHANGING YOUR EATING AND EXERCISE HABITS

- Go out for a stroll at lunchtime.
- Make it a rule not to drive distances shorter than a kilometre (if you live in the city, it is usually quicker to walk such distances than battle the traffic and find a parking spot).
- Encourage children to walk and walk with them if it is not safe for them to go alone.
- Avoid using a stroller at least some of the time and let toddlers walk.
- Go bushwalking on weekends.
- If you dislike the sweating that accompanies walking or other exercise, go for a walk before you have your morning shower.
- Try to fit in a walk every day.
- Always use stairs instead of escalators.
- If you have to go to a floor many storeys up, walk the first 6 floors and then take the lift.
- Walk at a comfortable pace for about 30 minutes, if possible, then increase the pace as your fitness increases.
- If you can't fit in a 30-minute walk, take three 10-minute walks during the day.
- Take the spot near the entrance to a carpark and walk to the exit. See it as an opportunity to fit in some movement.
- Walk briskly.
- Offer to get up and fetch things from another room or office and see it as an opportunity to move.
- Throw away the remote control for the television and get up to change channels at the set.

Some overweight women say that they will do some exercise once they have lost weight and feel more comfortable in shorts or clothes suitable for exercise. That's the wrong way to try. The more you accept your body the way it is, the easier it is to change it. Once women change their perspective from that of someone desperate to lose weight to one where they are looking after the health of something they value, they develop greater self-respect. Changing to a healthier way of eating and incorporating more activity can produce much greater self-esteem and health—and fat loss—than can ever be achieved with stringent dieting. Forget about weight and start thinking about healthy eating and more movement.

11

Planning your new habits

THERE ARE NO SET RULES ABOUT how you should divide your day's foods between meals and snacks. However, it is important to eat breakfast. It is better to 'breakfast like a king, lunch like a queen and dine like a pauper' than to skip breakfast, force the body to run on low power all day and then bombard it with a mass of food just before going to bed.

BREAKFAST

Breakfast helps 'break your fast'. It increases metabolic rate so you burn up more kilojoules for the whole day. One study compared the kilojoules used for metabolism when foods were divided in different ways throughout the day. When the subjects ate nothing during the day and ate their total amount of food in the evening, their metabolic rate decreased by 5.9 per cent. In theory, such a reduction in metabolism is enough to lead to weight gain.

When they skipped breakfast and consumed their food at lunch and dinner, their metabolic rate decreased by 4.8 per cent, still enough to allow a theoretical weight gain, which can add to a considerable total after a few years. All from skipping breakfast. Overnight, the body slows down its rate of metabolism so you can sleep. Breakfast gets it going.

A GOOD BASIC DAILY FOOD PLAN

- Plenty of vegetables—perhaps a large salad and hearty helpings of 3–4 different vegetables (more if desired).
- Three pieces of fresh fruit a day, of any type, but preferably whole fruit rather than juice.
- At least 4 slices of wholemeal bread plus wholegrain cereal, or more if you have a large frame and exercise more. If you do not like bread, substitute other grain foods for bread.
- Some dairy products, preferably low-fat varieties. 500 mL of low-fat milk would provide calcium, protein and other nutrients without contributing much fat.
- A serving of seafood, very lean meat or poultry, eggs, cheese or some type of legume or seeds.
- 6–8 glasses of water or more for those who are exercising heavily.

These foods can be arranged in any way that fits in with your lifestyle.

Babies almost always wake up feeling hungry and wanting food first thing in the morning. Many people continue to enjoy breakfast throughout life. Others decide after a few years that they would rather spend a little longer in bed than get up and make time for breakfast. After a while, many of these people decide that they do not enjoy breakfast. Some even say they would feel sick if they ate breakfast. We are all different and obviously some bodies take longer before they want to be speeded up for the coming day. However, at some stage—and preferably as soon after rising as possible—you should try to eat something.

Some people do not eat breakfast because they find they begin to feel hungry during the morning if they eat breakfast, but can last until lunchtime if they eat nothing. When you do not eat breakfast, your body may continue to go at its slower overnight pace. Eating breakfast speeds up metabolism and once you have digested and used your breakfast, your body is ready for more fuel. This is good and shows the body is functioning well. If you eat nothing and do not feel hungry, it is likely that your body is reducing its metabolic rate and will be burning up fewer kilojoules.

Breakfast does not need to take a long time. It does not need to be cooked. However, if you like having a cooked meal at this time of the day, go ahead. Just follow the general advice to cut back on fat and keep up the carbohydrates and dietary fibre, and you should have no problems.

> **A WALK BEFORE BREAKFAST**
>
> If you do not like breakfast, try getting up a bit earlier and going for a 20-minute walk in the mornings. Most people who try this find their body is soon ready for some food.

It is usually a good idea to have as much variety in your daily diet as possible. However, if you prefer the same breakfast each day, make sure you get variety in your other meals. The following information may help you make some healthy breakfast choices.

Cereals

I recently counted over 150 breakfast cereals in my local country town supermarket. Some have excellent nutritional value; some are more than half sugar. Read the label carefully and choose one of the many cereals with plenty of dietary fibre and a good content of starchy carbohydrate.

The best choices include porridge, made either from oats, rice flakes, wheatmeal or a mixture of any grains. I buy a mixture of oats, barley flakes, rye flakes, rice, corn, wheat and triticale which my local health food shop grinds so it will cook quickly.

> **PORRIDGE FOR POWER!**
>
> The easiest way to cook porridge is to mix your grain (such as rolled oats or other cereal) with some water or low-fat milk in a bowl and place the bowl in the microwave on HIGH for about 2 minutes. There is no mess, no dirty porridge saucepan to wash and the whole operation is fast. If you like a sweetener, try a few raisins, a small quantity of dark brown sugar (the stronger flavour means you can use less), or a teaspoon of honey. Serve with low-fat milk.

There are also many nutritious prepared cereals. Select from wholewheat breakfast biscuits, puffed wheat or many of the wheat-based products; oat bran, oat flakes or other oat-based products (preferably without lots of added sugar); bran products with or without dried fruit; soy and linseed products; or any of the better quality mixed cereals.

> ### WHEATGERM
>
> A spoonful of wheatgerm sprinkled over breakfast cereals or porridge adds some important vitamins, especially vitamin E. Keep wheatgerm in the refrigerator to preserve its flavour and vitamins.

Mueslis are a mixed lot. Some have a lot of added sugar while many of the toasted mueslis also have a lot of saturated fat. Check out the ingredient and nutritional information on the packet. Remember that the ingredients are listed in their order of prominence in the product. If some type of oil is listed in the top four or five ingredients, try another product. The oil used in toasted muesli is usually coconut or palm kernel—both highly saturated fats. A bowl of some brands of toasted muesli gives you as much saturated fat as fried egg and bacon.

Unprocessed bran is often eaten, in spite of its taste, for its dietary fibre. In small quantities (1–2 tablespoons), it causes no problems. Eating a large amount of unprocessed bran may interfere with the absorption of minerals such as calcium, iron and zinc. Choose a bran with large flakes as these absorb water and can help those with constipation. Small-flaked bran can form small hard stools and make constipation worse. A high-fibre diet needs a *variety* of different types of fibre, from products such as wholemeal bread, wholegrain cereals, fruits, vegetables and legumes.

Fruit

Any type of fruit adds nutrients to breakfast. Try to eat a piece of fruit rather than drinking juice as the fruit will give you important dietary fibre and is more filling than the juice. For example, eating an orange will give more satisfaction than drinking the juice from an orange (but all the kilojoules will go into the juice). In practice, most people drink the juice from several pieces of fruit, which can add many kilojoules without being very filling.

A banana is an excellent addition to a bowl of cold cereal. Or try peaches, apricots, melon, mango or any type of berry, according to season and price. If you prefer canned fruit, the best choice is one canned without juice or syrup. You can also use 'pie pack' fruit (unsweetened), or fruit canned in concentrated pear juice, although this has only marginally fewer kilojoules than syrup.

Dried fruits are simply fruits from which the water has been removed. No sugar is added but some have sodium metabisulphite (additive 223) added to hasten the drying process, prevent the fruit from going too hard and to help preserve the fruit's vitamins. If you are sensitive to this substance, choose 'natural' dried fruits.

Bakery products

Breads, toast, bagels, bread rolls, yeasted muffins or crumpets are all low-fat products which fit easily into a healthy eating pattern. As we have mentioned, bread is not the fattening product some people assume it to be. Neither are any of the other bakery products mentioned, unless they are topped with cheese and bacon, or filled with sweet custard cream.

White bread is a perfectly satisfactory food and has no more kilojoules than wholemeal. However, grain breads have a higher content of dietary fibre, vitamins and minerals. Wholegrain, wholemeal or wholegrain/wholemeal loaves have more fibre than multigrain, mixed grain or rye breads. Soy and linseed breads have a higher fat content, but their fat is 'good' fat. Loaves with increased fibre are usually similar in dietary fibre to multigrain breads. They are useful for those people who prefer white bread but want a higher level of dietary fibre.

Most cake-type muffins, including those which say they are low in fat, have a high content of added fat. Croissants are always high in fat. So are Danish pastries or other pastry-type products. One croissant has as much fat as 17 slices of bread.

Spreads

Any type of fat spread will add kilojoules. It is best to use as little butter or margarine as possible as every tablespoon contributes 615 kJ (145 Cals). Low-fat spreads have about half the fat level of regular butter or margarine.

Yeast extracts such as Vegemite are rich in vitamins of the B complex. A typical spread of Vegemite will supply from 40 to 70 per cent of the body's daily needs for several of these vitamins. Vegemite also contains salt, although the quantity of salt in a spread of Vegemite is less than that in the bread under it. Some other yeast extracts have a slightly higher salt content. All are very low in kilojoules.

Jams are usually 60 per cent sugar, but have no fat. A tablespoon spread on a slice of toast contributes 250 kJ (60 Cals). Home-made jams and honeys have about the same kilojoule level as bought jams. Low-kilojoule, unsugared jams are also available.

Spreads only create problems for those wishing to lose weight when large quantities or multiple spreads are used. For example, margarine and jam is obviously higher in kilojoules than jam on its own. It is an Anglo-Saxon habit to use butter (or now, margarine) on bread but it does not take long to get used to the taste of jam without a layer of fat between it and toast. It is also feasible to consider using smaller quantities of all spreads.

Below are some healthy breakfast ideas which fit the general guidelines. Some are suitable for every day; others are a little more exotic and a few are for times when you are running late. Add a beverage such as a glass of water, tea or coffee. Avoid using sugar in your beverage, but add milk if desired. The exact quantities depend on your size, level of physical activity and appetite. If you are small and/or inactive, have a small bowl of cereal and one slice of toast. If you are bigger and/or you exercise vigorously, have a larger bowl of cereal and several slices of toast.

HEALTHY BREAKFAST IDEAS

- A bowl of healthy, high-fibre cereal with a sliced banana and low-fat milk plus a slice of wholegrain toast with marmalade.
- A bowl of cooked porridge with raisins and wheatgerm, served with low-fat milk, plus a slice of multigrain toast with fresh sliced tomato and chopped basil.
- An apple, a boiled egg and a slice of wholemeal toast with a little low-fat spread and Vegemite.
- A glass of low-fat milk, half a cup of non-fat yoghurt, a couple of ice cubes, some fruit (for example, a banana, a piece of melon, some strawberries or half a cup of canned pie-pack peaches) and a tablespoon of wheatgerm. Blend the whole lot together to a thick smoothie.
- A glass of orange juice (or the flesh of an orange), an egg and half a cup of non-fat yoghurt blended with a teaspoon of honey.
- A wholemeal muffin, split, topped with tomato slices and low-fat cheese and grilled until bubbly.
- Half a grapefruit plus a bagel, toasted and served with a little light cream cheese and pure fruit jam.
- A small bowl of fresh fruit salad with some non-fat yoghurt.
- A piece of melon or some other fruit plus a wholemeal crumpet with a little light cream cheese and a teaspoon of honey.
- A toasted cheese and tomato sandwich (use fat-reduced cheese and skip the butter or margarine).
- Baked beans and grilled tomatoes on toast plus a glass of low-fat milk.

- Grilled tomatoes and mushrooms plus wholemeal toast.
- Poached egg served on puréed spinach plus a small hot bread roll.
- A bagel, toasted and spread with a little light cream cheese, some smoked salmon and cherry tomatoes.

LUNCH

Once your body has digested breakfast, it will give a hunger signal. If you do not feel hungry, it may mean that you ate too much breakfast, or too much morning tea. Most people will feel a hunger pang within 4 or 5 hours of eating. Hunger pangs will disappear after a few minutes and return about 45 minutes later. Take notice of your body's signals and try to have something to eat.

Like breakfast, lunch does not need to be large and it does not need to be cooked. A good sandwich and some fruit makes an ideal lunch. Salads, soups, seafoods and many light dishes are also suitable for lunch (see page 205 for ideas for restaurant lunches).

CRISPBREADS

Many slimmers avoid bread and eat crispbread. Some of these are fine for a change. Rye crispbread, for example, has no fat and is high in dietary fibre. Crispbreads come with or without salt and may have added sesame seeds, linseeds or cracked grains for extra fibre. Some crispbreads and crackers, however, have a surprisingly high fat content. Check the ingredient label on different brands.

Remember, too, that crispbreads are not very filling and have a large surface area. You may need to eat so many to feel satisfied that you end up covering them with heaps more high-kilojoule fillings than you would use in a healthy sandwich. However, crispbreads without fat can make a change occasionally.

Sandwiches

Any type of bread can be used for sandwiches. However, if your sandwich is to be a taste delight, a wholemeal, wholegrain, multigrain or rye bread may be more interesting than white sliced bread.

Other types of bread include flat breads such as lavash bread, pita bread or Lebanese bread. Flat breads can be rolled around a variety of fillings or, in the case of pita bread, split and filled with wonderful salads. Foccacia is also good for sandwiches, although it varies greatly, with some brands being quite fatty.

Don't forget the great range of rolls, too. They come in all shapes and sizes and can form the basis of wonderful, healthy lunches.

The most important aspect of bread is to try different varieties so that bread stays an interesting and delicious basis for lunch.

Sandwich fillings

Most people will not notice whether or not a freshly made sandwich contains butter or margarine. You might as well skip the spread. Alternatively, you can use a thin spread of light cream cheese or avocado, depending on the choice of filling.

Salad fillings are ideal for sandwiches. Any salad vegetable can be used including a variety of different lettuces, sliced cucumber, chopped celery, grated carrot, grated raw beetroot (or cooked sliced beetroot), sprouts (alfalfa, lentil, sunflower, mung beans or any other type available), sliced mushrooms, sliced tomatoes, asparagus, sliced roasted or raw red or green capsicum, char-grilled eggplant or zucchini, spring onions, sliced canned artichokes, shredded red or green cabbage, radish, avocado, sliced cold potato, fennel or watercress. Try to use lots of salad so your sandwich is filling.

Various protein foods can also be used on sandwiches without adding lots of fat. Try the following:

- sliced turkey breast
- cold chicken
- canned salmon or tuna
- shelled prawns or shredded crab meat
- turkey ham or turkey salami (both very low in fat)
- low-fat cheese
- cottage cheese

Combine protein fillings with salad rather than with each other, if possible. For example, have a ham and salad sandwich rather than ham and cheese together.

Condiments such as freshly ground pepper, mustard, chilli, chutneys and relishes are all suitable on sandwiches. Parsley, chopped mint, basil or any other herb can also liven up a sandwich.

Go easy on high-fat additives such as some peanut sauces, thick cream cheese, rich pâté or mayonnaise (try to use a low-fat variety or substitute a little low-fat natural yoghurt).

Salads

There are many ways to make an interesting salad and some of these are discussed above. Any combination of vegetables is good, and protein foods, as listed under 'Sandwich fillings', can be added. A little dressing is fine but some salads swim in a sea of fat. No-oil and low-fat mayonnaises are available, or you can use a few drops of balsamic or wine vinegar, some lemon juice mixed with Dijon mustard and a small amount of an extra virgin olive oil (the strong flavour means you can use less).

Use only enough dressing to flavour the vegetables, not so much that it lies in a puddle in the bottom of the salad. In potato salad, coleslaw and many mixed salads, some non-fat yoghurt mixed with fresh snipped herbs and a little lemon juice can substitute for mayonnaise. Every tablespoon of a rich mayonnaise can add up to 630 kJ (150 Cals).

TOASTED SANDWICHES

Toasted sandwiches are wonderful in colder weather. They can easily be made without a spread. Try these:

- salmon, tomato and chopped chives
- low-fat cheese, sliced celery and thinly sliced pineapple
- chopped chicken, sliced capsicum, a couple of basil leaves and some avocado
- sliced potato, chutney, sliced mushrooms and parsley
- light cream cheese, avocado, mung bean sprouts and chopped mint
- baked beans, sliced tomato and chopped celery.

Salad on its own may not be sufficient to last until dinner. Add a bread roll or a slice of bread.

Soups

There are many home-made soups which are filling, nutritious and low in fat. The basis of a good soup is usually a good stock. Buy some chicken bones (or save some from a meal), cover with water, add a couple of bay leaves, some parsley sprigs and a piece of rosemary. Bring to the boil, cover and simmer for an hour. Strain off the stock and refrigerate. When cold, skim off any fat and use stock for soups.

A veal or pork knuckle can be used instead of chicken bones. Cook for about 2 hours and remove any meat from the bones. Add this to the strained stock, if desired. Stocks can be frozen until required.

A basic vegetable soup can be made by heating the stock, adding a chopped onion, some mixed dried herbs (or a specific herb of your choice) and any vegetable which is available (pumpkin, carrot, zucchini, broccoli, potato, cauliflower, tomato, beetroot, mushroom, spinach, red capsicum or peas are ideal) and simmering until the vegetable is tender. As a guide, use one litre of stock and one kilogram of vegetable (one type or a mixture) to make six serves of soup. Once the vegetable is cooked, purée the soup in a food processor or blender. To make a creamy soup, add about three-quarters of a cup of dried skim milk powder and a pinch of nutmeg.

There are many variations on a basic vegetable soup and you can easily produce wonderful winter lunches. Soups can be frozen and reheated in a microwave or carried to work or school in a thermos flask. As with a salad, add a bread roll or some bread to complete the meal.

> ### A SUPERBLY SIMPLE LUNCH
>
> Various vegetable dishes are also suitable for lunch. For example, you can microwave a scrubbed potato until tender (pierce the skin with a skewer in several places first), cut a piece from the top, scoop out the contents and mash with a little non-fat yoghurt, some chopped herbs or mustard and a variety of other ingredients. Sliced mushrooms, finely chopped onions, corn kernels, capsicum, drained tuna or salmon, chopped chicken or turkey ham or whatever you have on hand can be added. Pile the mixture back into the potato 'shell', sprinkle with a little grated low-fat cheese and reheat in the microwave or a regular oven until piping hot. Served with a side salad, this makes a superbly simple lunch.

Light meals

Any kind of seafood is wonderful value for those wanting less fat but 'good' fat. As mentioned earlier, fish have a wonderful balance of the essential omega-3 fatty acids A recent study comparing the satiety value of fish and meat found fish was more filling than meat.

Eggs can also be used as a light meal. Poached eggs, an omelette (served with salad or vegetables) or scrambled eggs are a suitable lunch occasionally.

Rice and pasta can also form the basis of a light lunch. Pasta sauces can feature vegetables (onions, garlic, mushrooms, tomatoes, tomato paste and herbs cooked in red wine is delicious). Skip cream-based sauces.

Rice can be served with stir-fried vegetables, perhaps with sliced fish or other seafood. Heat a wok or large non-stick pan and add a small amount of oil, or stir-fry in concentrated chicken stock made by boiling some chicken stock until it is thick. Vegetables stir-fried in stock look shiny and taste delicious.

> **DRINKS AT LUNCH**
>
> The ideal beverage is water, soda water or mineral water. As long as you sip the water and do not use it to 'wash down' unchewed food, there is no reason not to drink water with meals. Tea or coffee are fine in moderation—say 3 or 4 cups a day. If you want to lose body fat, you need to drink less alcohol. If you want to achieve a good work output in the afternoon, it is best to avoid alcohol at lunchtime.

Recipe books with delicious low-fat recipes are listed on page 219.

DINNER

Trying to take in your food energy during the day rather than at night does not mean that dinner must disappear. However, the balance of dinner may need to change. Many people's evening meals revolve around meat. The meal is even described by the meat or other protein food being served. For example, when someone asks 'What's for dinner?' the answer is usually 'grilled steak' or 'roast lamb' or 'chicken'. Vegetables may be part of the meal but they do not rate much mention. It makes more sense to give a greater starring role to vegetables and let the protein food become the accompaniment. This changes the balance of the meal, decreasing the fat and kilojoules but not necessarily reducing the volume of the meal.

You can still relax and enjoy a wonderfully flavoured evening meal. You can even have several courses, if you like. For example, you might have a bowl of soup, a large plate of lightly-steamed vegetables with some fish, and a selection of fresh fruits. Such a meal will be filling, and high in nutrients, but light in kilojoules.

Many people now use takeaway foods or ready-prepared meals bought from the freezer cabinet for dinner. Most of these foods are high in fat and a healthy diet can only accommodate them occasionally.

There seem to be two major reasons for the high usage of convenience meals. One is that fewer people have the cooking skills which most women once had. The second is that most of the food preparation is still left to women. Since most women work outside the home for similar hours to men, they come home tired and do not want to have to think about preparing and cooking dinner. Taking something out of the freezer or buying takeaway are obvious options.

Until the food industry comes up with some more nutritious products, we may need to make some other changes within the home. If everyone took a turn at being responsible for preparing and cooking the meal, it might be that the sharing of the task would make it less onerous. Those who cannot cook may need to take some lessons, but this may be the only way to reduce the high usage of these high-fat products which are helping increase the national waistline. The recipe books listed in the Appendix on page 219 contain simple recipes which are suitable for those who have not previously cooked. Some women's magazines also include a difficulty rating with their recipes to make it easier for first-time cooks.

The evening meal does not need to be complex. Any of the suggestions for lunch can be used at dinner. Grilled or home-barbecued chicken, fish or very lean meat plus a simple tossed salad also makes for an easy meal.

SNACKS

There is continued debate about whether you should eat three meals with no snacks or whether it is better to divide foods into small meals plus snacks. The French rarely eat between meals and have less obesity than many parts of the world. This pattern allows you to eat, satisfy your hunger, burn up the food and become hungry again before the next meal. The alternative is to eat often and not allow the body time to feel hunger between snacks.

A major problem with snacks is the types of foods commonly consumed between meals. Biscuits, cakes, doughnuts, pastry, ice cream, lollies, chocolates, chips, crisps and sugary soft drinks have little nutritional value and lots of kilojoules. All except soft drinks are high in fat. There is also a problem for those who overeat every time they eat. The more snacks they include, the greater the total food intake.

Snacking itself may not be a problem. The study referred to earlier, looking at changes in metabolic rate with different distribution of food throughout the day, found that eating three meals and three snacks could increase metabolic rate by over 2 per cent. However, it is important to choose snacks carefully.

Some people find it works well to divide their meals into two portions, eating one at a designated mealtime and keeping the rest to eat as a snack an hour or two later. For example, if it is convenient, you could have some cereal and fruit for breakfast and save a slice of toast until morning teatime. Or have a sandwich for lunch and keep some fruit from lunch until mid-afternoon.

HEALTHY SNACK FOODS

- fresh fruit
- frozen fruit
- bread, rolls, yeasted muffins
- crispbread, preferably low-fat varieties
- unsweetened breakfast cereals
- non-fat yoghurt, plain or fruit-flavoured varieties without added sugar
- low-fat frothy milkshakes made by blending skim milk with a couple of ice cubes, some vanilla (or coffee) and artificial sweetener
- lavash bread baked in a moderate oven until crisp
- vegetables (for example, tomatoes or cherry tomatoes, celery, carrots, fresh asparagus, raw broccoli or cauliflower sprigs dipped in a little non-fat yoghurt flavoured with herbs or horseradish)
- freshly popped corn, made with an air popcorn maker (add some dried salad herbs for flavour)
- low-kilojoule jelly (can be made with half the regular water content, set in a shallow dish and cut into squares)

WEIGHT PLATEAU

Many people set out to lose weight, do so quite satisfactorily and then reach a plateau. There are several reasons why this occurs. If your weight is within the healthy weight range, it may be that you have now reached a weight which is right for you. After all, anyone losing excess body fat needs to reach a plateau at some stage. Some aim for a weight loss of a kilogram a week and take anything less to mean they are not getting anywhere. A loss of a kilogram a month is more reasonable; losing this much fat and keeping it off is a success in itself.

Sometimes a plateau occurs as a consequence of dieting as the body adapts to the new lower kilojoule intake. At first the reduction in kilojoules is significantly different from the previous level and fat is burned to supply the deficit. Gradually, however, the body reduces its metabolic rate to match the lower food intake. This occurs much more in those who have lost weight fast. Research has shown that the decrease in metabolic rate which accompanies weight loss is much less when weight is lost slowly. Of course, a smaller body requires less food than a larger one, so weight loss is always accompanied by some reduction in energy use. Exercise has a similar effect. It takes far more kilojoules for a heavy person to walk a given distance than it does for a lighter person. Once you lose weight, you therefore burn up fewer kilojoules in everyday activity as well as in exercise.

A weight plateau is frustrating to many people trying to lose weight. It is an inevitable consequence of fast weight loss. The best way to deal with it is to check that you are not eating more fat, sugar and alcohol and increase your exercise. Those who exercise a lot are never fat. There are no fat marathon runners. Do not be tempted to start some silly diet as your weight loss will be largely water—and that always returns. In many cases, the plateau represents not a further loss of fat but a return of previously lost water.

In all cases, stick with it. It may take some months, but sensible eating and exercise will start to produce results. Most people give up the first week their weight loss reaches a plateau. If you genuinely cannot get off your plateau, you may need to accept that you have reached a weight which is ideal for you.

BINGEING AND COPING WITH GUILT

Many people, especially women, feel guilty every time they eat. Usually this occurs in frequent dieters or in those who are striving for a very low body weight. Our society's obsession with extreme slimness in women also makes many women feel they can never achieve such impossible standards. They keep trying and feel guilty almost every time they eat.

Let's look at a common example. Almost everyone has seen a woman craving something sweet—chocolate cake, perhaps. In most cases, the woman in question is a 'restrained eater' who does not allow herself to eat regular-sized meals. Her cravings eventually win and she furtively takes a piece of chocolate cake, saying, or at least thinking, 'I shouldn't be eating this.' To hide her guilt, she eats the cake quickly, denying herself the right to enjoy it. After all, if she shouldn't be eating this, it is best to get the crime over and done with as quickly as possible. Often she will have grabbed the first chocolate cake she came across and, without stopping to consider whether it is even a good chocolate cake or not, eaten it. Afterward, she does not feel happy or satisfied. Sometimes she hates herself for her weakness and may repeat the episode with some other food soon after.

Of course, the food may not be chocolate cake, but if this sounds like you, here is some advice. There is nothing wrong with having an occasional piece of chocolate cake—or any other food, for that matter. If you eat chocolate cake all the time, you will get fat, so it makes sense to make it only a small part of your total diet. However, an occasional piece will do no harm.

HOW TO EAT CHOCOLATE CAKE

Next time you want some particular food, such as chocolate cake, allow yourself to have it. Don't settle for any old chocolate cake, though—search out the very best chocolate cake you can find. This removes the instantaneous gobbling effect of eating something just because it is there. When you find a slice of chocolate cake (don't make a cake unless you have plenty of people to share it with, or you will end up eating the whole thing), sit down and eat it slowly. Enjoy every mouthful and allow yourself the full delight of its richness. If you take this attitude, you will find that the chocolate cake is much more satisfying than the piece you guiltily gobble down.

Having allowed yourself a scrumptious piece of cake, and knowing that at some time in the future you can have a similar experience, you can get on with the rest of your life's activities. When you do not forbid chocolate cake, it is much easier to see it as one part of your life. When it is forbidden, the desire to sneak a piece becomes overriding. When you eat guiltily, you tend to continue craving the food because you have had no satisfaction from it.

Bingeing

Almost everyone has an occasional binge. It may happen at a party or at some time when you simply feel like eating more of a particular food. Or it may involve standing at the door of the refrigerator or pantry and looking for something to eat. It may be a way to get relief from tension or anger. If it happens only on rare occasions and you automatically eat less for the next meal or two, it is probably of little consequence. There is a continuum from normal eating to overeating or bingeing.

Many women constantly restrain their natural desire to eat even normal quantities of food. Frequently they will binge in an abnormal

PLANNING YOUR NEW HABITS

fashion, to the point where their bingeing dominates their lives. Some do it within reason and merely appear to be large 'weekend eaters', reimposing their control on Monday mornings. Others suffer from bulimia and binge excessively and in secret, sometimes taking laxatives or vomiting to 'get rid of' the food. Even while they are sitting on the toilet or being sick, they are thinking about the next food they will eat. And every time they eat, they are thinking about how they will get rid of the food.

This is abnormal and destructive behaviour and generally requires help from someone who specialises in eating disorders. However, all bulimics begin somewhere and constantly practising very strict eating restraint from Monday to Friday and then overindulging on weekends is not a healthy or necessary practice. Most women who do this are striving for extreme thinness.

Bingeing occurs much more easily in restrained eaters, not only in humans but also in other animals. An animal which is underfed will often eat more than its normal requirement when food is readily available. This is thought to be a survival response. If you have not had much food and then food becomes available, you eat more in case there is none later.

Some particular foods may also trigger a feeding response. When animals are underfed and are then given either sugar, alcohol or water before being given a normal meal, those which have been given sugar or alcohol will eat much more than those given water.

A well-known study had women college students, both normal and restrained eaters, take part in what they were told was a test of taste perception. All students were asked to describe the flavour, texture and taste characteristics of different ice creams. Unknown to them, the quantity of ice cream they ate was being measured. Before being given the ice cream, they were asked on one occasion to drink one milkshake, on another, two milkshakes and, on another, nothing. After drinking one milkshake, the normal eaters ate much smaller portions of the ice cream. After two milkshakes, they ate even less ice cream. The restrained eaters did just the opposite. Once they had broken their normal restraint by having a milkshake, they ate more of the ice cream. After two milkshakes, they ate even more ice cream. The psychological explanation for their behaviour was that, having been forced to break their usual restraint, they found it difficult to reimpose control.

12

The overweight child

THERE HAVE ALWAYS BEEN SOME CHILDREN who were fat. In every school class there was perhaps one fat child, but usually not more than one. In the past, most children took part in enough physical activity to ensure that whatever they ate, the kilojoules were used up. Excess body fat was rare. Recent Australian surveys, however, show that one child in four is now too fat, and the number of children who are actually obese has increased significantly since the 1980s.

Hereditary factors play a part in weight gain in children. But genes cannot make you fat—you must actually consume food and drink to gain fat. Some children, like some adults, simply need less food than others. If they all eat the same amount, some will end up normal-sized; others will be fat.

Most children need large numbers of kilojoules for growth as well as for physical activity. Their appetites usually match their needs. However, the appetite control mechanisms only seem to work with a certain level of physical activity. Those who are very active need more food and eat more; those who are inactive need less food but tend to eat more.

A lack of physical activity is a major cause of excess weight in children. Children no longer walk much, and are now driven distances which earlier generations would have walked. In many areas it is not considered safe for children to go off riding their bicycles, and many sports are now so organised and competitive that only those children who excel tend to participate. Society's patterns of saving energy are also established early in life. Even shopping has changed. Children no longer run errands; their parents drive.

Television and computers are also to blame. Not only do children sit in front of a screen instead of playing more energetically, but during children's viewing hours on television there are many advertisements for foods—usually foods high in fat and sugar. By contrast, there are no advertisements for carrots or potatoes or other vegetables and very few for fruits. Tap water is not advertised. A recent study in the United States found that for each hour children watch television, they see an average of 12 food advertisements depicting foods with almost 11 000 kilojoules, 74 grams of fat and 418 grams of carbohydrate. One hour's viewing shows more kilojoules, fat, carbohydrate and salt than the child needs for the whole day.

SPECIAL FOODS FOR CHILDREN

The kinds of food children eat must shoulder some of the blame for excess fat. Foods which were once kept for special occasions are now regular fare. Most mothers also work outside the home and many, to make up for their absence, make sure lots of 'treats' are left for the children to eat.

From an early age, children are taught that they will be given special foods. This begins in infancy with baby foods and establishes a pattern of feeding children foods which are different from regular family foods. After baby foods come junior foods, special drinks and a variety of items designed to appeal to the toddler.

This leads to the idea that children do not eat regular foods. Whereas young children once ate smaller portions of whatever the family was eating, they now learn at an early age to expect foods bought especially for them. It does not take long before they learn to demand these foods, leading parents to say 'she won't eat anything else', as they give in to their children's tactics. Surveys have shown that in many homes, children's wishes are a major consideration not only in the kinds of foods bought but even in the brands of different items.

Various snack foods, including dozens of different ice confections, crunchy, fatty snack foods and sweets, are marketed predominantly to children. Food manufacturers and advertisers strive to find ways to appeal to this young market. Adding sugar and suggesting the food is full of 'fun' seem to be the most popular ploys for the pre-schooler. Sex, sophistication and peer group pressure take over when the target is teenagers. When you are thirsty, you are encouraged to go to the refrigerator, not the tap. Most of the drinks advertised are high in sugar, whether this is from added sugar or that present naturally in fruit juices.

Fast foods are also marketed to children. Indeed, in contrast to many conventional restaurants, most fast-food outlets welcome children. Children begin going to fast-food restaurants because they like the welcoming atmosphere and many promotional attractions. The food does not start off being the prime attraction. However, the foods are bland, can be eaten in the fingers (which appeals to children of all ages) and few children dislike anything about them. As they become accustomed to the blandness of the food and enjoy the 'eating out' experience, they frequently ask their parents to take them again.

Gradually, any sense of adventure about trying different foods is lost and children come to prefer the familiarity of fast food. Adults often report that they do not especially like fast foods but they eat them 'because the kids like it'. Fast foods are also popular because most working women are too tired at the end of a day's work to come home and start preparing dinner from scratch. Fast foods offer an easy and relatively cheap solution. From the nutritional viewpoint, however, almost all fast foods could more accurately be described as 'fats' foods.

New habits

Many of the foods once kept for special occasions, but now used as everyday items, are higher in kilojoules than the traditional foods they have replaced. For example, afternoon tea was once bread with jam or Vegemite, or toast, or some kind of fruit. If you were thirsty, you drank milk or water. Now, many children have bowls of ice cream, potato crisps, chocolate bars, biscuits and fatty snack foods—all washed down with sugary soft drinks.

For older school children, the traditional lunch is disappearing too. Many teenage girls skip lunch altogether in an attempt to stay slim. Teenage boys are usually too hungry to go without and less inclined to see themselves as fat. Once teenage boys would take a pile of sandwiches to school for lunch. These days they take one sandwich (or none) and make up the deficit with ice blocks, chips, chocolate bars and drinks. The girls who have skipped lunch are usually so hungry after school that they eat sweets, chocolates and chips. The replacement foods have far more fat and kilojoules than the healthy pile of sandwiches of the past. Almost half of Australian children take a packet of crisps or similar snack food to school each day. Those who do so have the lowest consumption of fruit.

DOES OVERWEIGHT MATTER?

There have been many studies showing that children of fat parents have a strong chance of becoming fat themselves. This is almost certainly a combination of genetics and family eating habits. There are also studies which show that a significant percentage of overweight children become overweight adults.

THE OVERWEIGHT CHILD

Fat children are less healthy than their thinner peers. Many are also less happy. The cruel taunts of their classmates lead many fat children to opt out of games and various activities. Fat children are often less popular, are picked last for sporting events and are treated differently from thinner children. Many never recover from the psychological damage. To rid themselves of feelings of isolation, many turn to eating even more. Food becomes a comfort.

Parents who establish eating and exercise habits which make a fat life easy for their children are not doing them any kindness. Those who go to the opposite extreme also cause difficulties. Children should be active, healthy and not overweight. They should not have their lives made a misery by either excessive or restrictive diets.

HOW EXCESS WEIGHT BEGINS

In the first year of life, a child's body fat level depends on genetics and on what is consumed. Breast or formula milks make up most of the diet, at least for the first 7–8 months. If these are fed too often (in the case of breast milk) or at the wrong concentration (for formula), the child can become overfat. It is important to distinguish between normal fat levels in an infant and excessive amounts of fat. Almost all babies lay down some extra fat in the last few months of their first year, presumably to last them over the next year when they will be so busy discovering how to walk, talk and explore their new exciting world that many will not bother too much with food. Most children are not excessively fat in their first year. Those who are too fat can find learning to walk difficult. A lack of exercise can then make fatness almost inevitable.

With babies and young children, some carers interpret every cry as a need for food. Most babies cry when they are hungry and most toddlers start to whinge when it is time for a meal. They may also cry when they are wet, cold, hot, tired, thirsty or if they need company or attention. Parents and carers need to learn to distinguish between a child's different needs.

Sometimes parents do not understand children's changing appetite and need for food. Adults tend to eat much the same sized serving of foods from day to day. Children are growing and their appetites reflect the spasmodic spurts in growth. Just before a growth spurt, they may be very hungry. Afterwards, their hunger abates and they do not want much food. They may sometimes want half a slice of bread and at other times 4 or more. Children do not have any instinctive knowledge about *what* to eat (if humans ever had any instinct about what their bodies needed, it has been ruined by advertising). But initially, children do know *how much* they need to eat. When they have had enough, they stop. If we smile and praise them when they eat everything, they soon learn to eat for the praise and lose their natural ability to eat when they are hungry and stop when they feel satisfied.

> **SWEET SILENCERS**
>
> Toddlers are demanding of their carers' time. Many busy people 'palm off' children with food. The phone rings, you want a little peace, the children are cranky—so you give them something to eat. They may not be hungry but a biscuit or something sweet goes down easily without hunger. Many people also bribe and reward children with sweet foods when what the child really wants is time and attention. Instead they get something to eat.

A carer's dislike of messiness can also contribute to weight gain in a young child. By around 10–12 months of age, most infants are trying to feed themselves. They are not very good at it and much of the food ends up in places other than the mouth. Most infants thoroughly enjoy the whole messy business and the amount they eat soon matches their needs. When they are sick of eating, they stop—whether they have eaten everything or not. In practice, few parents allow young children to go through this process of learning about food by touching it, eating it and deciding for themselves when they do not want any more. Instead, the parent very efficiently spoons the food into the child, not stopping until it has all gone. This happens so quickly that some children do not realise they are full. They soon learn to eat automatically.

Some parents try to encourage reluctant eaters by adding sugar to foods. This is useless and can lead to weight problems. All children will eat when they are hungry, if food is available to them. There is no need to bribe them with sweetness. Problems with toddlers who do not want to eat are discussed in my book *Food for Under 5s*.

DRINKS

I have long been convinced that what children drink is related to their weight. Water has no kilojoules. Thirsty children will drink water, but not if they have learned that thirst is quenched with juice or cordial or soft drink. Children also follow adults' eating habits, especially those of their father. If Daddy always drinks tea or coffee or beer or soft drink and seldom drinks water, the children will follow suit.

THE OVERWEIGHT CHILD

> **DOS AND DON'TS FOR PARENTS OF OVERWEIGHT CHILDREN**
> - Do not blame the child.
> - Check the kitchen.
> - Keep the diet balanced.
> - Check your cooking methods.
> - Avoid diets and mention of diets.
> - Encourage physical activity.
> - Keep special foods for special occasions.
> - Buy foods with less fat, sugar and salt.

Many well-meaning parents buy fruit juice for their children, often taking care to choose varieties with no added sugar. However, whether sugar is added to fruit juice or not, the products still contain a lot of fruit sugar. This contributes just as many kilojoules as any other sugar. Fruit itself has fibre with its sugar. In making fruit juice, the fibre is removed and it then becomes easy to take in far more kilojoules than would be possible from eating the fruit.

Freshly squeezed orange juice is a delightful and healthy addition to breakfast. But few people squeeze oranges several times a day so there are few cases of overconsumption of fresh orange juice. But the availability of ready-prepared juices of many flavours means that juice consumption has increased dramatically. It is not uncommon for many children to have 4 or 5 glasses a day. Many teenagers drink even more. Juices contribute a large number of kilojoules, without being very filling. One glass of juice a day provides a valuable source of vitamin C, but drinking juice every time you are thirsty is unnecessary. Cordials and soft drinks are even worse as they contain just as many kilojoules and do not even contribute any vitamins.

Parents often complain that their children will not drink water. They will—if they are thirsty and if you do not have juice, cordial or soft drinks sitting in the refrigerator. Children are more likely to drink water if they see adults doing so. For older children, it also helps if you keep water in the refrigerator in a clear flask which looks attractive. Those who were not introduced to syrups as babies are also more likely to drink water.

WHAT TO DO ABOUT EXCESS WEIGHT IN CHILDREN

Do not blame the child

Many parents blame their children for their excess fat. Even the parents of 3-year-olds will sometimes tell me that their child will not stop eating the wrong foods. Basically children eat the foods available. If sweet and fatty foods are not a regular part of the household eating pattern, the child will not have a problem.

> **HEALTHY SNACKS FOR KIDS**
> - breads (there are many varieties, including wholemeal, wholegrain, mixed grain, high-fibre, white, rye, raisin, corn)
> - bread products such as muffins, rolls, toast, flatbreads
> - crispbreads
> - cereals (great for snacks as well as breakfast)
> - fruits (fresh, frozen or dried)
> - vegetables
> - milk, cheese or yoghurt
> - lean meats, chicken, fish or vegetarian alternatives such as baked beans
> - freshly popped corn or nuts (according to the age of the child).

Check the kitchen

It is not fair to expect a child of any age to look at chocolate biscuits or cakes or whatever and not have any. It makes much more sense for the foods available to include healthy items. For example, you might have on hand any or all of the items listed in the box above.

There are also many healthy foods which can be available for the child, such as soups, rice or pasta dishes, pizza, some wholegrain fruit loaves or frozen yoghurt. You do not need to emphasise the healthiness of these foods. Simply having them available and not buying the others is all that is necessary for most children.

Avoid diets and mention of diets

No child should be put on a diet. Children are growing and even those who are overweight should not aim to lose weight but to hold their weight steady while they grow taller. Encourage children to become 'healthy eaters' rather than 'dieters'. There is no need to weigh them. Scales can be embarrassing for children and may encourage some to manipulate their weight through sweating or not drinking water. Weight is unimportant. Too much body fat is the real problem.

Encourage physical activity

Physical activity is the key to successful fat loss. Many fat children are reluctant to walk or exercise much because it is uncomfortable for them to do so. By all means, encourage those who still like sports and physical activity to continue. For others, swimming, riding a bicycle or having active family fun may be more suitable than actual sports—at least until the child has 'grown into' his or her weight.

Keep the diet balanced

There are a few important considerations for younger children to ensure the diet remains balanced. A child under the age of 2 should have regular milk, not skim milk. This is important to provide vitamin A. However, children do not need more than 500–600 mL of milk a day. Some 2-year-olds who still love frequent bottles of milk have twice this much. If you cannot get rid of the bottle, dilute 500 mL of milk with water. Do not switch to using a large volume of skim milk, as this contributes too much protein. Few young children drink too much milk from a cup.

Over the age of 2, a reduced-fat milk can be used for overweight children. Try to make sure the child also eats plenty of green and orange vegetables to supply extra vitamins. Once teenage children have stopped growing, low-fat or skim milks are the most suitable, whether the child is fat or not.

The general principles of healthy eating as outlined in Chapter 10 are important for children. Remember, too, that just because a food is nutritious, it does not necessarily follow that eating more is an advantage. Too much of healthy foods such as meat or cheese, for example, is unwise for an overweight child.

Check the cooking

Fats in food easily become body fat. Many people use a lot of fat in cooking and food preparation without realising how many extra kilojoules they are consuming. Try to grill, barbecue, cook in a non-stick pan, bake on a rack, make casseroles ahead so that fat can be removed, and cook in a microwave oven without fat, rather than frying.

Fast foods and many prepared foods are high in fat, so use these as seldom as possible. Many people also add plenty of margarine or butter, or cream or mayonnaise to their cooking. Avoid these where possible, and use low-fat spreads (or no spread), yoghurt or low-fat evaporated milk in cooking and food preparation. Low-fat cheeses can also be used in many recipes.

Keep special foods for special occasions

There is no reason why an overweight child should not have some birthday cake. Nor is there any reason why he or she should not

THE DIET DILEMMA

occasionally have a fast-food meal or some other 'treat'. Banning a food generally increases anyone's desire to have that food. Better to adopt a habit of using special foods for special occasions.

Most children accept the fact that their parents will not buy a birthday cake anytime they spot a delicious-looking one in a cake shop. They accept the fact that birthday cakes are for birthdays. Children can understand the idea of different menus. For example, you can have a party menu, a menu when Grandma is visiting and an everyday menu. This always happened in the past and was well accepted by children. They knew that soft drinks were for birthdays and Christmas, chocolates were bought only for celebrations and cream or chocolate biscuits only appeared for very special visitors. This approach means no foods need be forbidden but foods with a lot of fat and sugar do not become everyday items.

Buy 'lite'

There are now many foods which are available with less fat, sugar or salt. For example, you can buy cheese with 7 per cent fat (instead of the usual 33 per cent), jams without sugar, breakfast cereals with no or minimal sugar levels (including the biggest-selling variety), spreads with half the usual fat content, light cream cheese with half the usual fat level, and a wide range of other products. Choose these for the whole family, not just for anyone who is fat.

13

Coping with eating out and other distractions

EATING OUT

You keep to a sensible eating plan when you are at home. But as soon as you eat out or go on holidays or to parties, all your good intentions fly out the window. Sound familiar? Many people's eating habits change dramatically as soon as they do anything out of the ordinary. If you eat out only rarely, it does not matter too much what you choose to eat as it will have little effect on your overall diet and weight. If you eat out or entertain often, however, you may need to follow a few guiding principles for good choices. Many healthy choices have wonderful flavour.

How much to eat

First of all, think about how much you want to eat. Almost everyone sets some limit on what they eat and drink. Healthy and enjoyable eating involves knowing the appropriate limits for your body and level of physical activity. Restaurants serve everyone the same-sized portion. For some it is appropriate, for others it is too much. But you don't have to eat it all. You can let the chef know that you left some simply because there was too much.

It is not difficult to enjoy delicious foods without gaining extra fat. The common idea that healthy eating and enjoyable eating are mutually exclusive is a myth. The secret lies in knowing where the nutritional nasties lurk and learning which delectable foods you can indulge in freely. You can eat almost as much of any vegetable as you please, and take a good few liberties with seafoods, but for most other items of food and drink there is an appropriate quantity. If you are tall, large-framed and lean, or if you exercise a lot, you can usually eat much more without adding to your body fat than if you are small or inactive.

> ### HOW MANY COURSES?
>
> Three courses is too much for most people who eat out often. Aim for two, or try to dine with a kindred spirit with whom you can share—one dessert, two spoons, makes great sense after a big meal. You could also order two entrées instead of an entrée and a main course. Remember that good eating means enjoying superb-tasting foods. It does not necessarily mean stuffing yourself with vast quantities of everything.

Some basic principles

Most restaurant meals contain more fat and kilojoules than many home-cooked meals. However, it is now much easier for healthy eaters to get a better deal in a variety of restaurants than it used to be. Simple, healthy foods are popular and wise restaurateurs know it. Many ethnic eateries have always offered a healthy selection of foods—if you know what to choose.

Basically, it's up to the diner to make good choices. Often it's not the meal choices which cause problems but the 'extras', such as the butter that automatically comes with the roll or is pre-soaked into garlic bread, the chips which accompany many meals, the chocolates served with the coffee. Eliminate these and you have greater freedom with the basic menu items.

A sane approach to eating out also means taking care that everything you do eat is a positive taste delight. Don't waste your kilojoules. Try the 'I only eat quality' approach too. Ask yourself if a food is worth the kilojoules and fat. This makes it easy to decline anything which is likely to be fairly ordinary. You can then indulge in some of the more brilliant of the chef's creations, having saved so much by skipping the ordinary.

Eating out healthily also means asking a few questions about what is in the foods and having the self-confidence to make a few requests. Too often we sit there smouldering because we didn't really want our grilled fish smothered in butter or some rich sauce. Ask what is in various dishes and if you want your food served without some additions, or the sauce 'on the side', say so when giving your order. You are paying. Few chefs mind accommodating people who have special requirements. It helps if you're reasonable about it too.

COPING WITH EATING OUT AND OTHER DISTRACTIONS

> **ASK YOUR WAITER**
>
> If you really want foods cooked with less fat, ask the waiter which items on the menu could most easily be adapted. In other instances, it is easy to request small changes. For example, you can ask for sauces and dressings to be served separately so you can have just a little. You can also ask for your vegetables to be served without butter or fresh fruits to be served without cream. You can ask a waiter to remove the butter from the table rather than have it sit tempting you throughout the meal.

Different types of restaurants are either wonderful or woeful for the healthy eater. In general, those establishments which serve good quality foods, simply prepared, present few problems. They rely on the quality of the basic produce rather than some gluggy, buttery or battered attempt to hide inferior food.

What to choose

At a 'modern Australian' café or restaurant, you can usually find plenty of healthy offerings.

Look for superb soups where the beauty of the ingredients is subtly found in a wonderfully flavoured stock—a fish soup, one brimful of pumpkin and leek or an oxtail or duck consommé, perhaps. They are far less fattening than the butter/flour/cream concoctions with their vaguely indiscriminate flavour.

Vegetables and seafoods are a healthy eater's best friends. And what an array of both we now have available. Oysters, prawns, bugs, marron, succulent squid and octopus or freshly-caught crab are all low in fat. As long as they're not served deep-fried, they make a great choice. Go for the char-grilled versions, carpaccio (of any type), warm salads or the superb flavour of sugar-cured trout or smoked salmon.

With pasta, avoid rich sauces and choose those which feature seafoods, tomatoes, mushrooms, eggplant or any other vegetable and herbs rather than the waist-expanding cream-based types.

Salads and vegetables are superbly healthy and the trend towards unusual seasonal vegetables, often served on a coulis of some complementary cousin, is ideal. Many restaurants are now serving delightful salads and vegetable dishes which are as good for you as they taste.

Thankfully, many restaurants have stopped serving overcooked, tasteless vegetables and are providing great-tasting products such as witlof, radicchio or rocket, lamb's lettuce, mizuna or other interesting salad greens, fresh asparagus, eggplant, semi-dried tomatoes, fennel, delicate baby vegetables of all kinds, big, flat, flavourful field mushrooms, watercress and coriander. Salads can be sensational—or, if you don't request otherwise, they may be drowned in a fatty dressing.

For main courses, look for those which feature fish or other seafoods or any type of game meat, or lean meats such as turkey or chicken breast or fillets of lamb, pork or beef. Fried foods and some sauces may be heavily laced with butter or cream. Sauces made from flavoursome stock reductions or vegetables, herbs, spices and wine are above nutritional reproach.

Desserts present problems. The only healthy solution for frequent diners is to choose any fresh fruits and try to avoid the cream that so often accompanies them. The next best dessert—and an ideal one in the heat of summer—is sorbet. After that, desserts are suitable for occasional indulgences only. Sharing dessert helps a bit. So does a long, vigorous walk later.

Cheeses are, sadly, so rich in fat that they do not sit well in the full stomach of someone trying to be healthy. Better to keep your cheese for a simple lunch along with bread, fruit and salad. That way, you can enjoy it, in moderation, without guilt.

WHAT YOU EAT IS WHAT YOU GET

Take a look at the people who eat various types of foods and you will notice that some nationalities tend to be slim. It's a good sign that their diet is above reproach. For example, there are few fat Asians; if we ate similar foods, they would be unlikely to make us fat. Unfortunately, some Asian restaurants in western countries change their basic foods in a way they think will fit the western palate. This usually results in higher fat levels. Westerners often order more meat dishes than most Asians. When sharing with several people, make sure your choices include plenty of vegetable dishes.

GUIDE TO DIFFERENT CUISINES

Australian

Modern Australian cafés and restaurants usually serve fresh simple food which is ideal for those watching their weight. Choose any salads, char-grilled meat, poultry or seafood, pasta or noodle dishes without cream-based sauces, grilled or oven-roasted vegetables, grilled bread topped with eggplant, tomatoes or other vegetables. Fresh fruit is usually available.

COPING WITH EATING OUT AND OTHER DISTRACTIONS

Cajun

The spices themselves and the fiery charcoal cooking do not add fat but servings are often large. Try to share portions if possible. Choose seafood dishes, chowders, gumbo, rice-based Creole dishes and any modest-sized serves of charcoal-grilled meats. Avoid the enormous plates of ribs served in some restaurants, unless you are sharing with friends. It could take some weeks of sober eating to make up for indulging in rich sundaes, pies and other desserts.

Chinese

Choose vegetable, rice, noodle, tofu, seafood, chicken, pork or beef dishes, but avoid anything which has been dipped in batter and/or deep-fried. Ask for steamed rice rather than fried.

French

Choose bouillon, vegetable or seafood soups (without cream); any seafoods (not fried or in rich sauces); game, poultry or meat dishes without rich sauces; interesting vegetables (ask for no butter); fresh fruit.

German

Try to avoid fatty pork and high-fat sausages. Portions are often huge, so sharing makes sense. Some soups, potato dishes, cabbage, and any other vegetables are good choices. Desserts are often so rich that it is best to skip them.

Greek

Some Greek restaurants use a lot of olive oil, a healthy product but, like all fats, high in kilojoules. At least it is good for you, but you might want to resist the temptation to mop up excess oil with your bread. Instead of fried foods and foods wrapped in pastry, try stuffed vine or cabbage leaves, stuffed vegetables, any seafood dishes, spinach dishes, lamb (it is usually lean), Greek salads (ask for the dressing to be served separately) and souvlaki. Eat the bread but avoid the pastry desserts. Fresh fruit is almost always available or simply settle for Greek coffee.

Indian

Rice and curries are suitable foods. However, many curries contain a lot of ghee (clarified butter) and coconut milk, both of which raise the fat level. In India, vegetable curries, lentils and various legumes predominate and supply dietary fibre and starch. Australians have a tendency to order mainly meat dishes. Choose some vegetable, legume and seafood curries. Choose naan rather than paratha and avoid too many samoosas and other deep-fried foods. Fruit or a small serve of kulfi (an ice cream made from concentrated milk rather than cream) are usually available.

Indonesian

The rice and vegetable dishes are suitable. Sate poultry and meats are generally very lean, although the accompanying sauces may have coconut milk. Avoid eating too many dishes cooked in coconut cream as it is high in fat and kilojoules.

Italian

The major problem is the quantity of oil used, and also butter and cream in Northern Italian cuisine. Choose grilled seafoods or meats, pasta with sauces featuring seafood or vegetables, or osso buco. Most veal dishes are fried and many have added cheese, giving a high total fat content. Parmesan cheese is usually used sparingly in keeping with its strong flavour and presents few problems. There are usually interesting vegetables and delicious salads available. Gelato is a low-fat (but high-sugar) dessert.

Japanese

The Japanese are the world's longest-living people and they are almost never overweight. When you look at what they eat, it is not so surprising. Rice, seafoods, the leanest of meats and chicken and a variety of vegetables make up the bulk of their meals. Sushi, sashimi and most dishes are eminently suitable for a healthy eater. The only foods to avoid are tempura and anything deep-fried.

Lebanese

Many of the foods feature vegetables and legumes. The major problem is the large quantity of olive oil which covers so many dishes. Olive oil is the healthiest oil but too much provides a lot of kilojoules. Try to avoid very oily dishes. Eat the excellent Lebanese bread. Skip desserts which are heavy with butter, sugar and nuts.

Malaysian

Eat plenty of rice and try some vegetable dishes. Take care not to order too many dishes with coconut cream. Like Indonesian and Indian food, most of the foods only cause problems when eaten in large quantities.

COPING WITH EATING OUT AND OTHER DISTRACTIONS

Mexican

The gigantic size of the portions served in many Mexican restaurants makes sharing dishes a good idea. Tacos, tortillas and enchiladas are fine and the use of beans is excellent, but you will need to avoid the heavy-handed approach with cheese, meat and sour cream.

Spanish

Seafoods, rice dishes, chicken and vegetable dishes are the best choices. Many dishes are rich with tomato, garlic and onion-based sauces. These are generally fine. Most of the dessert flans have a lot of cream but fresh fruit is usually available.

Swiss

In Switzerland, many people walk, climb mountains, ski and are generally very active. Although they choose dishes made with meats, cream, sauces, butter and cheese, most people choose small portions and eat much more bread and potato dishes. Most Swiss restaurants serve fairly high-fat foods to English-speaking westerners. You may need to climb a mountain after eating them!

Thai

Most foods are fine except for deep-fried filled pastry foods. Sour soups, seafood dishes, chilli sauces, steamed dishes, lean beef and chicken dishes and various hotpots are all low in fat. Rice, of course, has no fat and is an excellent choice. Try to avoid too many oily, coconut-based sauces. Sometimes there are many fried entrées, although some salad-based items are also served. Fruit is usually eaten for dessert.

Vegetarian

In theory, vegetarian restaurants sound as if they should ooze health. In many cases they do and you can eat your fill of vegetables, salads and other high-fibre, healthy delights without fear of fat. But some vegetarian menus are so laden with cheese, butter and cream that you could have a much healthier meal eating meat or fish. The same principle can hold for desserts. Tofu ice cream may not contain dairy products but it usually has as much fat, sugar and kilojoules as the real thing. If you're trying to cut down on fat and kilojoules, check what is in some of the vegetarian combinations available. Go for the vegetables, lentils and wholegrain products but steer clear of rich creamy sauces, dollops of cream, lots of cheese, and large serves of nuts. For dessert, at least fruits are usually on offer.

Vietnamese

Like most Asian cuisines, the use of rice, steamed noodles, vegetables, seafoods, chicken and lean meat makes for healthy choices. Avoid deep-fried items.

THE TRUTH ABOUT ORANGE JUICE

Many people think that orange juice will be less fattening than alcoholic drinks. A single glass of juice may have some advantages as it contributes vitamin C and some other important nutrients. However, that does not mean that more orange juice is better. As we discussed earlier, few people will overconsume fruit because the fibre is filling. Fruit juices, on the other hand, can easily contribute many kilojoules. A 250 mL glass of pure orange juice has as many calories as 2 slices of bread. It won't give you a hangover, but if you drink a lot, your body will not get round to burning fat. Tomato and vegetable juices have few kilojoules and are fine.

DRINKS

In dollar terms, drinks can easily cost 30–40 per cent of the total restaurant bill. Their kilojoules follow suit. Try to drink lots of water, soda water or icy cold mineral water before you have anything else to drink. The water will quench your thirst, and you will then find it much easier to sip everything else slowly. The longer a drink lasts, the less you will drink. Waiters only refill your glass when it is empty, so the healthy solution is to drink slowly. If you lunch out frequently, you should aim to have at least some alcohol-free occasions.

Drinks are not filling, so we have little inbuilt safeguard against overconsuming them. Drinks are a major problem in the summer, at parties and all social occasions. The reality is that drinks often contribute more kilojoules than foods and because your body burns their kilojoules first, any accompanying fat may not be used for energy but will be converted to body fat.

A standard glass of wine, middy of beer, nip of spirits or a liqueur have similar quantities of alcohol and kilojoules. Choose whichever you can drink in the least quantities. Some beer drinkers find they will down 10 middies of beer but will be happy with 2 whiskies. You also need to be realistic about how much you drink. Many people share a bottle of wine and then report that they usually drink 2 glasses of wine. Since a bottle of wine contains 7.5 standard glasses, in reality they are drinking more than 3 glasses. How much you drink is up to you but you will lose fat faster if you drink less.

At a restaurant or when entertaining, have iced water, mineral or soda water available. Those wanting to drink less alcohol can use these as an alternative or top up a glass of whisky or wine with soda if they choose. Iced tea with lime or lemon can also give some respite from high-kilojoule drinks. Or try fresh lime juice and soda, or a few drops of bitters in soda water for a pretty pink drink that won't give you a hangover.

ENTERTAINING

When you are the cook, it is much easier to serve low-fat foods without your guests even knowing. The abundance of fruits and vegetables available today is a healthy eater's dream. Baby vegetables of a dozen or more different varieties, richly flavoured winter vegetables and the delicious soups, vegetable pâtés and sauces you can make are all low in kilojoules and fat.

Make the most of vegetables such as crisp, pale green endive, snow-white mushrooms, golden baby squash, rich red capsicums, crunchy honey-snap peas, tiny purple eggplant, smooth-flavoured celeriac, large full-flavoured field mushrooms, the new teardrop or blood tomatoes, crisp watercress or fragrant basil as well as the wonderful selection of seasonal vegetables that grace our vegetable shops.

Turn them into entrées, stuff them, simmer them with herbs in full-flavoured chicken stock for soups, thread them onto skewers for barbecues, toss them into salads with dressings made from wonderfully flavoured vinegars and just a touch of walnut or extra virgin olive oil, or serve them microwaved, steamed or stir-fried as an accompaniment to your main course. You can really let your head go with quantities—no one ever grew fat on vegetables.

PARTIES

Think of all the foods and drinks you consume at parties even though the taste really isn't worth the fat or kilojoules. Remember the soggy savouries, the limp pastry, the half-cold chips, the ordinary orange juice, the fake cream, the artificial-tasting ice cream, the standard chocolates and crisps, the mundane mayonnaise. All solid sources of kilojoules and hardly a taste delight among them. Most of the time we eat these foods simply because they are there. Start

THE DIET DILEMMA

> by skipping these foods and you have more leeway to indulge in the foods which really taste good—with appropriate limits, of course.
>
> With some foods—vegetables, for example—you need not bother with limits. It's almost impossible to eat too much fresh asparagus or too many teardrop tomatoes, or even too many potatoes, for that matter. Vegetables are wonderfully nutritious, and they can taste terrific if properly prepared. They'll never make you fat.
>
> Fruits need some limit, but also offer a fair degree of flexibility. As you sink your teeth into the delights of a perfectly ripe peach, a succulent mango or a bunch of deep purple cherries, you can feel virtue as well as pleasure.
>
> The health benefits of seafoods also give plenty of scope for indulgence. Eat them fresh and succulent, simply char-grilled or barbecued. If they are battered and fried, you gain a stack of fat.
>
> If you are going to a party and you have a fair idea that most of the foods served are likely to be fatty salty snacks, make sure you do not arrive in a state of semi-starvation. Most people are far less discriminating than usual when they are really hungry.

Fruits fit into the same category. They can appear at breakfasts, brunches and lunches, before dinner or as the ultimate dessert. There are few things to equal the taste sensation of a perfectly ripe fresh fig or a bowl of fresh raspberries, the smooth texture of a brown-skinned pear or the crispness of a beautiful apple. And then there are the luscious tropical fruits which are guaranteed to bring praise from guests. As long as you eat fruit with its natural fibre, you're unlikely to overconsume it.

Seafoods can be served simply grilled, barbecued or baked wrapped in foil with some lemon thyme, a few sliced mushrooms and a slice or two of lemon. If you live in a large city, take a trip to the fish markets and discover the delights of the variety of fish and seafoods now available. Baby octopus, prawns (try them flamed in a little brandy and orange with a hint of dill), lobster or any shellfish are low in fat and kilojoules. Oysters are the ultimate first course, with a bare 40 kilojoules (about 8 Cals) each, and loads of iron and zinc.

Healthy eating does not mean you need give up meat, just avoid big fatty steaks. Game meats are very low in fat, veal and new-fashioned pork have very little fat and a small serve of lean beef or lamb fillet is perfectly healthy.

COPING WITH EATING OUT AND OTHER DISTRACTIONS

Sauces accompanying meats or seafoods should emphasise flavour, which can come from using a good stock with herbs, vegetables and wine (all the kilojoules from wine evaporate during cooking).

Desserts which contain pastry or cream or a heavy hand with sugar pose a hazard. The only real solution is to settle for fresh fruit—or restrict your dessert eating to just a few special occasions.

HOLIDAYS

Holiday eating falls into two categories: events such as Christmas and Easter, and holidays away from home with either lots of takeaways or plenty of restaurant meals.

Groaning stomachs and holidays seem to go hand in hand. Many people relax, eat more, put on weight—and afterwards wish they had been more careful. Trips at home or abroad may involve lots of eating in hotels and restaurants, where many foods are high in fat and the servings are much greater than at home. Also, having paid for a meal, many people feel compelled to eat it all, even when they are full. Remember that you are not charged any more for leaving some—and you may be glad later.

Christmas and New Year holidays are times when many people overeat and drink more than usual. February sees a spate of new diets to undo the damage. However, a little planning can leave you without extra fat after holiday times.

The bulk of available foods in many holiday areas or towns on travel routes are greasy, fatty offerings. The situation is starting to change, however, and many places now boast some establishments with fine fresh foods. The greasy joints are still there, but at least you sometimes have a choice.

If you are in an area where there seems to be no choice, you can at least make up a good picnic meal with some fresh crusty bread, salads, avocado, seafoods or cold chicken or turkey, vegetables and fruit.

FAST FOODS

Almost all foods commonly regarded as fast foods are high in fat and kilojoules. Fat is cheap, reheats well and the smell of hot fat has a magnetic attraction for many people.

If you cannot avoid fast foods, at least try for salads, fruit salads or, in the hot food department, go for a quality pizza or Lebanese bread with kebabs or lean meat cooked on the spit. Most fish

> shops will also grill a piece of fish if you ask. Few people think of sandwiches and rolls as fast foods but they are quick and many delightful varieties are beginning to appear at takeaway food outlets. They have much less fat than any fried offerings. Fresh fruit is the ultimate fast food.

Christmas

The major problem with Christmas eating is the quantity of food and drinks which most people consume. Extra exercise will help a little, but there is no substitute for eating small portions and taking care with choices.

Just as they are wonderful in restaurants or at parties, seafoods are a saviour. Crabs, prawns, oysters, fresh fish, octopus or squid can be barbecued or char-grilled, or wrapped in foil and baked. Marinades based on wine, garlic, a very small amount of extra virgin olive oil and some fresh herbs will add lots of flavour.

If you are choosing ham for Christmas, make sure it is one of the new super-lean hams and eat it with lots of fresh salads which will supply the potassium to balance the sodium from the salt in the ham.

If you are a traditional turkey lover, you can remove any fatty pads and the skin at the rear, stuff the bird with some steamed rice, perhaps with a few brandy-soaked dried apricots and a few toasted pine nuts added, roast it, skim the fat from the pan drippings and add a little brandy and fresh orange juice for a sauce—and you have a delicious low-fat meal. It is the trimmings which often cause the problems. Avoid heavy stuffings, rich sauces and large slabs of plum pudding to follow.

Provided they are not fat-logged, vegetables help balance a meal. Using some unusual vegetables adds to a special meal. Steam vegetables briefly, microwave them, or serve them in salads. Roast potatoes by rolling in a very small quantity of hot olive oil in a well-used baking dish and baking in a hot oven until crisp.

For dessert, it is hard to beat fresh raspberries, perfectly ripe mangoes, fresh juicy peaches, richly coloured apricots, tangy kiwi fruit or beautiful blueberries. Serve them chilled without any accompaniment.

GIVING UP SMOKING

Many people put on weight when they stop smoking. The usual weight gain is a couple of kilograms, although some people do not gain anything. Some women keep smoking, or even take it up, as a means of controlling their weight. They ignore the health risks associated with smoking because they feel it will decrease their appetite and give them an alternative to eating. The greatly increased risk of cancer of the cervix, the possibility of heart disease or lung cancer, chest complaints, asthma, even the extra risk to their children's health, all pale into insignificance beside the thought of gaining 2 or 3 kilograms of weight. It shows the distorted value systems many people have.

If you are a smoker and you want to give up, you do not have to gain weight. There is no magic to it. Most ex-smokers gain weight because they eat more. It may help to understand the reasons why this weight gain sometimes occurs.

Smoking depresses the appetite, so some smokers eat less. Smoking also decreases taste sensations. Without cigarettes, food starts to taste better and some people begin to eat more. Smoking can also increase metabolic rate in some people, so they burn up fewer kilojoules when they quit. However, by far the most common reason for ex-smokers gaining weight is that they eat whenever they would previously have had a cigarette. Usually they eat sweets. To make matters worse, a cigarette also signifies the end of a meal. Without their cue to stop eating, ex-smokers sometimes keep on eating.

None of these reasons is good enough to justify smoking. It is better to taste the wonderful flavours in foods. The urge to enjoy their greater taste, and so eat more, soon settles down. The decrease in metabolic rate in ex-smokers is easily compensated for by an increase in exercise. Since exercise becomes much easier without the impaired lung function which goes with smoking, this is no problem. Many ex-smokers discover that being able to exercise without running out of breath is a real joy.

SNACK EATING FOR SMOKERS

The hardest problem is learning to do something other than eating at times when you would once have had a cigarette. The easiest way to start to change the habit is to adopt an eating pattern of 6 to 8 small meals or snacks a day. This stimulates metabolic rate and increases the number of kilojoules burned. As long as the snacks are planned to include healthy foods, frequent eating is not a problem.

A 'small and often' eating plan helps many people giving up smoking and is especially useful for the first few weeks after giving up smoking. This eating plan is intended to prevent weight gain rather than cause weight loss. *It is not intended as a permanent way of eating.*

Each day, the choices are as follows:

Breakfast

Choose any one from:

- 1 cup cooked rolled oats, 1 tablespoon sultanas, non-fat or skim milk
- 1 boiled egg, 1 slice wholemeal toast with low-fat spread, 1 kiwi fruit
- 200-gram carton low-fat fruit yoghurt (without added sugar) and a banana or some other fruit
- 1 slice wholemeal toast with 1 slice cheese, a few sliced mushrooms and grilled tomato
- 2 wholewheat breakfast biscuits with non-fat milk, 2 apricots (fresh or canned without sugar)
- 1 glass skim or non-fat milk blended with a banana (or some other fruit), 1 teaspoon honey and 2 tablespoons low-fat yoghurt
- ½ grapefruit with 1 teaspoon brown sugar (grill until sugar melts), 1 slice wholegrain toast with low-fat spread, Vegemite, 1 glass skim milk

Daytime snacks

Choose up to 4, preferably eaten separately, during the morning and afternoon:

- ½ cup buttermilk mixed with ½ cup apricot nectar
- small tub coleslaw or vegetable salad
- small can (110 g) baked beans
- 1 cup vegetable soup
- small carton plain or fruit non-fat yoghurt (no added sugar)
- 200 mL non-fat milk blended with 2 ice cubes, a sachet of sweetener and a few drops of vanilla or some instant coffee powder
- 1 slice bread, raisin toast or ½ muffin spread thinly with ricotta cheese and low-kilojoule jam (if desired)
- 2 wholemeal or rye crispbreads spread lightly with light cream cheese and sprinkled with cinnamon
- a large crisp carrot
- 1 dozen natural oysters
- small cone frozen soft-serve made from fruit juice (such as Vitari)

Lunch

Choose any one from:

- wholemeal bread sandwich with canned or smoked salmon and salad (no butter, margarine or mayonnaise)

COPING WITH EATING OUT AND OTHER DISTRACTIONS

- average bowl of pea or other thick soup, 2 rye crispbreads
- ½ small avocado (or ¼ large one), large vegetable salad with low-kilojoule dressing
- pita bread with salad
- mushroom omelette (2 eggs, cooked in a non-stick pan), sliced or cherry tomatoes
- 1 cup fresh fruit salad, 200-gram carton non-fat yoghurt
- 1 slice rye or multigrain bread with wedge of camembert or brie cheese, asparagus, celery, lettuce, snow peas, cherry tomatoes (or other salad vegetables)

Dinner

Choose one from:

- grilled or barbecued fish, jacket potato with non-fat yoghurt, green vegetables, salad with low-kilojoule dressing
- chicken breast fillet stir-fried in 1 teaspoon olive oil with vegetables such as onions, bean sprouts, carrot, zucchini, mushrooms, broccoli, capsicum, snow peas and ½ cup steamed rice
- small piece of lean grilled steak, potato, vegetables (no butter)
- 1 cup fettuccine noodles with marinara sauce (made from fish or other seafood in a sauce of tomato, herbs, mushrooms and wine)
- grilled or barbecued kebab with lean cubes of lamb, capsicum, pineapple
- grilled or barbecued chicken breast, small cob corn, large vegetable salad with low-kilojoule dressing
- vegetable curry, ½ cup steamed rice, chutney, 2 or 3 grilled pappadams

After dinner

Choose one, or a portion of one, from:

- 1 cup hot skim milk with low-kilojoule chocolate topping (if desired)
- 1 slice hot raisin toast with scrape of low-fat spread
- 1 cup fresh fruit salad or melon
- 2 kiwi fruit
- baked apple (remove core and stuff centre with 2 prunes or a few raisins, microwave for 5 minutes)
- 1 scoop light ice cream or 1 ice cream slice
- ½ muffin, toasted, spread with light cream cheese and sprinkled with cinnamon
- 1 cup freshly popped corn
- 2 water cracker biscuits with 15 grams low-fat cheese
- 1 scoop frozen yoghurt
- ½ small rockmelon sprinkled with orange juice

At any time

- water (try to have at least 6 glasses a day)
- low-kilojoule soft drinks
- mineral or soda water
- low-kilojoule jelly (not more than one packet a day)
- 3 or 4 cups tea or coffee (no sugar)
- any crisp vegetables
- chewing gum, preferably with artificial sweetener

Appendix

Useful books

Good Fats, Bad Fats, Rosemary Stanton, Allen & Unwin, 1997
    Puts fats into perspective.

Growing Up, Not Out. A weight management guide for families, Dr Kate Steinbeck, Simon & Schuster, 1998
    A book that addresses the problems of overweight children and their families.

Real Gorgeous, Kaz Cooke, Allen & Unwin, 1994
    An important book for all teenage girls and women to read. Good for self-esteem.

Rosemary Stanton's Fat and Fibre Counter, 2nd edition, Information Australia 1999
    Lists the fat and fibre content of thousands of foods and also signals whether each food is high in 'good' or 'bad' fats.

Recipe books

GutBuster Recipes, Rosemary Stanton, Allen & Unwin, 1994
    Simple but filling low-fat recipes designed for those with little previous cooking experience.

Low Fat Cookbook, Loukie Werle, Gore & Osment Publications 1997
    An inexpensive, magazine-style recipe book with good-tasting recipes, all approved by The Heart Foundation.

Rosemary Stanton's Easy Diet Cookbook: The Low Fat Way, Murdoch Books, 1995, reprinted 1998
    Another small inexpensive recipe book with low-fat, high-fibre recipes. Available in supermarkets or from Murdoch Books (45 Jones Street, Ultimo 2007 Australia).

THE DIET DILEMMA

Rosemary Stanton's Healthy Cooking, Murdoch Books, 1993, reprinted 1997
　　Over 150 low-fat recipes in an attractive large-format book.

Rosemary Stanton's Healthy Living Cookbook, Rosemary Stanton, Pan Macmillan, 1998
　　Healthy low-fat recipes.

Rosemary Stanton's High Energy Cookbook, Murdoch Books, 1998
　　A small inexpensive recipe book with low-fat, high-fibre recipes. Available in supermarkets or from Murdoch Books (45 Jones Street, Ultimo 2007 Australia).

Simply Healthy: The Victor Chang Cardiac Research Institute Cookbook, Sally James, J.B. Fairfax Press, 1999
　　Excellent recipes and attractive photography.

Simply Lite, Australian Women's Weekly quarterly magazine
　　Good low-fat recipes.

Index

acupuncture, 158
Acuslim, 158
advertising, 9, 29
Air Force Diet *see* Drinking Man's Diet
alcohol, 43, 47, 80, 81, 82, 166, 174–5, 210
aloe vera, 55, 151
alpha lipoic acid, 55
amino acids, 10, 52–3, 80, 81
amphetamines, 67, 155
antioxidants, 10, 50, 52, 63, 98, 117, 172
appetite, 33, 85, 110, 155
appetite suppressants, 155
'apple' shape, 38–40
arginine, 52–3
arthritis, 40, 46–7
athletes, 16, 18
Atkins, Dr, 125–6
Australian Association for the Study of Obesity, 4
Australian Competition and Consumer Commission, 9
Australian Nutrition Foundation, 89

babies, 197
basal metabolic rate (BMR), 77, 78
'beer gut', 24, 90
Beverley Hills Diet, 128–9
Beyond Pritikin, 123–5
bingeing, 71, 75, 92, 167, 191–3
bioelectrical impedance, 18
bioflavonoids, 23
blood pressure, 39, 40, 41, 42
blood sugar, 42–3
body builders, 15
body image, 4–7
body mass index (BMI), 13–18, 21, 40
body wrap, 9, 23
branched chain amino acids, 52
bread, 35, 182, 184–5
breakfast, 119–20, 178–84
brindleberry *see* hydroxycitric acid
brown fat, 124
bulimia, 193

Cabot, Dr Sandra, 104–08
caffeine, 62

cancer and body weight, 40, 44–5
capsaicin, 61–2
carbohydrate, diet low in, 2–3, 35–7
carbohydrates, 35, 81, 82, 83, 109, 114, 117, 166, 172; loading, 77
carnitine, 52, 53–4, 55
Cellasene, 4, 23
cellulite, 22–3, 64, 73, 102, 145
cereals, 180–1
children, 29, 33; overweight, 26, 194–202
chillies, 61–2
chitosan, 51–2, 154
chocolate, 43
cholecystokinin, 156
cholesterol, 31, 41, 51, 70, 96, 114, 168
choline, 55–6
chromium picolinate, 55, 57–8
cleansing diet, 3
clover, 23, 64
collagen, 9, 54–5, 149
Complete F-Plan Diet, 102–03
conjugated linoleic acid (CLA), 65
Conley, Rosemary, 101
Cooke, Kaz, 6
cramps, 36
crispbread, 184
croissant, 27
CT scans, 18

dairy products, 65
dehydration, 36
dehydroepiandrostenone (DHEA), 60–1
depression, and weight, 66, 155
diabetes, 39, 42–4, 110, 111, 116
diet merry-go-round, 69–87
diet products, 7–11, 21
diet program, how to pick a good, 76

Diet That Works, The, 93–4
dietary fibre, 45, 63, 80, 82, 103
Dietary Supplement and Health Education Act (DSHEA), 2, 50
dietitians, 74–5, 110, 145
Dietitians Association of Australia, 89, 150
diets, 35–7; good, 88–97
digestion, 79, 80–2, 118
dinner, 188–9
diuretics, 66, 143–4, 157
Dr Atkins Diet revolution, 3
Dr Atkins Super Energy Diet, 125–6
Drinking Man's Diet, 127–8
drinks, 210–11; for children, 198–9
drugs, for obesity, 34, 152–7
Duncanson, Kerith, 91–2

Eat More, Weigh Less (Ornish), 96–8
Eat More, Weigh Less (Shintani), 98–100
eating out, 30–2, 203–10
Egg Diet, 127
Egger, Dr Garry, 90, 91
eggs, 74, 168
eicosanoids, 113
endorphins, 62
energy, 80–1, 118
entertaining, 211
enzymes, 67, 105
ephedrine, 62, 67
escin, 64
evening primrose oil, 23, 64
exercise, 22, 32, 81–2, 84–7, 90, 94, 146, 175–7; *see also* physical activity
Eyton, Audrey, 103

fast foods, 10, 27, 30, 31, 34, 43, 168, 195, 213–14
fasting, 71, 160-2

INDEX

fat, body, 16, 18, 26-7, 35, 37, 82, 83
fat metabolisers, 49; products, 50–68
fat-reduced foods, 165
fats, blood, 41–2; dietary, 27–8, 83, 105, 107, 109, 115, 166, 167; essential, 104; fake, 165; fish, 96, 166, 167; monounsaturated, 43; omega–3, 46, 64, 81, 105, 123, 170; omega–6, 64, 123; saturated, 39, 43, 115, 168; trans, 125, 168; unsaturated, 81, 168
female hormones, 5
Fen/phen, 153
fertility, 20
fibre *see* dietary fibre
fidgeting, 85–7
filling foods, 172
fish, 102; fish oil, 23, 96
Fit For Life, 79, 115, 117–20
fluid levels, 16, 64, 111, 164
food combining, 3, 118
foods, healthy, 34
foods, processed, 28–30
French eating habits, 31
fruit, 118–19, 121, 172–3, 181–2
fruit and vegetable extracts, 173
fruit juice, 199, 210
Fucus vesiculosis see kelp

gallstones, 39, 40, 44
gamma linolenic acid, 64, 125
Garcinia cambogia see hydroxycitric acid
gastric banding, 159
genes, and obesity, xi, 6, 7, 10, 11, 26, 33–4, 86, 164
Genic Hunter-Gatherer diet, 94
Ginkgo biloba, 23, 61
Gittleman, Anne, 123
glands, 34

Gloria Marshall Figure Shaping Salons, 141–2
glucagon, 115
glucomannan, 49
glucose, blood 36, 43, 52, 81, 82, 83; *see also* blood sugar
glucose tolerance, 65
gluten, 124
glycaemic index, 3, 94, 115, 116, 120, 121
glycaemic load, 43, 115–16
glycogen, 35, 36, 37, 59, 76, 77, 81, 83, 116, 128, 164, 172
gout, 39, 40, 46–7
grains, 112, 172
grapefruit, 74
Grapefruit Diet, 132–3
grapeseed, 23, 63
growth hormone, 53
guar gum, 63
guarana 62–3
guilt, about food, 75, 191–2
GutBuster program, 3, 138–9; Waist Loss Guide, 90–1

halitosis, 126
Hall, Tim, 127
Hay Diet, 121
Hayes, Dr Mileham, 93–4
healthy weight range, 14, 15
heart disease, 39, 40, 41–2
height weight charts, 17
Herbalife, 143–5
herbs, 66–7; Chinese, 65, 143–4
High Sexuality Diet, 133
Hip and Thigh Diet, 100–02
holiday foods, 213–14
horse chestnut *see* escin
hunger, 80, 155
hydroxycitric acid (HCA), 50–1, 55

If Not Dieting, Then What?, 89–90
inositol, 64–5

insulin, 42–3, 52, 96, 109, 110, 111, 112. 114, 121
Internet, 1, 8, 60, 113, 154; quackwatch site, 149
intestinal bypass, 159–60
iodine, 56, 155
Israeli Army Diet, 127

jaw wiring, 158–9
Jenny Craig Weight Loss Centres, 139–41
junk foods, 29

Katahn, Martin, 129
Kausman, Dr Rick, 6, 89–90
kelp, 23, 50, 56–7
ketones, 37, 126, 161
ketosis, 150, 161
kilojoules, 166–7

lactic acid, 59
Last Chance Diet, 148
laxatives, 66, 156–7
lean tissue, 10, 16
lecithin, 23, 50, 55–6
Licence to Eat, 91–2
Linn, Robert, 148
linseed, 46, 96, 105, 167
lipoprotein lipase, 37
liquorice, 66
Livatone, 108
Liver Cleansing Diet, 104–08
LSA mixture, 105
lunch, 184-8

McDonalds, 10
ma huang, 66
Mazel, Judy, 128
meal replacement products, 143, 147–52
meals, light, 187–8
meat fat, 169, 170
Mediterranean diet, 111, 115
men, 90; body image, 6, 24–5; body shape, 39

menopause, 38, 45–6, 47, 101
menstruation, 7, 16
metabolic rate, 62, 76–7, 82, 84, 155, 161
metabolism, 9, 10, 21, 34, 35, 56, 77–8, 83, 115, 152, 178
monoamine oxidase inhibitors, 66
Montignac, Michel, 114, 120–2
muesli, 27, 181
multi-level marketing companies, 1, 48–9, 60, 66
muscle, 17, 33, 35, 57, 76

National Nutrition Survey, 14
Negative Calories, 131–2

obesity, 15–18; environmental factors, xi; and health problems 5, 14; and prevention of, x; socioeconomic status, 13
oestrogen, 44, 45–6, 47
olive oil, 168, 169
O'Neill, Matthew, 91
Orlistat *see* Xenical
Ornish, Dr Dean, 96–8
ornithine, 52
osteoporosis, 13, 14, 16, 45–6
overweight, incidence of 13, 15–18, 26

papain, 67
passive exercise machines, 142
pasta, 30, 35
pawpaw, 67
'pear' shape, 38–40, 101
pectin, 63
physical activity, xi, 11, 21, 34, 39, 78, 87, 200–01; lack of 12, 32–3, 41, 44, 194–5
phytoestrogens, 46, 64
pinch test, 18
potatoes, 30, 35
Powter, Susan, 122–3
prawns, 168

INDEX

pregnancy, 16
prepared meals, 146–7
prevention of obesity, 163
Pritikin Program, 3, 94–6, 99, 112
proanthocyanidins, 63
Proietto, Dr Joe, 4
proteins, 10, 52–3, 115, 117, 166
psychological problems and obesity, 41
pyruvate, 55, 58–60

quiche, 27

recipe books, 219–20
recommended reading, 219
relaxation, 86
restaurant meals, 205–10
restrained eaters, 193
rhubarb, 66
rice, 35, 116
Rotation Diet, 129–31

salads, 185–6
salt, 120, 174
satiety, 27
Scarsdale Diet, 126
school canteens, 34
seafood, 171
Sears, Barry, 109
seaweed, 100
self-esteem, 6, 7, 71–3
shape, 18–20
Shintani, Dr Terry, 98–100
skinfold measurement, 18
sleep apnoea, 39, 40
slimming products, 49–50
smoking and body weight, 39, 214–18
snacks, 31, 169, 189–90, 195; healthy, 200, 215–18
soft drinks, 29, 82
soups, 186–7
spirulina, 108, 150
sports people, 15, 61
spreads, 182–3

St Johns Wort, 66
starch, 50, 82
starch-blocker pills, 50
starving, 161
stomach stapling, 159
Stop the Insanity, 122–3
sugar, 27, 28, 29, 43, 82, 114, 116, 166, 173, 195; sugars, 80, 81
Sugar Busters!, 3, 114–17
supplements, 37, 48, 68, 108
surgery for obesity, 158–9
'sweet tooth', 156
sweets, 29
Swiss Slimming Clinic, 9

takeaway foods, 30
Tarnower, Dr Herman, 126
tea, 108; herbal weight loss, 49, 66–7
teenagers, 29; and weight, 14
Therapeutic Goods Act, 2
Therapeutic Goods Authority, 50
thyroid gland, 56, 68, 155
toxic wastes, 80, 102, 117
triglycerides, 42, 114, 170
Trim for Life, 91
trimethylamine, 56
'tummy', 38, 47, 73
Tupling, Hilary, 92–3

uric acid, 47

varicose veins, 40
vegetables, 172
vegetarian diet, 113
vervain, 66
vinegar, 50
visceral fat, 39
vitamin B6, 50, 56, 68
vitamin B_{12}, 170
vitamin E, 52
vitamins, 68; fat-soluble, 52

waist fat, 5, 138
waist to hip ratio, 17, 39
walking, 33, 176–7
water, 36; loss, 35
weight, 16–18; fluctuations, 16
weight chart, 15
weight loss, 35; fast, 37, 47, 69–70, 74, 77, 111; and health, 40
weight loss pills, 1, 2
weight loss products, 50–68
weight loss programs, 134–47
weight loss tips, 169–72
Weight off Your Mind, A, 92–3
weight plateau, 190–1

Weight Watchers, 5, 9, 69, 70, 135–8
women, body image, 6, 71–2; body shape, 19–22, 23–4, 39, 73; thighs, 5, 19, 21, 47, 73, 105; weight, 1, 4, 12, 14, 44, 47, 73, 78–9
wild yam, 60

Xenical™, 153–4

Yen, Dr Samuel, 60–1
yo-yo dieting, 69–70

Zone Diet, The, 3, 108–13